YOUR TOTAL SOLUTION FOR READING

GRADE 2

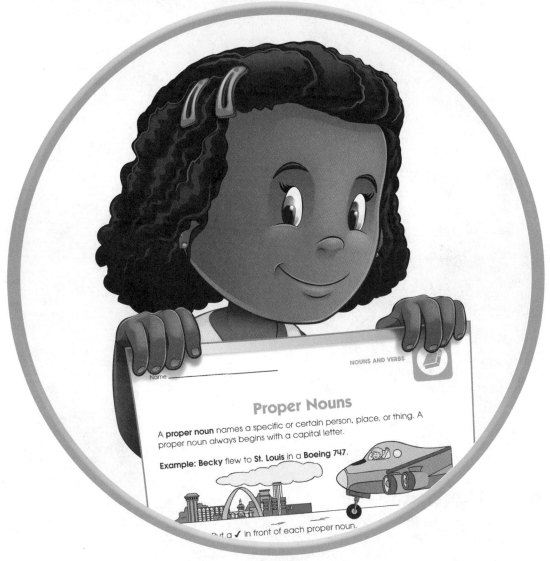

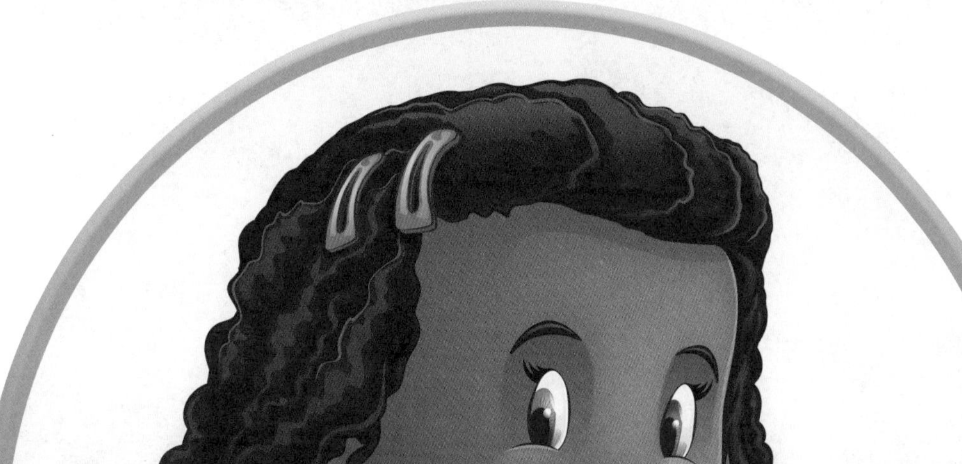

An imprint of Carson-Dellosa Publishing LLC
P.O. Box 35665
Greensboro, NC 27425 USA

Carson-Dellosa Publishing LLC
P.O. Box 35665
Greensboro, NC 27425 USA

ISBN 978-1-4838-0715-7

01-097147811

Table of Contents

Name ________________________________

Batter Up!

What did Bobby yell to the batter?

Directions: To find out, say the name of each picture. On the line, write the letter that you hear at the beginning of each picture.

_____ _____ _____ _____

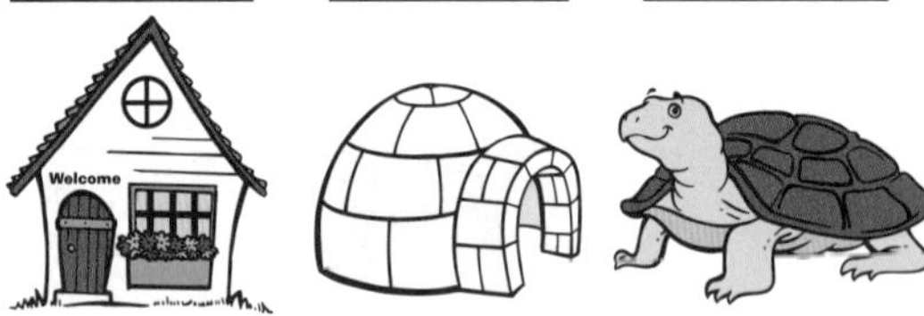

_____ _____ _____ _____ _____ _____ _____ !

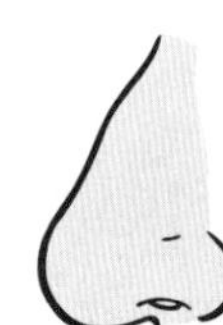

Name ______________________

Bats and Balls

Directions: Look at the baseball words below. Use the letters from the word box to make new words. **Hint:** Some letters can be used for both sets of words.

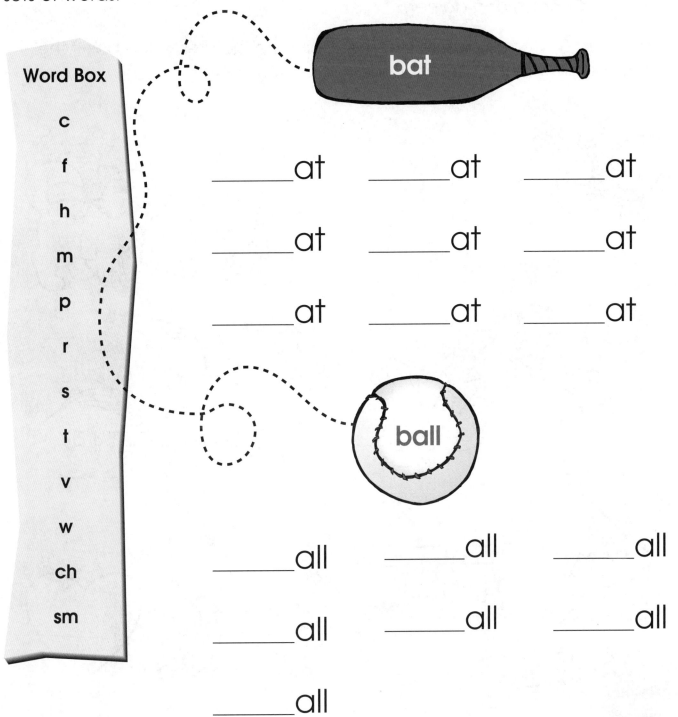

Word Box

c
f
h
m
p
r
s
t
v
w
ch
sm

bat

_____at _____at _____at

_____at _____at _____at

_____at _____at _____at

ball

_____all _____all _____all

_____all _____all _____all

_____all

Name ________________________

Sounds the Same

Different words may begin with the same sound.

Example: Box and **boy** begin with the same sound.
Cat and **dog** do not.

Directions: Say each picture's name. Color the pictures in the box if their names begin with the same sound.

RUFF

Name ______________________

Tic-Tac-Toe

Directions: Find the three pictures in each game whose names begin with the same sound. Draw a line through them.

Name ______________________

Beginning Consonants: b, c, d, f, g, h, j

Directions: Fill in the beginning consonant for each word.

Example: __c__ at

_____ ox

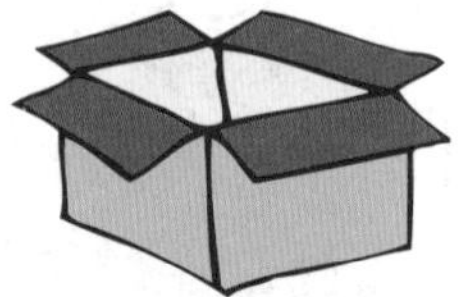

_____ acket

_____ oat

_____ ouse

_____ og

_____ ire

Name ______________________________

Beginning Consonants: k, l, m, n, p, q, r

Directions: Write the letter that makes the beginning sound for each picture.

 ______

 ______

 ______

 ______

 ______

 ______

 ______

 ______

 ______

 ______

 ______

 ______

 ______

 ______

 ______

 ______

Name ______________________

Beginning Consonants: s, t, v, w, x, y, z

Directions: Write the letter under each picture that makes the beginning sound.

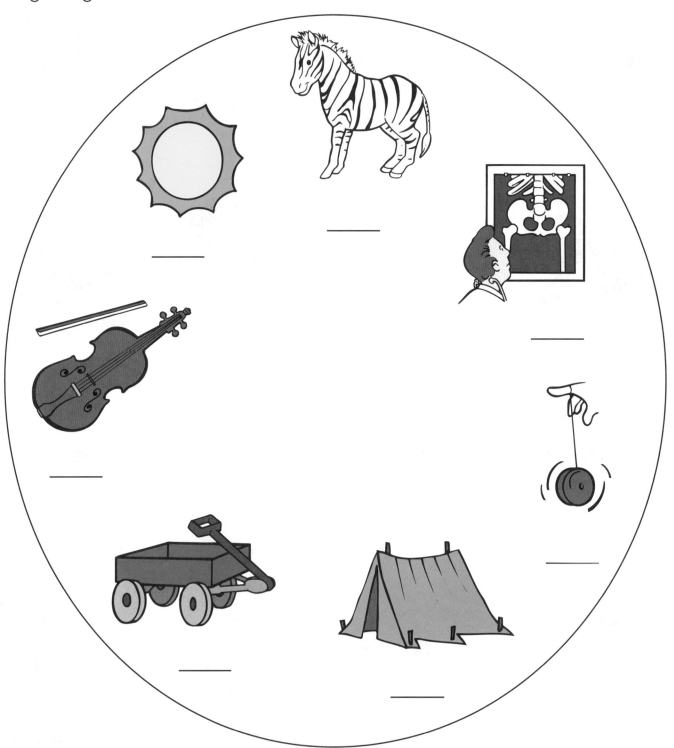

Name ____________________________

Ending Consonants: b, d, f, g

Directions: Fill in the ending consonant for each word.

ma ____

cu ____

roo ____

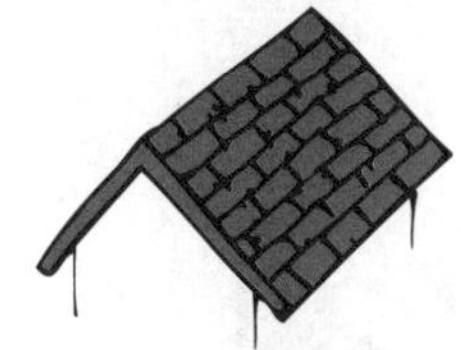

do ____

be ____

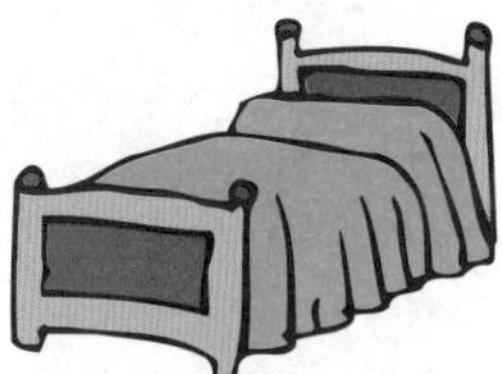

bi ____

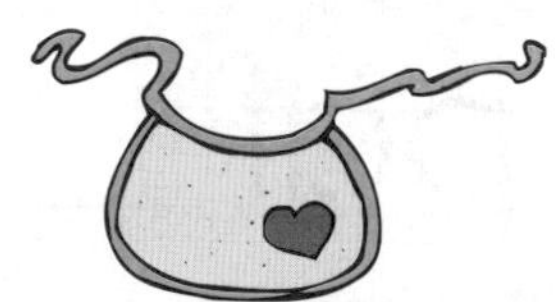

Name ______________________

Ending Consonants: k, l, m, n, p, r

Directions: Fill in the ending consonant for each word.

nai ____

ca ____

gu ____

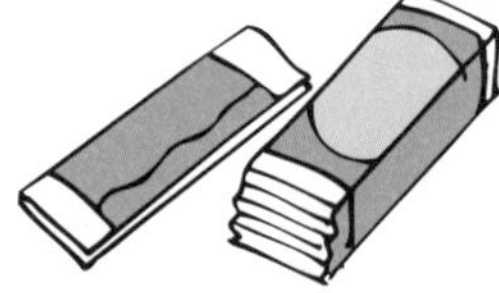

ca ____

truc ____

ca ____

pai ____

Name ______________________

Ending Consonants: s, t, x

Directions: Fill in the ending consonant for each word.

ca ____

bo ____

bu ____

fo ____

boa ____

ma ____

Name ______________________________

Blends: fl, br, pl, sk, sn

Blends are two consonants put together to form a single sound.

Directions: Look at the pictures and say their names. Write the letters for the beginning sound in each word.

________	________
________	________
________	________
________	________
________	________
________	________

Name ____________________

Blends: bl, sl, cr, cl

Directions: Look at the pictures and say their names. Write the letters for the beginning sound in each word.

______ own

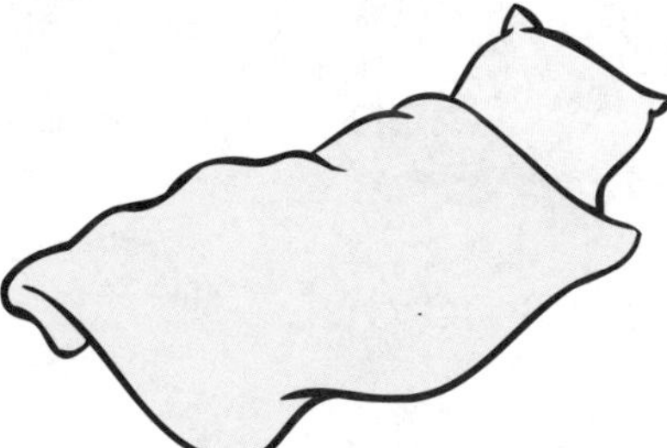

______ anket

______ ayon

______ ock

______ ide

______ oud

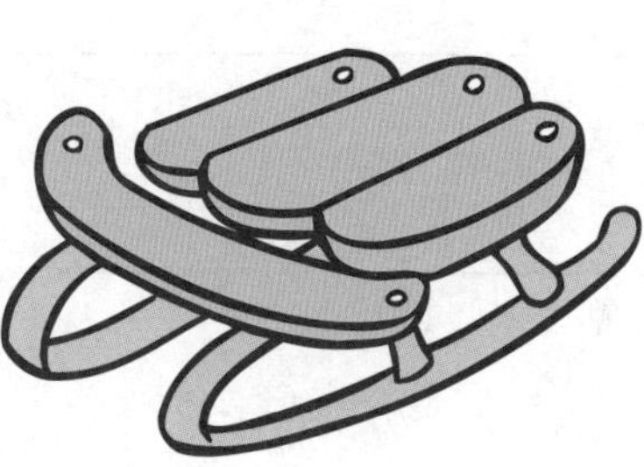

______ ed

______ ab

______ ocodile

Name ____________________

Consonant Blends

Directions: Write a word from the word box to answer each riddle.

clock	glass	blow	climb	slipper
sleep	gloves	clap	blocks	flashlight

1. You need me when the lights go out. **What am I?** ____________________
2. People use me to tell the time. **What am I?** ____________________
3. You put me on your hands in the winter to keep them warm. **What am I?** ____________________
4. Cinderella lost one like me at midnight. **What am I?** ____________________
5. This is what you do with your hands when you are pleased. **What is it?** ____________________
6. You can do this with a whistle or with bubble gum. **What is it?** ____________________
7. These are what you might use to build a castle when you are playing. **What are they?** ____________________
8. You do this to get to the top of a hill. **What is it?** ____________________
9. This is what you use to drink water or milk. **What is it?** ____________________
10. You do this at night with your eyes closed. **What is it?** ____________________

Name ______________________

Nothing But Net

Directions: Write the missing consonant blends.

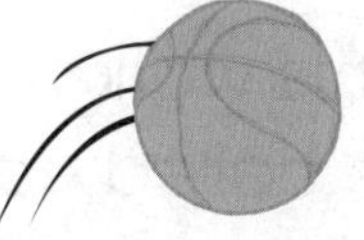

scr	mp	dr	lp	nk	ss	st	sk	nd	gr	sn	nt	fr	sl

1. "My ___ ___ eakers he ___ ___ me run very fa ___ ___!" exclaimed Jim Shooz.
2. "I really like to ___ ___ ibble the ball," announced Dub L. Dribble.
3. Team captain ___ ___ y-High Hook can easily ___ ___ am du ___ ___ the basketball into the net.
4. Will Kenny Dooit make an extra poi ___ ___ with his ___ ___ ee throw?
5. Harry Leggs can ju ___ ___ at lea ___ ___ 4 feet off the ___ ___ ound.
6. Wow! Willie Makeit finally caught the ball on the rebou ___ ___!
7. "Watch me pa ___ ___ the ball!" yelled Holden Firm.
8. He ju ___ ___ ___ ___ opped the ball, and now they all will ___ ___ ___ amble to get it.
9. "I cannot tell which team will win at the e ___ ___ of the game," decided Ed G. Nerves.
10. "You silly boy! Of course, the team with the mo ___ ___ poi ___ ___ s will win!" explained Kay G. Fann.

Name ______________________

Consonant Digraph th

Some consonants work together to stand for a new sound. They are called **consonant digraphs**. Listen for the sound of consonant digraph **th** in **think**.

think

Directions: Print **th** under the pictures whose names begin with the sound of **th**. Color the **th** pictures.

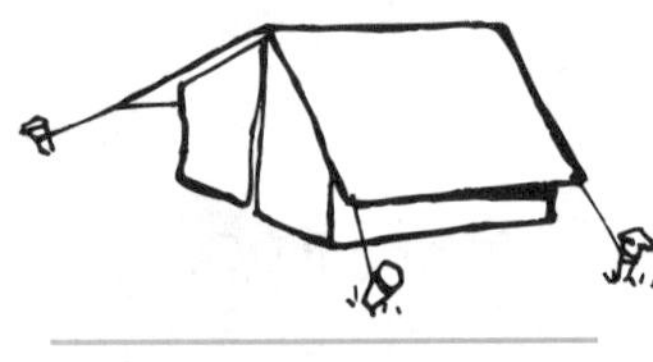

Think About th

Directions: Say the name of each picture. Fill in the missing letter or letters.

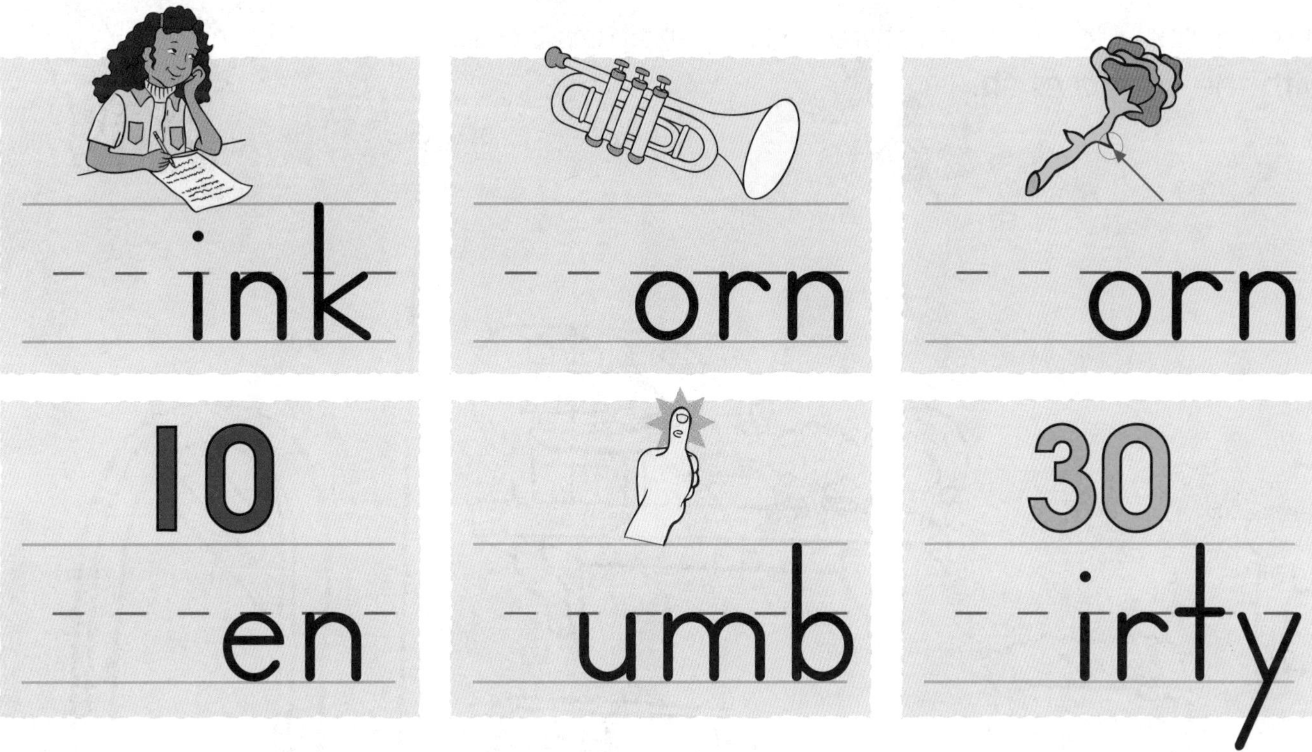

Directions: Find and circle these **th** words in the puzzle. The words may go **across** or **down**.

think	thorn	thumb	thirty

T	T	H	I	R	T	Y
T	H	I	N	K	H	J
H	O	B	H	N	U	L
O	R	N	E	H	M	X
J	N	H	R	T	B	Y

Name ______________________________

Consonant Digraph sh

Listen for the sound of consonant digraph **sh** in **sheep**.

Directions: Color the pictures whose names begin with the sound of **sh**.

sheep

Name ______________________

Change a Word

Directions: Make a new word by changing the beginning sound to **sh**. Write the new word on the line.

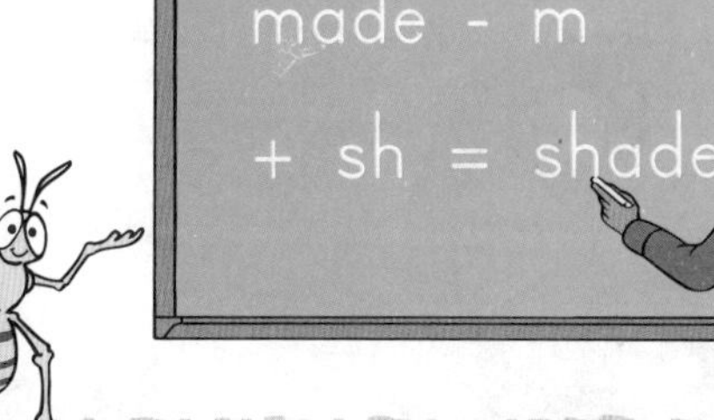

zip	sell	beep
________	________	________
tin	**line**	**lift**
________	________	________
red	**cape**	**cave**
________	________	________
top	**bake**	**feet**
________	________	________

Name ____________________

Consonant Digraph wh

Directions: Write **wh**, **th**, or **sh** to complete each word.

____eel  ____ale  ____eep

____ink 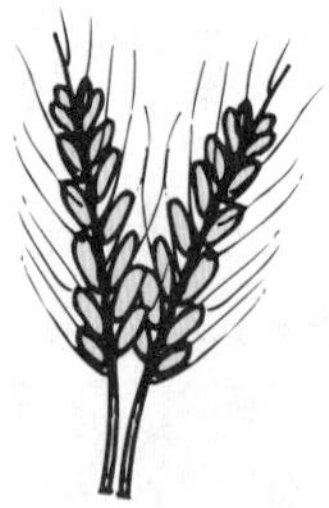 ____eat 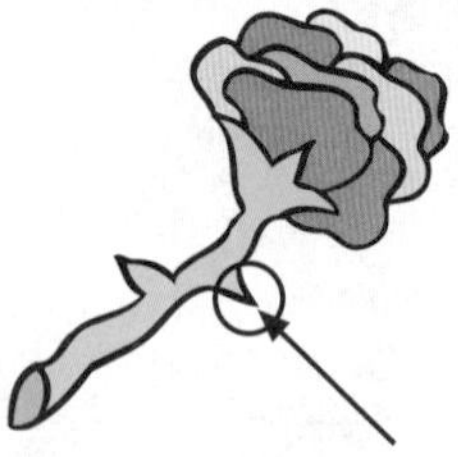 ____orn

____ip  ____irty 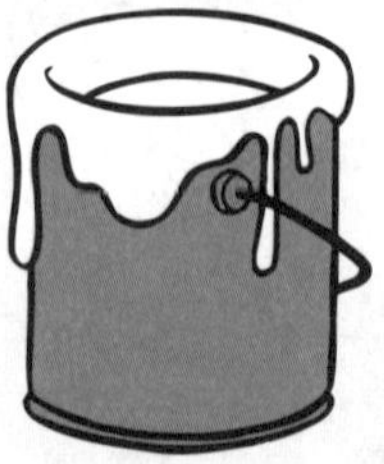 ____ite

Wheel of Fortune

Listen for the sound of consonant digraph **wh** in **whale**.

whale

Directions: Color the pictures whose names begin with consonant digraph **wh**.

wh

30

Name ______________________

Consonant Digraph ch

Listen for the sound of consonant digraph **ch** in **cherry**.

cherry

Directions: Trace the cherry if the name of the picture begins with the **ch** sound. Use a red crayon.

Name ______________________

Read and Write Digraphs

Directions: Write a word from the box to label each picture.

chest	**check**	**sheep**
chimp	**cherry**	**thirty**
chain	**cheese**	**wheel**

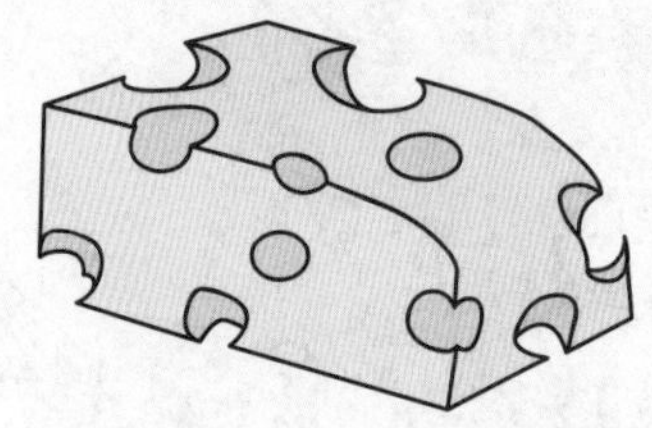

30

Name ______________________________

Consonant Digraph kn

Listen for the sound of consonant digraph **kn** in **knot**.
The **k** is silent.

knot 

Directions: Color the pictures whose names begin with the **kn** sound. Connect all the colored pictures from the knight to his horse.

Name ______________________________

Knocking Around in Knickers

A long time ago, golfers wore knickers when they played. **Knickers** are short, loose trousers gathered just below the knee. **Kn** at the beginning of a word makes the same sound as **n**.

Directions: Look at each picture and write **kn** or **k** at the beginning to complete the words.

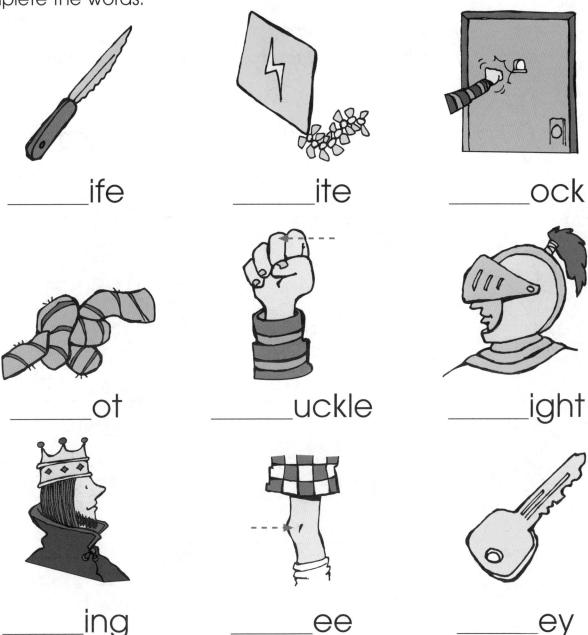

______ife ______ite ______ock

______ot ______uckle ______ight

______ing ______ee ______ey

Name ____________________

Consonant Digraph wr

Listen for the sound of consonant digraph **wr** in **wren**. The **w** is silent.

wren

Directions: Write a word from the box to label each picture. Color the pictures whose names begin with **wr**.

web	**wrist**	**wring**	**wrap**	
worm	**write**	**wreath**	**wink**	**wrench**

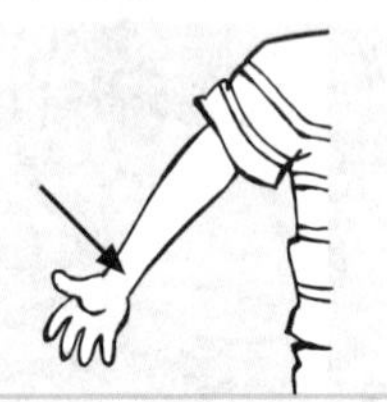

At the Pool

Directions: Write the correct letters from the word box to complete the word for each picture.

Word Box
wh
bl
sw
cl
st
ch

_____ istle

_____ ipboard

starting _____ ock

_____ opwat _____

_____ im cap

Name ________________________________

Ending Digraphs

Some words end with consonant digraphs. Listen for the ending digraphs in **duck**, **moth**, **dish**, and **branch**.

du**ck**  mo**th** 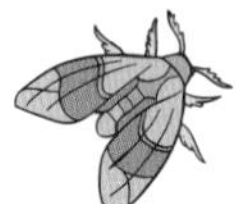 di**sh** 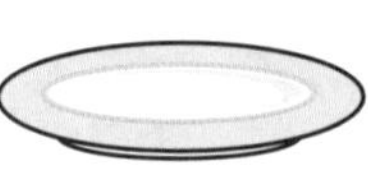 bran**ch** 

Directions: Say the name of each picture. Circle the letters that stand for the ending sound.

ck
th
sh
ch

ck
th
sh
wh

ck
th
sh
ch

ck
th
sh
ch

ck
th
sh
ch

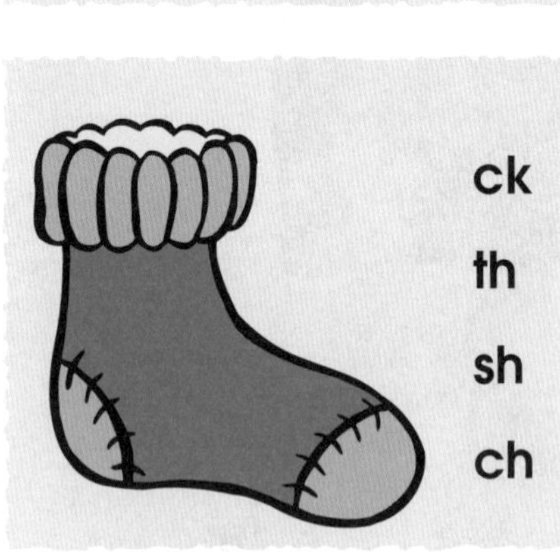

ck
th
sh
ch

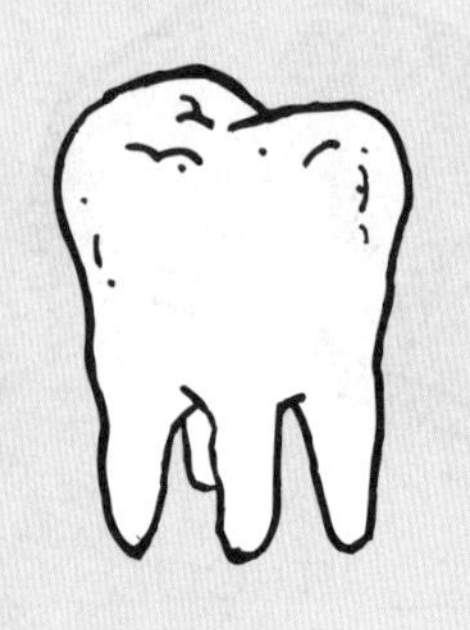

ck
th
sh
ch

ck
th
sh
ch

ck
th
sh
ch

Name ____________________

Hear and Write Digraphs

Directions: The name of each picture below ends with **ck**, **th**, **sh**, or **ch**. Write each word on the lines below.

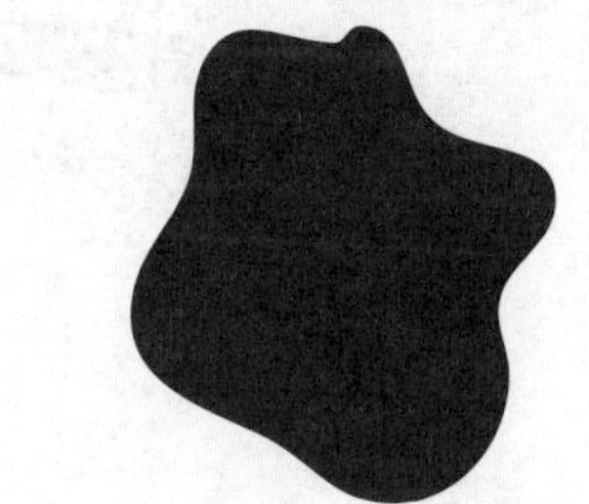

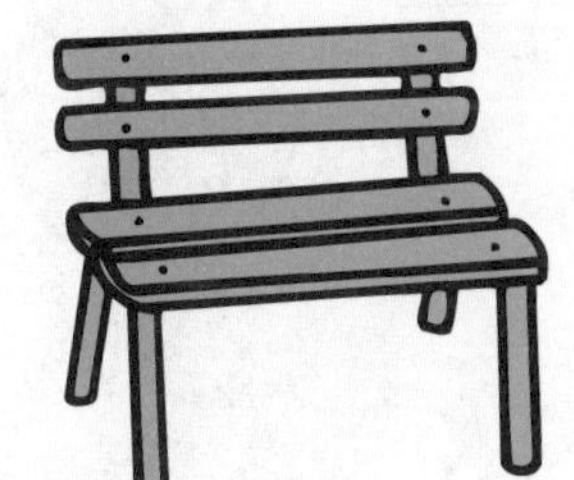

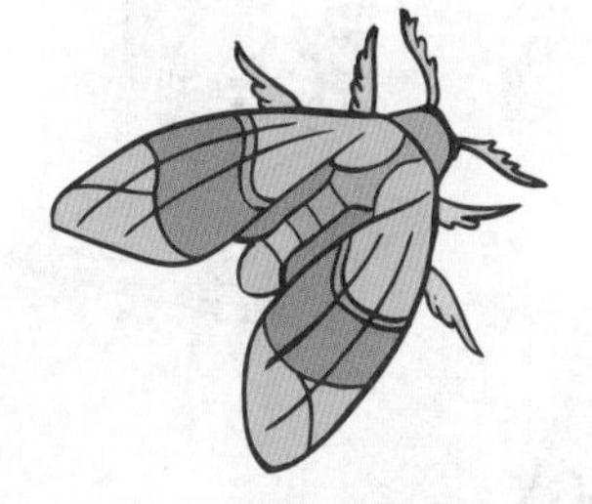

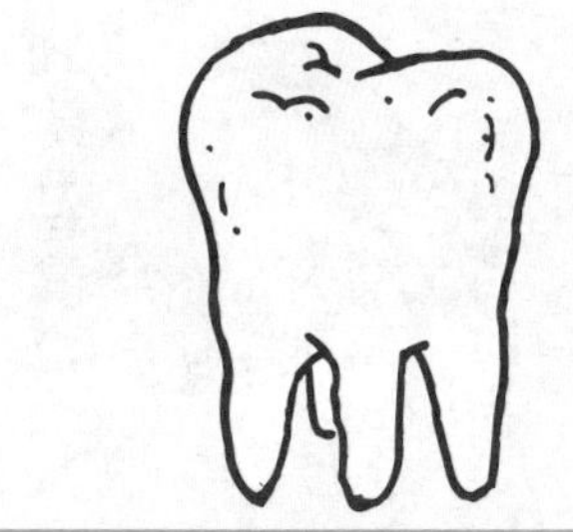

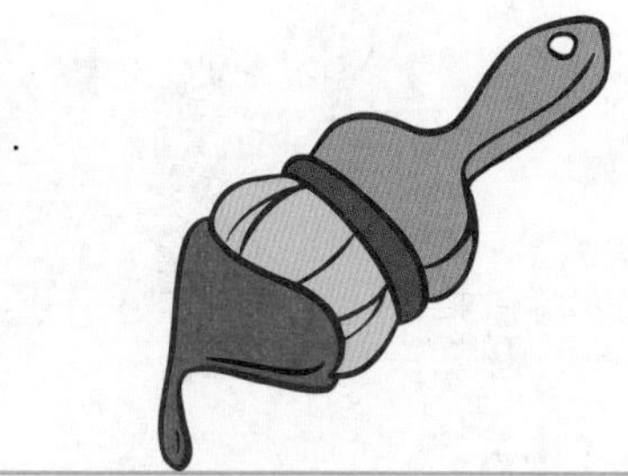

Name ___________________________

Missing Digraphs

Directions: Fill in the circle beside the missing digraph in each word.

___ale	pea___	___ife
○ **wh** ○ **wr** ○ **ch**	○ **ck** ○ **th** ○ **ch**	○ **kn** ○ **ch** ○ **wr**
___imp	___ell	clo___
○ **ck** ○ **kn** ○ **ch**	○ **ch** ○ **sh** ○ **ck**	○ **ck** ○ **ch** ○ **kn**
___ite	fi___	___orn
○ **kn** ○ **wr** ○ **th**	○ **ch** ○ **sh** ○ **th**	○ **th** ○ **wr** ○ **ch**

Name ______________________

Missing Digraphs

Directions: Fill in the circle beside the missing digraph in each word.

so___ ○ **ck** ○ **ch** ○ **kn**	___ain ○ **th** ○ **ch** ○ **sh**	___eath ○ **wr** ○ **wh** ○ **kn**
___ip ○ **th** ○ **sh** ○ **ck**	ben___ ○ **ck** ○ **th** ○ **ch**	___eel ○ **sh** ○ **th** ○ **wh**
___ight ○ **kn** ○ **th** ○ **wr**	too___ ○ **ch** ○ **ck** ○ **th**	___ench ○ **kn** ○ **wr** ○ **th**

Name ______________________

Silent Letters

Some words have letters you cannot hear at all, such as the **gh** in **night**, the **w** in **wrong**, the **l** in **walk**, the **k** in **knee**, the **b** in **climb**, and the **t** in **listen**.

Directions: Look at the words in the word box. Write the word under its picture. Underline the silent letters.

knife	**light**	**calf**	**wrench**	**lamb**	**eight**
wrist	**whistle**	**comb**	**thumb**	**knob**	**knee**

__________ __________ __________ __________

__________ __________ __________ __________

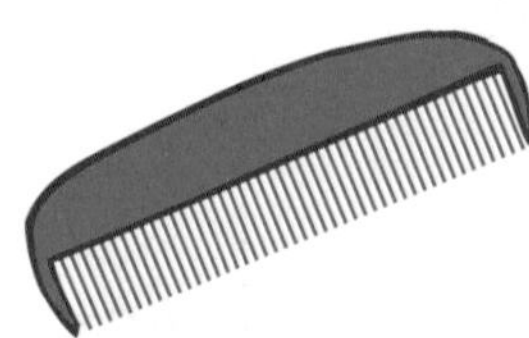

__________ __________ __________ __________

Name ______________________

A Flying Saucer?

A **discus** is a flat circle made mostly of wood with a metal center and edge that looks a bit like a plate. A men's discus is about 9 inches across and weighs a little over 4 pounds. A women's discus is about 2 inches smaller and about 2 pounds lighter. The men's world record throw is 243 feet, but the women's world record is even greater—252 feet!

Directions: Read the word in each discus. Write its silent consonant in the center.

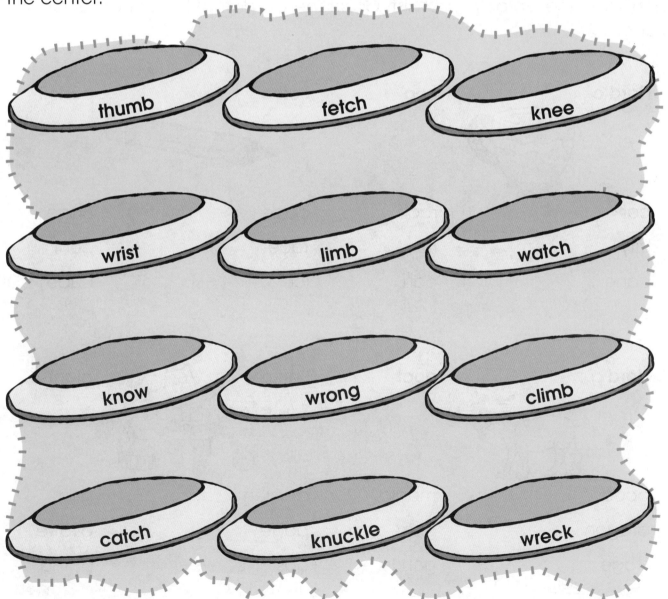

thumb | fetch | knee

wrist | limb | watch

know | wrong | climb

catch | knuckle | wreck

Name ______________________________

Sounds of c and g

Consonants **c** and **g** each have two sounds. Listen for the soft **c** sound in **pencil**. Listen for the hard **c** sound in **cup**.

Listen for the soft **g** sound in **giant**. Listen for the hard **g** sound in **goat**. **C** and **g** usually have the soft sound when they are followed by **e**, **i**, or **y**.

Directions: Say the name of each picture. Listen for the sound of **c** or **g**. Then, read the words in each list. Circle the words that have that sound of **c** or **g**.

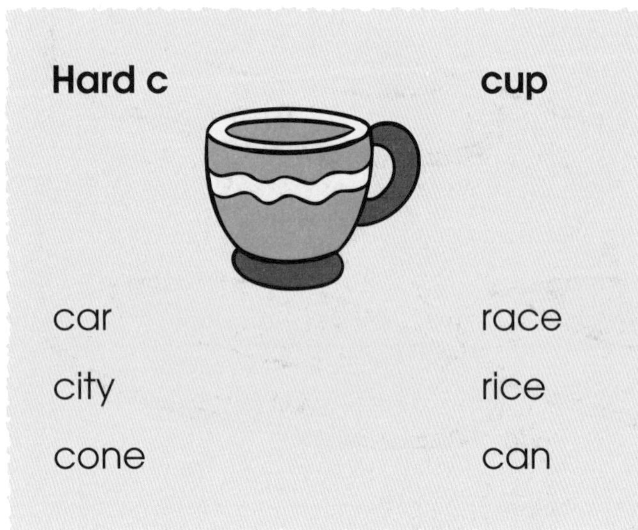

Hard c **cup**

car race
city rice
cone can

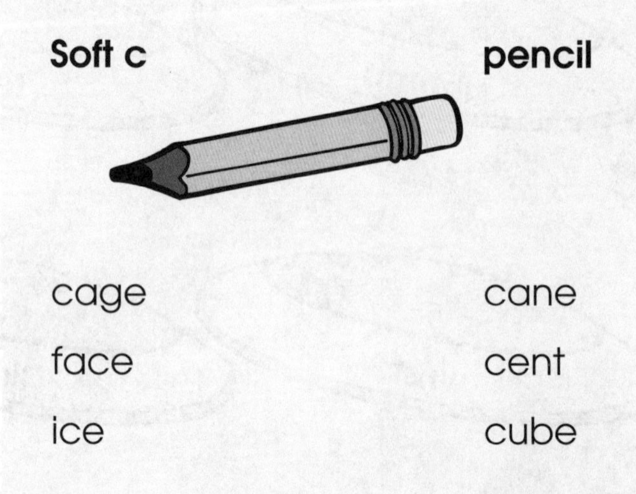

Soft c **pencil**

cage cane
face cent
ice cube

Hard g **goat**

good magic
dragon gum
stage gentle

Soft g **giant**

garden gem
page giraffe
gas gorilla

Name ___________________________

Hard and Soft c and g

Directions: Underline the letter that follows the **c** or **g** in each word. Write **hard** if the word has the hard **c** or hard **g** sound. Write **soft** if the word has the soft **c** or soft **g** sound.

car	wagon	cup
pencil	gym	cot
giant	gem	celery
gum	cymbals	goat

Name ______________________

Kick It In!

Directions: Write a vowel to complete each word below.

Name ______________________________

Short a Picture Match

Directions: Cut out the cards. Read the words. Match the words and the pictures.

hat	**van**	**bat**	**ham**
bag	**man**	**map**	**fan**

Name ____________________

The Donkey's Tail

Directions: Find the donkey tails with pictures whose names have the short **i** sound. Cut them out. Glue those tails onto the donkeys.

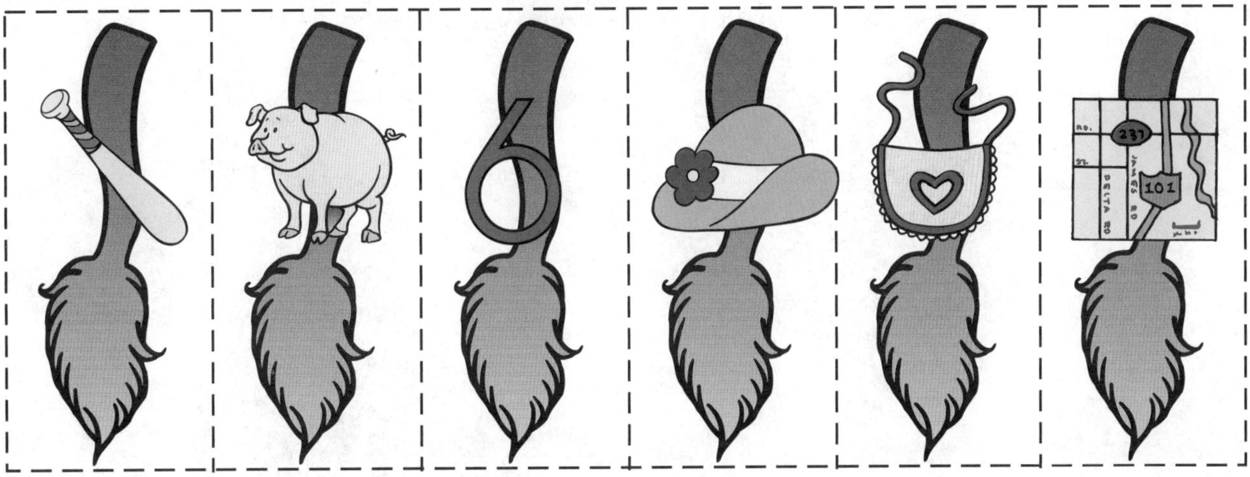

Name ________________________________

Feed the Pup

Directions: Cut out the picture cards. Say the name of each picture. If the name has the sound of short **u**, glue the card in the pup's bowl.

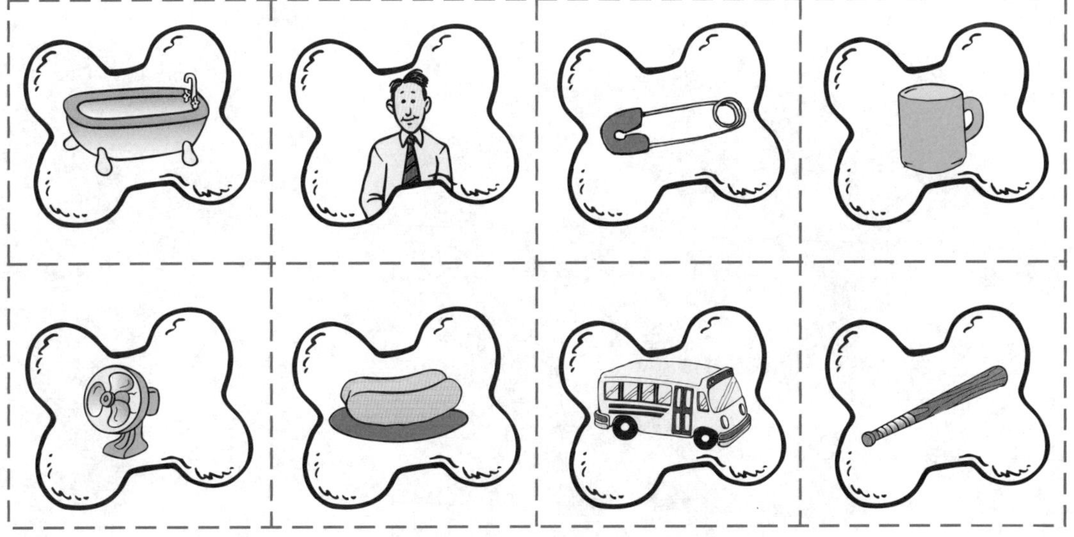

Name ______________________

Short o Puzzles

Directions: Cut out the puzzle pieces. Match each picture with its name.

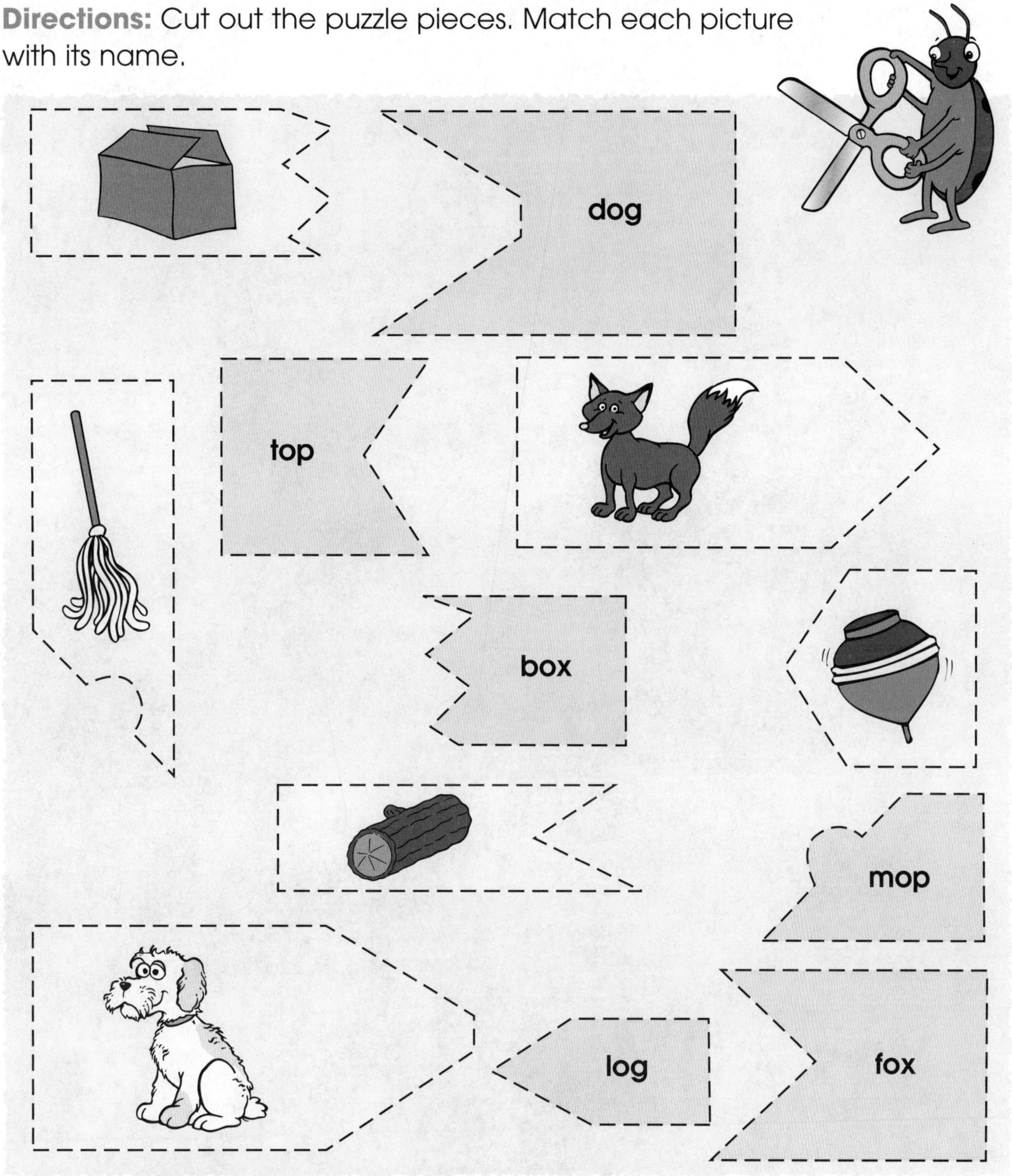

dog

top

box

mop

log

fox

Short Vowel Scrapbook

A Cut-and-Fold Book

Directions: The pages of your Cut-and-Fold Book are on the back of this sheet. First, follow the directions below to make the book. Then, follow the directions on the small pages of your Cut-and-Fold Book. Show your Short Vowel Scrapbook to a family member or friend. Think of other words you could draw for each short vowel sound.

1. Tear the page out of the book.

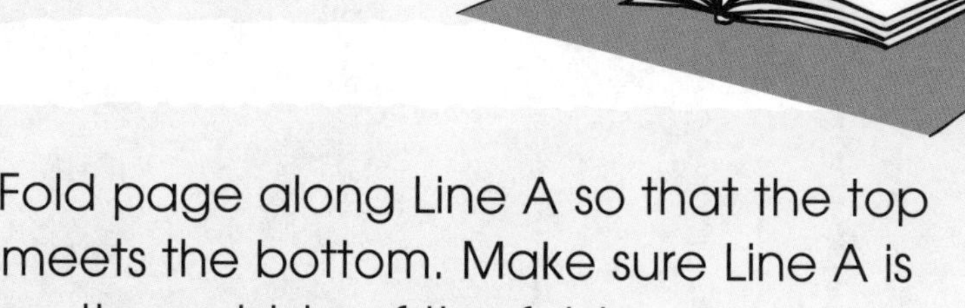

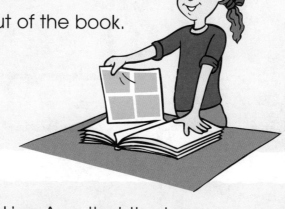

2. Fold page along Line A so that the top meets the bottom. Make sure Line A is on the outside of the fold.

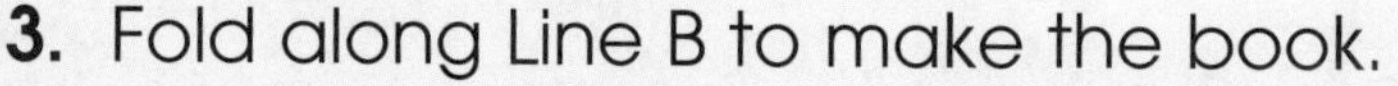

3. Fold along Line B to make the book.

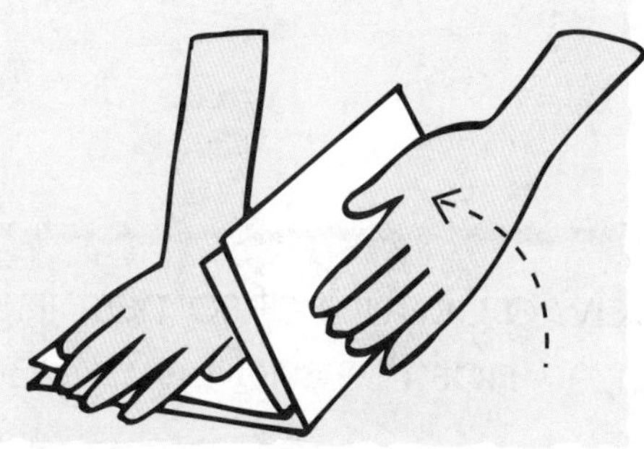

Draw a picture of something whose name has the short **a** sound.

Draw a picture of something whose name has the short **u** sound.

Draw a picture of something whose name has the short **i** sound.

Draw a picture of something whose name has the short **o** sound.

Draw a picture of something whose name has the short **e** sound.

Line A

Line B

Name ______________________

Super Silent e

Long vowel sounds have the same sound as their names. When a **Super Silent e** appears at the end of a word, you cannot hear it, but it makes the other vowel have a long sound. For example: **tub** has a **short** vowel sound, and **tube** has a **long** vowel sound.

Directions: Look at the following pictures. Decide if the word has a short or long vowel sound. Circle the correct word. Watch for the **Super Silent e**!

can cane

tub tube

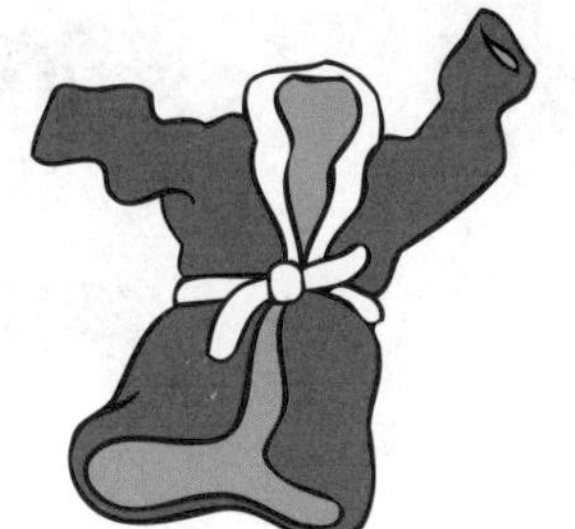

rob robe

rat rate

pin pine

cap cape

not note

pan pane

slid slide

dim dime

tap tape

cub cube

Name ____________________

Long Vowels

Long vowel sounds have the same sound as their names. When a **Super Silent e** comes at the end of a word, you cannot hear it, but it changes the short vowel sound to a long vowel sound.

Examples: rope, skate, bee, pie, cute

Directions: Say the name of the pictures. Listen for the long vowel sounds. Write the missing long vowel sound under each picture.

c ___ ke

h ___ ke

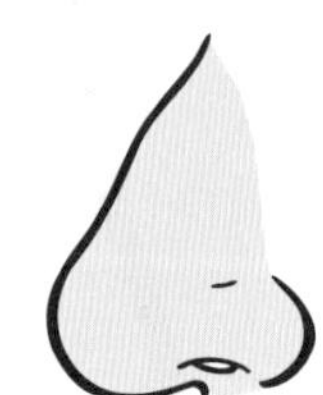

n ___ se

___ pe

c ___ be

gr ___ pe

r ___ ke

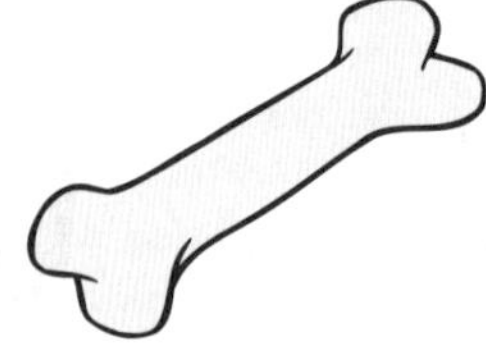

b ___ ne

k ___ te

Name ______________________________

Short and Long a e i o u

Directions: Color the correct pictures in each box.

˘ means short vowel sound ¯ means long vowel sound

ă blue ā orange	
ĕ red ē yellow	
ĭ green ī purple	
ŏ yellow ō blue	
ŭ green ū orange	

Name ______________________

Tricky ar

When **r** follows a vowel, it changes the vowel's sound. Listen for the **ar** sound in **star**.

Directions: Color the pictures whose names have the **ar** sound.

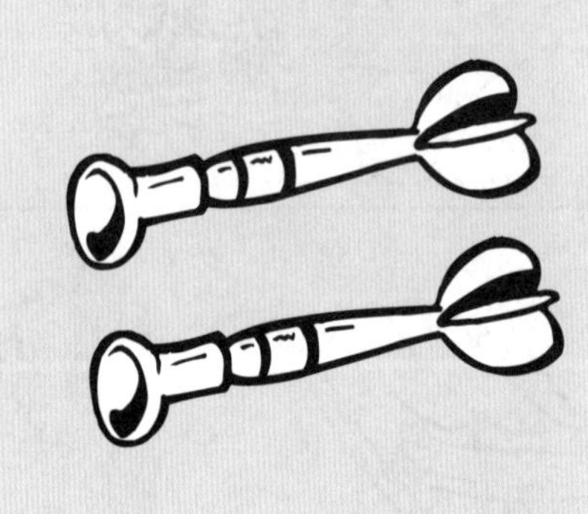

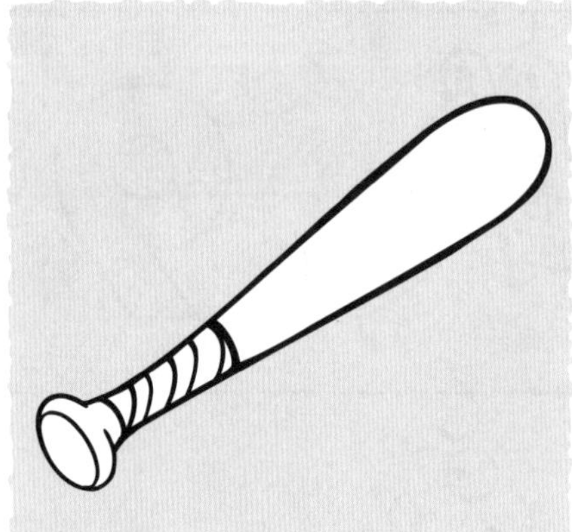

Name ______________________

Write ar or or

Listen for the **or** sound in **horn**. h**or**n

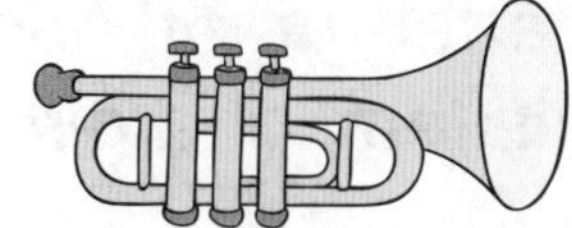

Directions: Write **ar** or **or** to complete each word.

th ___ n

c ___ t

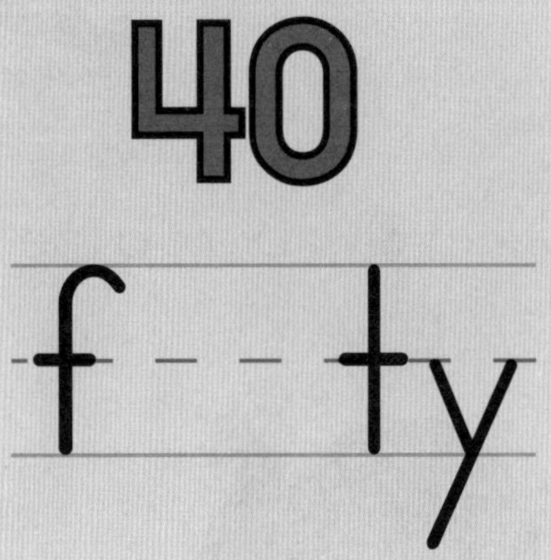

f ___ ty

st ___ k

c ___ n

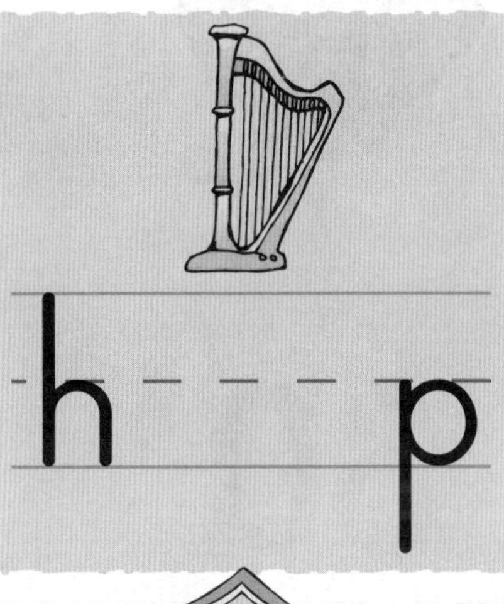

h ___ p

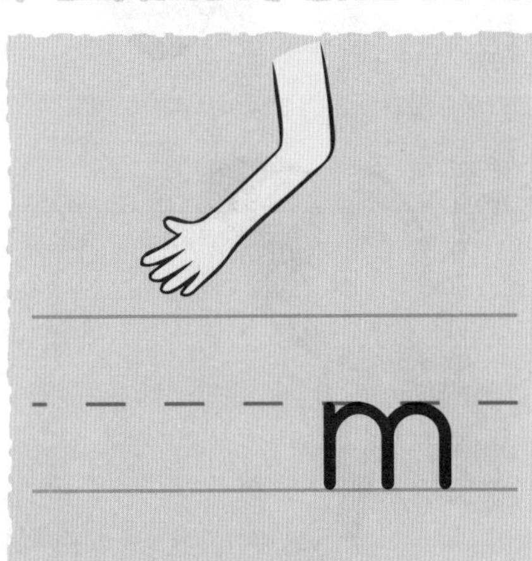

___ m

st ___

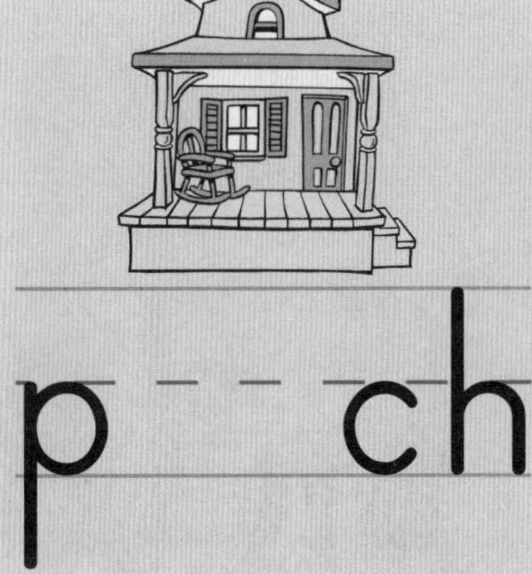

p ___ ch

Name ______________________

Mix and Match

The letters **ur**, **er**, and **ir** all have the same sound. Listen for the vowel sound in **surf**, **fern**, and **girl**.

s**ur**f  f**er**n  g**ir**l 

Directions: Draw a line from each word in the circle to the picture it names.

herd

turkey

clerk

thirty

purse

bird

30

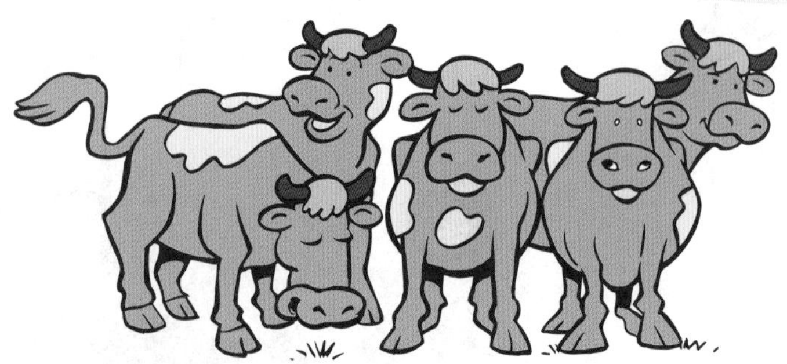

Name ____________________

Write ur, er, and ir

Directions: Find a word from the box to name each picture. Write it on the line below the picture.

turkey	**clerk**	**dirt**	**fern**	
girl	**herd**	**purple**	**surf**	**thirty**

30

Name ____________________

Vowel Pairs ai and ay

You know that the letters **a_e** usually stand for the long **a** sound. The vowel pairs **ai** and **ay** can stand for the long **a** sound, too. Listen for the long **a** sound in **train** and **hay**.

Directions: Say the name of each picture below. Look at the vowel pair that stands for the long **a** sound. Under each picture, write the words from the box that have the same long **a** vowel pair.

cage	**chain**	**gate**	**gray**
mail	**pay**	**snail**	**skate**
play	**snake**	**stay**	**tail**

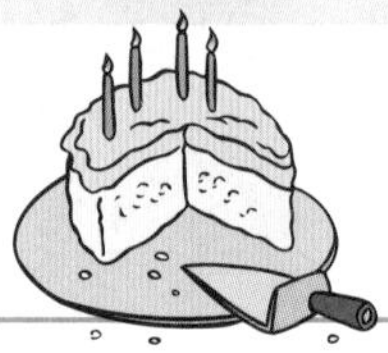

c**ake** | tr**ai**n  | h**ay**

Vowel Pairs oa and ow

You know that the letters **o_e** and **oe** usually stand for the long **o** sound. The vowel pairs **oa** and **ow** can stand for the long **o** sound, too. Listen for the long **o** sound in **road** and **snow**.

Directions: Find and circle eight long **o** words. The words may go **across** or **down**. Beside each picture, write the words that use the same long **o** vowel pair.

Z	L	I	A	C	R
B	O	C	R	O	W
S	W	R	J	A	G
O	G	O	A	L	R
A	L	A	G	X	O
P	Y	K	N	O	W

road

snow

Name ______________________

Vowel Pair ui

You know that the letters **u__e** and **ue** usually stand for the long **u** sound. The vowel pair **ui** can stand for the long **u** sound, too. Listen for the long **u** sound in **cruise**.

cr**ui**se

Directions: Circle the name of the picture. Then, write the name on the line.

mall
male
mule

sun
Sue
say

fruit
flat
frame

sun
sit
suit

cubes
cubs
caves

Jake
juice
just

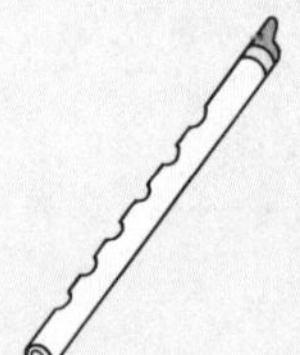

fly
flute
fleece

globe
gull
glue

blue
black
ball

Name ________________________

Vowel Pair ie

You know that the letters **i_e** usually stand for the long **i** sound. The vowel pair **ie** can stand for the long **i** sound, too. Listen for the long **i** sound in **butterflies**.

butterfl**ie**s

Directions: Write **i_e** or **ie** to complete each word. Draw a picture for one **i_e** word and one **ie** word.

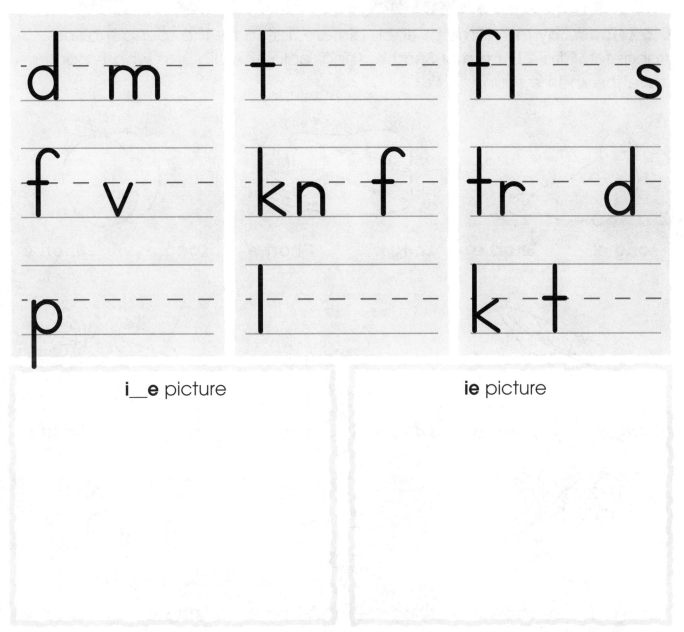

d __ m __	t __	fl __ s
f __ v __	kn __ f __	tr __ d
p __	l __	k __ t __

i_e picture

ie picture

Name ____________________

Vowel Pair ea

Some vowel pairs can stand for more than one sound. The vowel pair **ea** has the sound of long **e** in **team** and short **e** in **head**.

t**ea**m  h**ea**d 

Directions: Say the name of each picture. Listen for the sound that **ea** stands for. Circle **Long e** or **Short e**. Then, color the pictures whose names have the short **e** sound.

Long e **Short e**

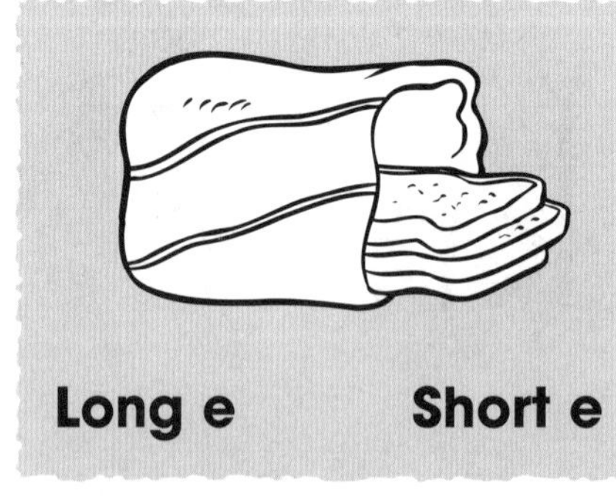

Long e **Short e**

Long e **Short e**

Long e **Short e**

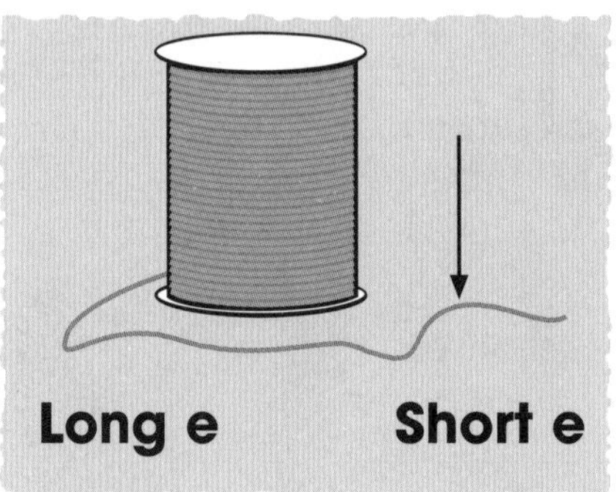

Long e **Short e**

Long e **Short e**

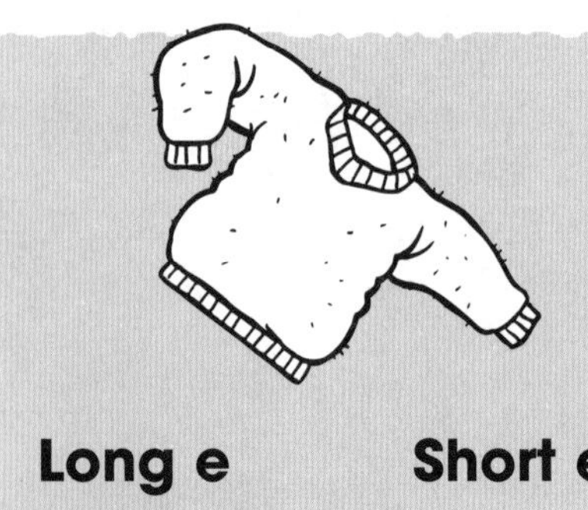

Long e **Short e**

Long e **Short e**

Long e **Short e**

Name ______________________

Vowel Pair oo

Listen for the difference between the sound of the vowel pair **oo** in **moon** and its sound in **book**.

m**oo**n 

b**oo**k 

Directions: Say the name of the picture. Circle the picture of the moon or the book to show the sound of vowel pair **oo**.

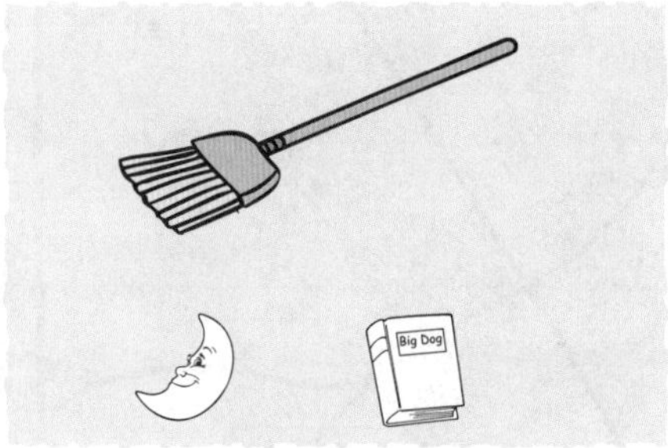

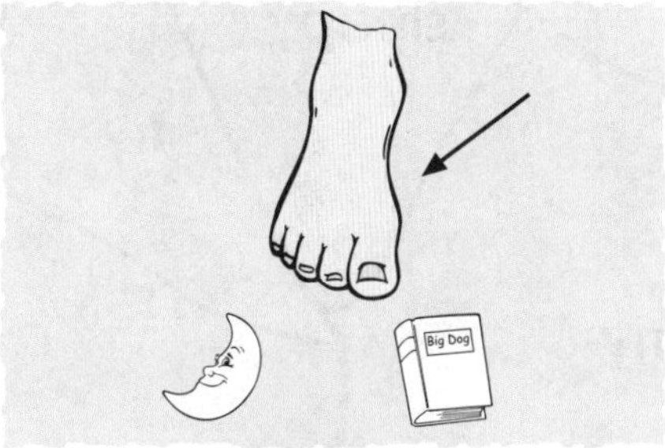

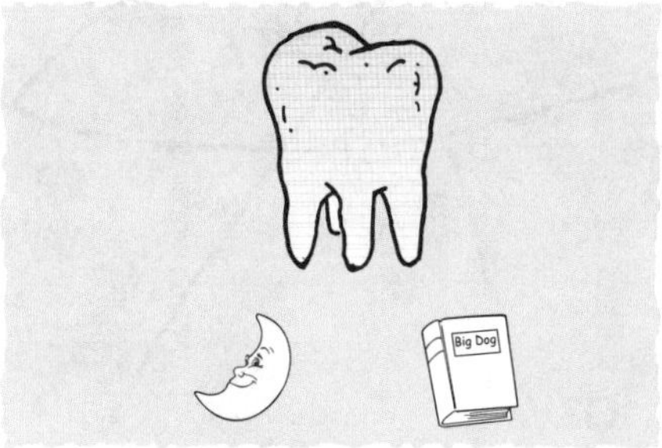

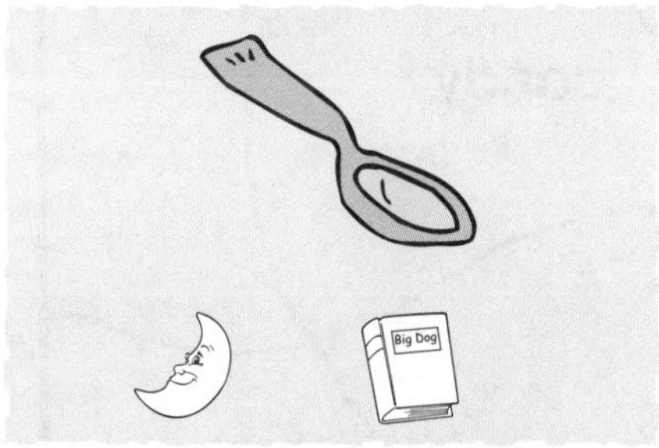

Name ______________________________

Y as a Vowel

Y as a vowel can make two sounds. **Y** can make the long sound of **e** or the long sound of **i**.

Directions: Color the spaces:
purple – **y** sounds like **i**.
yellow – **y** sounds like **e**.

What is the picture? ________

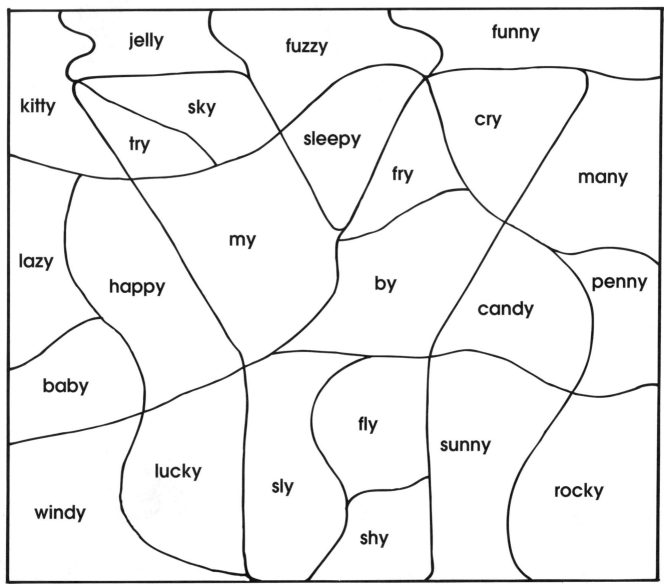

jelly fuzzy funny
kitty sky
try sleepy cry
fry many
my
lazy
happy by
penny
candy
baby
fly
sunny
lucky
sly rocky
windy
shy

Name ______________________

Missing Vowel Pairs

Directions: Fill in the circle beside the missing vowel pair in each word.

h___	tr___n	s___p
◯ **ui** ◯ **ow** ◯ **ay**	◯ **oa** ◯ **ai** ◯ **ie**	◯ **oa** ◯ **ai** ◯ **ui**
j___ce	p___	cr___
◯ **ai** ◯ **ui** ◯ **ie**	◯ **ui** ◯ **oa** ◯ **ie**	◯ **ui** ◯ **ay** ◯ **ow**
g___t	fr___t	sn___l
◯ **ai** ◯ **oa** ◯ **ui**	◯ **ai** ◯ **ow** ◯ **ui**	◯ **ow** ◯ **ai** ◯ **ie**

Name ______________________

Compound Your Effort

A **compound word** is made from two shorter words. An example of a compound word is **sandbox**, made from **sand** and **box**.

Directions: Find one word in the word box that goes with each of the words below to make a compound word. Write the compound words on the lines. Cross out each word that you use.

Word Box

board	**room**	**thing**	**side**	**bag**
writing	**book**	**hopper**	**toe**	**ball**
class	**where**	**work**	**out**	**basket**

1. coat ______________________
2. snow ______________________
3. home ______________________
4. waste ______________________
5. tip ______________________
6. chalk ______________________
7. note ______________________
8. grass ______________________
9. school ______________________
10. with ______________________

Look at the words in the word box that you did **not** use. Use those words to make your own compound words.

1. ______________________
2. ______________________
3. ______________________
4. ______________________
5. ______________________

Word Magic

Maggie Magician announced, "One plus one equals one!" The audience giggled. So, Maggie put two words into a hat and waved her magic wand. When she reached into the hat, Maggie pulled out one word and a picture. "See," said Maggie, "I was right!"

Directions: Use the word box to help you write a compound word for each picture below.

ball	door	rain	star	shirt	bell	fish	shoe	book	foot	basket
bow	lace	box	ball	light	sun	cup	mail	tail	cake	worm

____

____

____

____

____

____

____

____

____

____

____

Name ____________________

Prefix re

A **prefix** is a word part. It is added to the beginning of a base word to change the base word's meaning. The prefix **re** means "again."

Example:

Refill means "to fill again."

Directions: Look at the pictures. Read the base words. Add the prefix **re** to the base word to show that the action is being done again. Write your new word on the line.

read

____

write

____

paint

____

use

____

build

____

pay

____

Prefixes un and dis

The prefixes **un** and **dis** mean "not" or "the opposite of."

Unlocked means "not locked."

Dismount is the opposite of "mount."

Directions: Look at the pictures. Circle the word that tells about the picture. Then, write the word on the line.

tied
untied

like
dislike

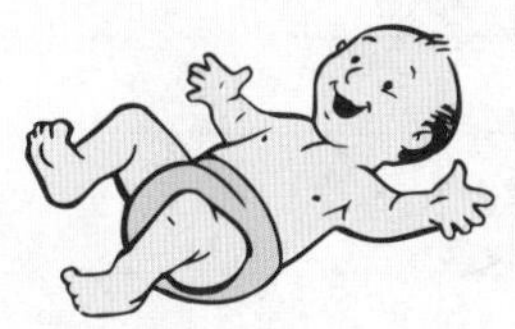

happy
unhappy

obey
disobey

safe
unsafe

honest
dishonest

Name ______________________

Suffixes ful, less, ness, ly

A **suffix** is a word part that is added at the end of a base word to change the base word's meaning. Look at the suffixes below.

The suffix **ful** means "full of." **Cheerful** means "full of cheer."

The suffix **less** means "without." **Cloudless** means "without clouds."

The suffix **ness** means "a state of being." **Darkness** means "being dark."

The suffix **ly** means "in this way." **Slowly** means "in a slow way."

Directions: Add the suffixes to the base words to make new words.

care + ful = ______________________

pain + less = ______________________

brave + ly = ______________________

sad + ly = ______________________

sick + ness = ______________________

Suffixes er and est

Suffixes **er** and **est** can be used to compare. Use **er** when you compare two things. Use **est** when you compare more than two things.

Example: The puppy is small**er** than its mom.
This puppy is the small**est** puppy in the litter.

Directions: Add the suffixes to the base words to make words that compare.

Base Word	+ er	+ est
1. loud	louder	loudest
2. old		
3. neat		
4. fast		
5. kind		
6. tall		

Name ______________________

Scale the Synonym Slope

Synonyms are words that have almost the same meaning. **Tired** and **sleepy** are synonyms. **Talk** and **speak** are synonyms.

Directions: Read the word. Find its synonym on the hill. Write the synonym on the line.

1. glad ______________________
2. little ______________________
3. begin ______________________
4. above ______________________
5. damp ______________________
6. large ______________________

wet

big

happy

over

small

start

Name ____________________

Bored Belinda!

Belinda is bored with using the same words all the time. Help her figure out a new word for the **boldfaced** words in each sentence.

Directions: Read each sentence and then circle the correct new word below.

I hope my grandma will like this **gift**.

present toaster

I always **laugh** when I watch my silly kitten.

chuckle worry

My friend loves to **talk** on the telephone.

draw chat

The little boy was **charming** to his grandparents.

delightful naughty

Can you please **sew** this fabric together?

hitch stitch

Name ______________________

Amazing Antonyms

Antonyms are words that have opposite meanings. **Old** and **new** are antonyms. **Laugh** and **cry** are antonyms, too.

Directions: Below each word, write its antonym. Use words from the word box.

stop

____

happy

____

right

____

up

____

wet

____

Who's Afraid?

Help Frog and Toad escape from the snake.

Directions: Read the two words in each space. If the words are antonyms, color the space **green**. Do not color the other spaces.

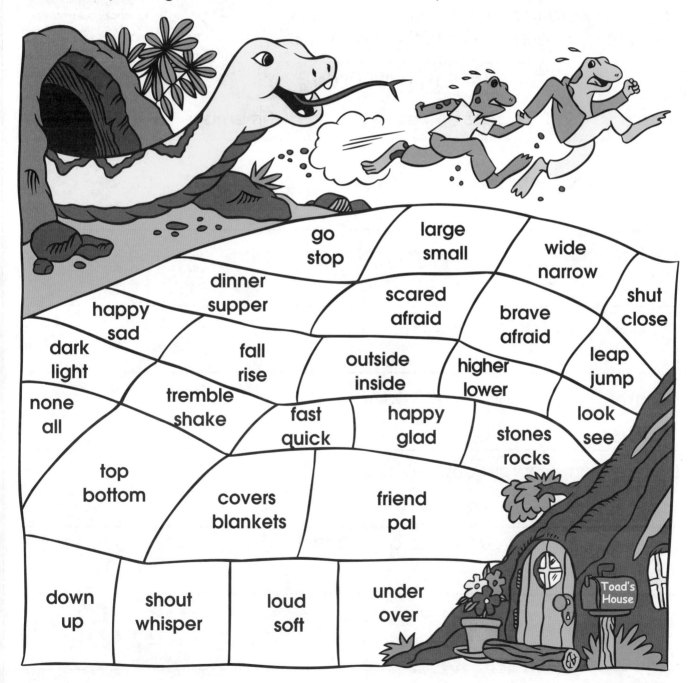

go
stop

large
small

wide
narrow

dinner
supper

scared
afraid

happy
sad

brave
afraid

shut
close

dark
light

fall
rise

outside
inside

higher
lower

leap
jump

none
all

tremble
shake

fast
quick

happy
glad

stones
rocks

look
see

top
bottom

covers
blankets

friend
pal

down
up

shout
whisper

loud
soft

under
over

Toad's
House

Name ____________________

I Meant to Say!

Molly meant to say the **opposite** of what she said in the sentences below.

Directions: Help Molly fix her mistakes by circling the incorrect word in each sentence. Then, choose a word from the word list to replace it. Rewrite the sentence using the new word.

My name is Molly,
not Polly. Molly wants
a cracker. No, not Polly!
My name is Molly!

Word List						
cold	sad	raise	everything	remember	old	soft

It is always hot in the Arctic.

____

The hard cushion was very comfortable.

____

We ate nothing at Thanksgiving.

____

It makes people happy when you frown.

____

It is important to forget people's birthdays.

____

Lower your hand if you want to ask a question.

____

My great-great-grandma is very young.

____

Name ____________________

Antonym or Synonym?

Directions: Use **yellow** to color the spaces that have word pairs that are **antonyms**. Use **blue** to color the spaces that have word pairs that are **synonyms**.

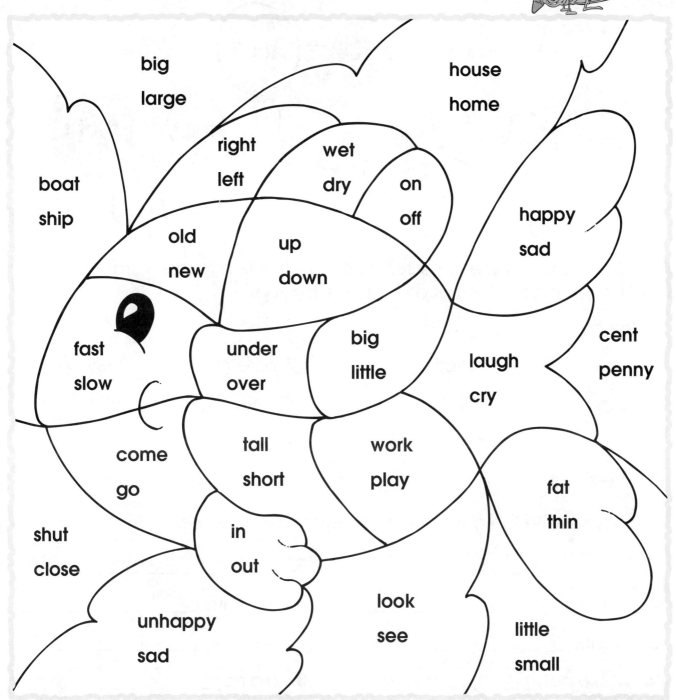

Name ____________________

Contractions

A **contraction** is a word made up of two words joined together with one or more letters left out. An **apostrophe** is used in place of the missing letters.

Examples: I am—**I'm**
do not—**don't**
that is—**that's**

Directions: Draw a line to match each contraction to the words from which it was made. The first one is done for you.

1. he's	we are	6. they'll	are not
2. we're	cannot	7. aren't	they will
3. can't	he is	8. I've	you have
4. I'll	she is	9. you've	will not
5. she's	I will	10. won't	I have

Directions: Write the contraction for each pair of words.

1. you are ____________________
2. does not ____________________
3. do not ____________________
4. would not ____________________
5. she is ____________________
6. we have ____________________
7. has not ____________________
8. did not ____________________

Something Is Missing!

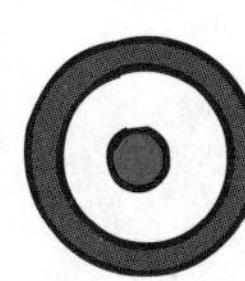

doesn't it's she's
don't aren't who's he's
didn't that's isn't

Directions: Write the correct contraction for each set of words. Then, circle the letter that was left out when the contraction was made.

1. he is ______________________
2. are not ______________________
3. do not ______________________
4. who is ______________________
5. is not ______________________
6. did not ______________________
7. it is ______________________
8. she is ______________________
9. does not ______________________
10. that is ______________________

Directions: Write the missing contraction on the line.

1. ______________________ on her way to school.
2. There ______________________ enough time to finish the story.
3. Do you think ______________________ too long?
4. We ______________________ going to the party.
5. Donna ______________________ like the movie.
6. ______________________ going to try for a part in the play?
7. Bob said ______________________ going to run in the big race.
8. They ______________________ know how to bake a cake.
9. Tom ______________________ want to go skating on Saturday.
10. Look, ______________________ where they found the lost watch.

Name ______________________________

Tooth Tales!

Directions: Read the following information about your teeth.

Did you know that your teeth are made of enamel? Enamel is the hardest material in your entire body. It makes your teeth strong.

There are four different types of teeth in your mouth. Your front four teeth on the top and front four teeth on the bottom are called incisors. Ouch! They are sharp teeth used for biting (for biting food that is, not for biting your brother!).

You have two very pointy teeth on the top and two on the bottom called canines. They are used for foods that are hard to chew.

In the very back of your mouth, you have twelve wide teeth called molars. They are used for grinding food. (These are worth a lot to the Tooth Fairy!)

Finally, you have eight teeth called bicuspids for crushing food.

Adults have thirty-two permanent teeth! That's a lot of teeth, so keep smiling!

Tooth Tales, cont.

Directions: Answer the questions from the story about your teeth.

What are your teeth made of? ____________________
Highlight where you found the answer.

What is the hardest material in your body? ____________________
Highlight where you found the answer.

How many different types of teeth are in your mouth? ____________________
Highlight where you found the answer.

What are your two very pointy teeth called? ____________________
Highlight where you found the answer.

What teeth are used for grinding food? ____________________
(Hint: The Tooth Fairy likes this type of tooth!)
Highlight where you found the answer.

How many teeth do adults have? ____________________
Highlight where you found the answer.

What teeth are used for biting? ____________________
Highlight where you found the answer.

How many molars do people have? ____________________
Highlight where you found the answer.

Name ______________________________

Something's Fruity!

Directions: Find and circle twelve things that are wrong with this picture.

Name ______________________

Clue Caper!

Directions: Read the clues below. Write each child's name under the correct picture. Color the hats using the following clues.

______________ ______________ ______________ ______________

- Anna is tall and wearing a green top hat. There is a red baseball cap on top of her top hat!
- Sara is short and wearing a blue polka dotted hat.
- Talia has long hair and is standing between Anna and Sara. Talia is wearing a pretty ribbon in her hair with a flower on it.
- Kessia is standing next to Sara. She is wearing a white baker's hat with a purple veil!

How many hats do you count on the page? ______________________

Name ____________________

Make the Touchdown!

Directions: Read the directions. Draw a line as you move from space to space.

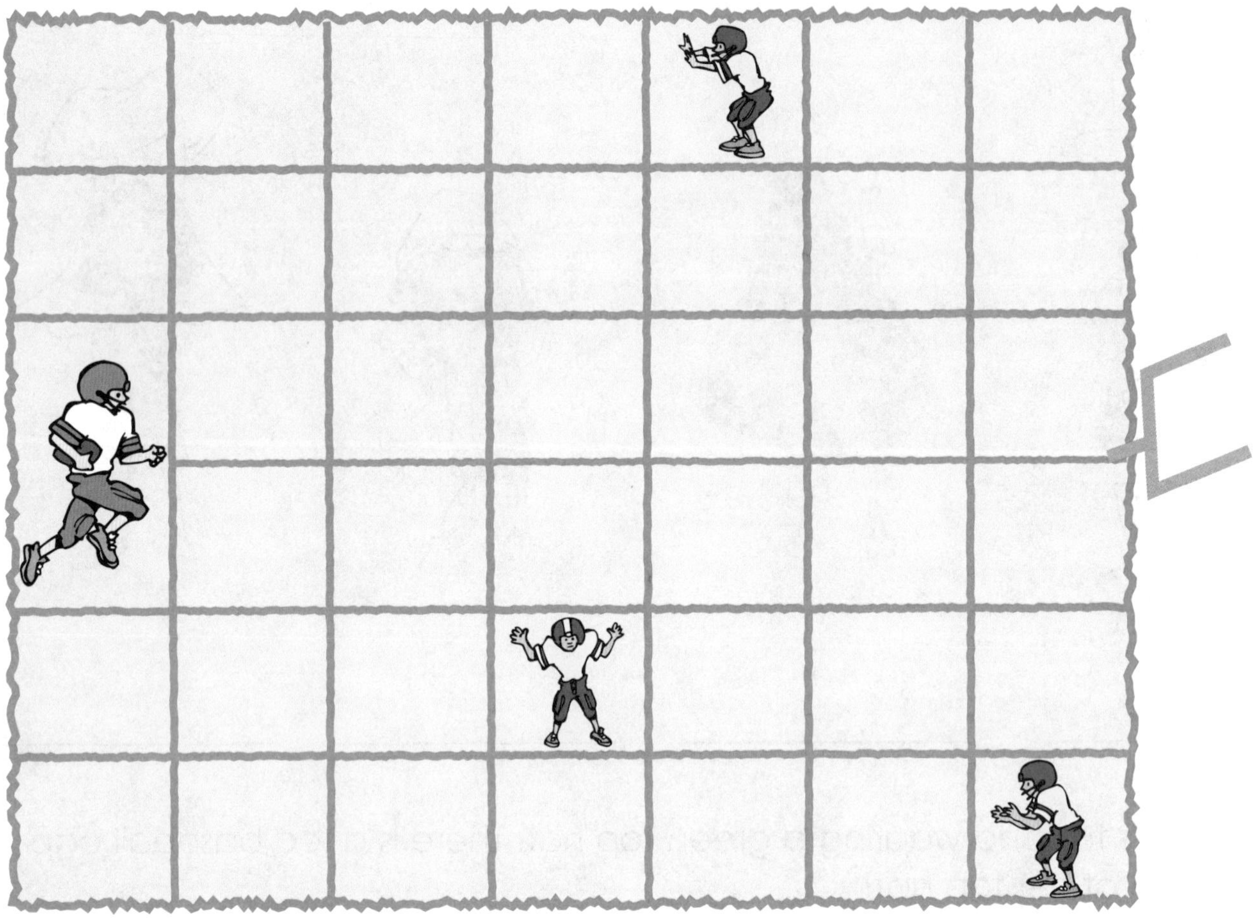

1. Start at the football player running with the football.
2. Go up 2 spaces.
3. Go right 3 spaces. Oops!
4. Now, go down 3 spaces.
5. Hurry and go left 1 space.
6. Turn and go down 2 spaces.
7. Now, quickly turn right and go 3 spaces.
8. You were almost tackled. Go up 3 spaces.
9. Move quickly to the right 1 space.
10. Hurray! You made the touchdown!

Directions: Draw a brown football under the goalpost.

Coach's Call

Directions: Follow the directions to draw and color the football player's uniform.

1. Color the pants yellow with a thin, blue stripe down the outside of each leg.
2. Color the top part of Teddy's socks blue, but leave the bottom part white.
3. Color a large yellow number 83 on the chest of the jersey and two yellow stripes on each sleeve. Then, color the rest of the shirt blue.
4. Draw and color black shoes with white stripes. Draw cleats on the bottom of the shoes.
5. Draw a yellow helmet on his head with a blue stripe down the center. Add a face mask.
6. Draw a brown football in Teddy's left hand. Now he's ready to play!

Name ______________________________

Game Story

Directions: Put the basketball story in order. Write the numbers **1–5** on the blanks to show when each event happened.

_______ At the end of the regulation game, the score was tied.

_______ The teams warmed up before the game.

_______ The score at the half was Cougars, 25; Lions, 20.

_______ Kim made the first basket of the game.

_______ When the overtime ended, the Lions had won the game 50–49.

Name ________________________________

Story Sequence

Look at picture number 4. What do you think happened before Donna went to the beach? What might happen when she is at the beach?

Directions: You get to decide how the story will go from beginning to end. Write a number in the empty square in each of the other pictures. Choose any number from 1 through 7 (except 4). Number 1 will be what happened first. Number 7 will be what you think happened last.

4

SMACKY FLAKES

Name ____________________

Same/Different: Shell Homes

Read the story about shells.

Shells are the homes of some animals. Snails live in shells on the land. Clams live in shells in the water. Clam shells open. Snail shells stay closed. Both shells keep the animals safe.

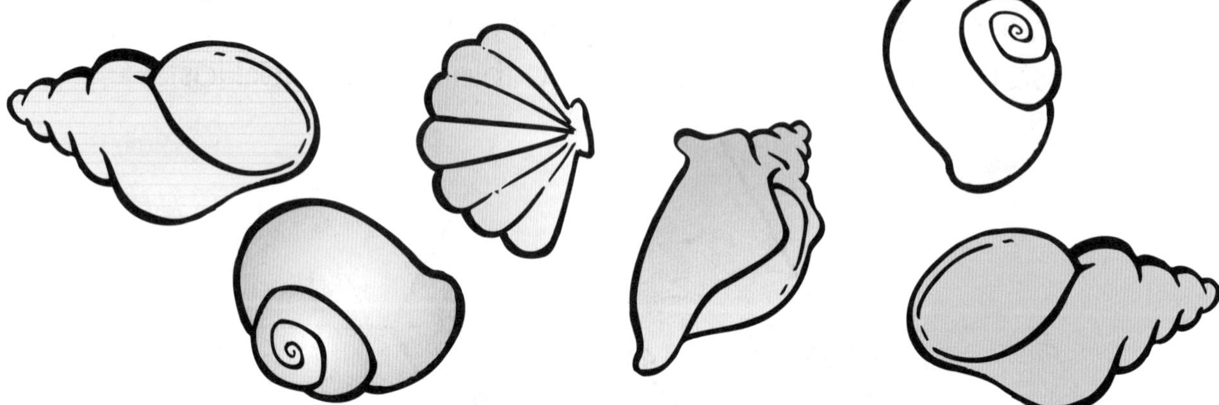

Directions: Answer the questions. For numbers 1 and 2, circle the correct answer.

1. Snails live in shells on the
   water. land.

2. Clam shells are different from snail shells because
   they open.
   they stay closed.

3. Write one way all shells are the same. ____________________

____

____

Name ______________________

Same/Different: Venn Diagram

A **Venn diagram** is a diagram that shows how two things are the same and different.

Directions: Choose two outdoor sports. Then, follow the instructions to complete the Venn diagram.

1. Write the first sport name under the first circle. Write some words that describe the sport. Write them in the first circle.
2. Write the second sport name under the second circle. Write some words that describe the sport. Write them in the second circle.
3. Where the 2 circles overlap, write some words that describe both sports.

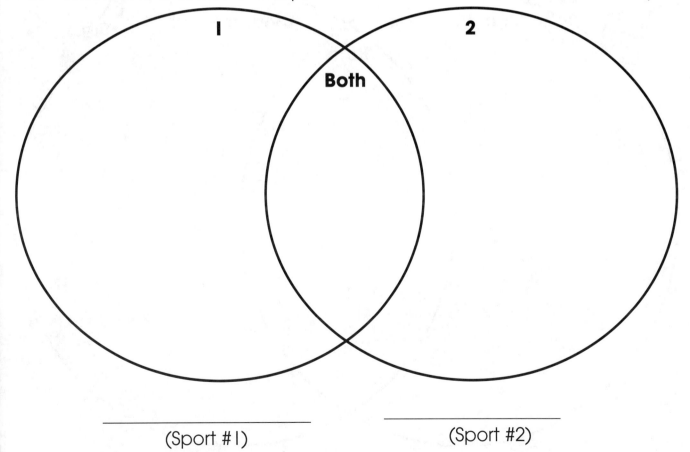

1

Both

2

____

(Sport #1)

____

(Sport #2)

Name ______________________________

Same/Different: Dina and Dina

Directions: Read the story. Then, complete the Venn diagram, telling how Dina, the duck, is the same or different than Dina, the girl.

One day in the library, Dina found a story about a duck named Dina!

My name is Dina. I am a duck, and I like to swim. When I am not swimming, I walk on land or fly. I have two feet and two eyes. My feathers keep me warm. Ducks can be different colors. I am gray, brown, and black. I really like being a duck. It is fun.

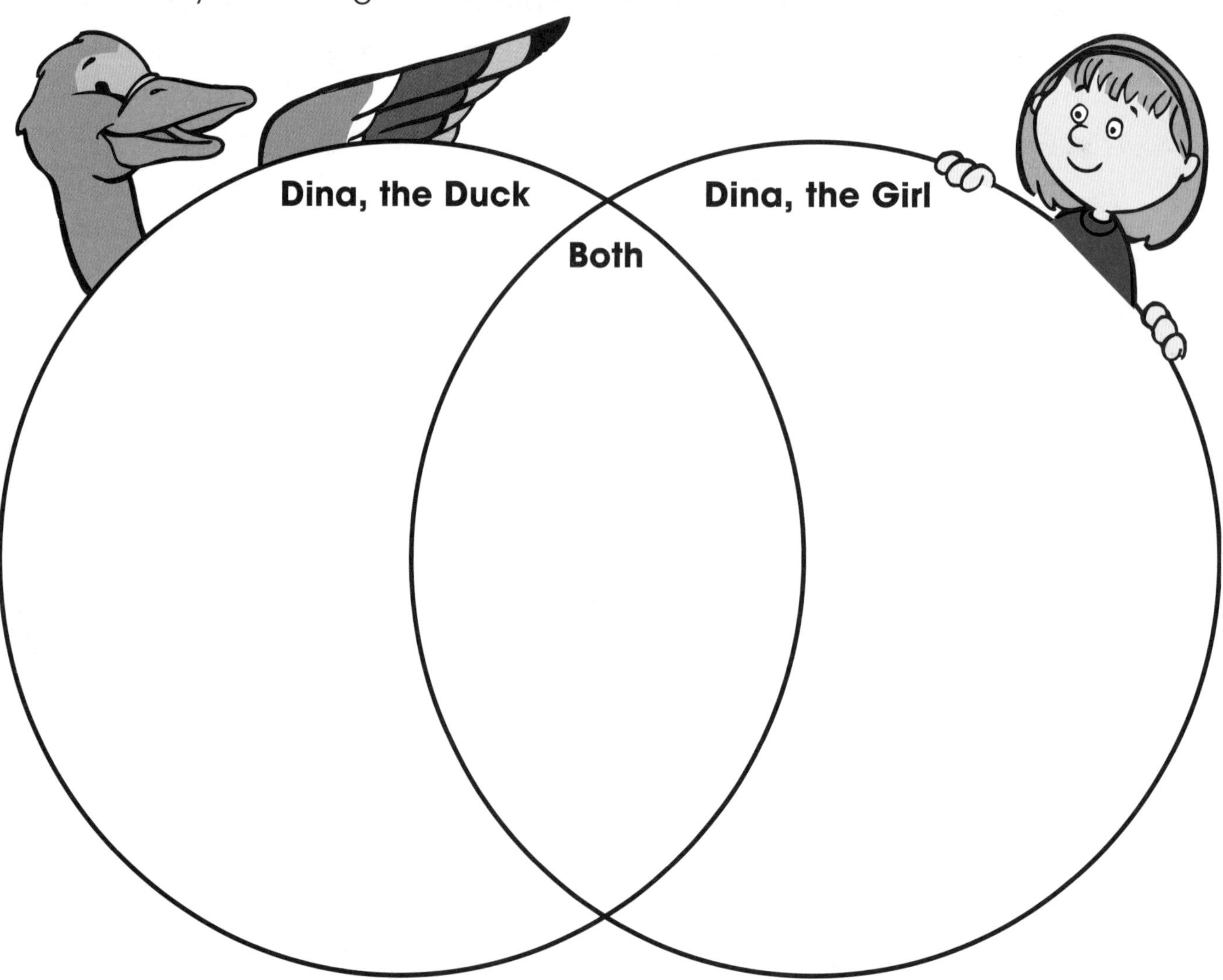

Same/Different: Marvin and Mugsy

Directions: Read about Marvin and Mugsy. Then, complete the Venn diagram, telling how they are the same and different.

Marcy has two dogs, Marvin and Mugsy. Marvin is a black-and-white spotted Dalmatian. Marvin likes to run after balls in the backyard. His favorite food is Canine Crunchy Crunch. Marcy likes to take Marvin for walks, because dogs need exercise. Marvin loves to sleep in his doghouse. Mugsy is a big, furry brown dog, who wiggles when she is happy. Since she is big, she needs lots of exercise. So, Marcy takes her for walks in the park. Her favorite food is Canine Crunchy Crunch. Mugsy likes to sleep on Marcy's bed.

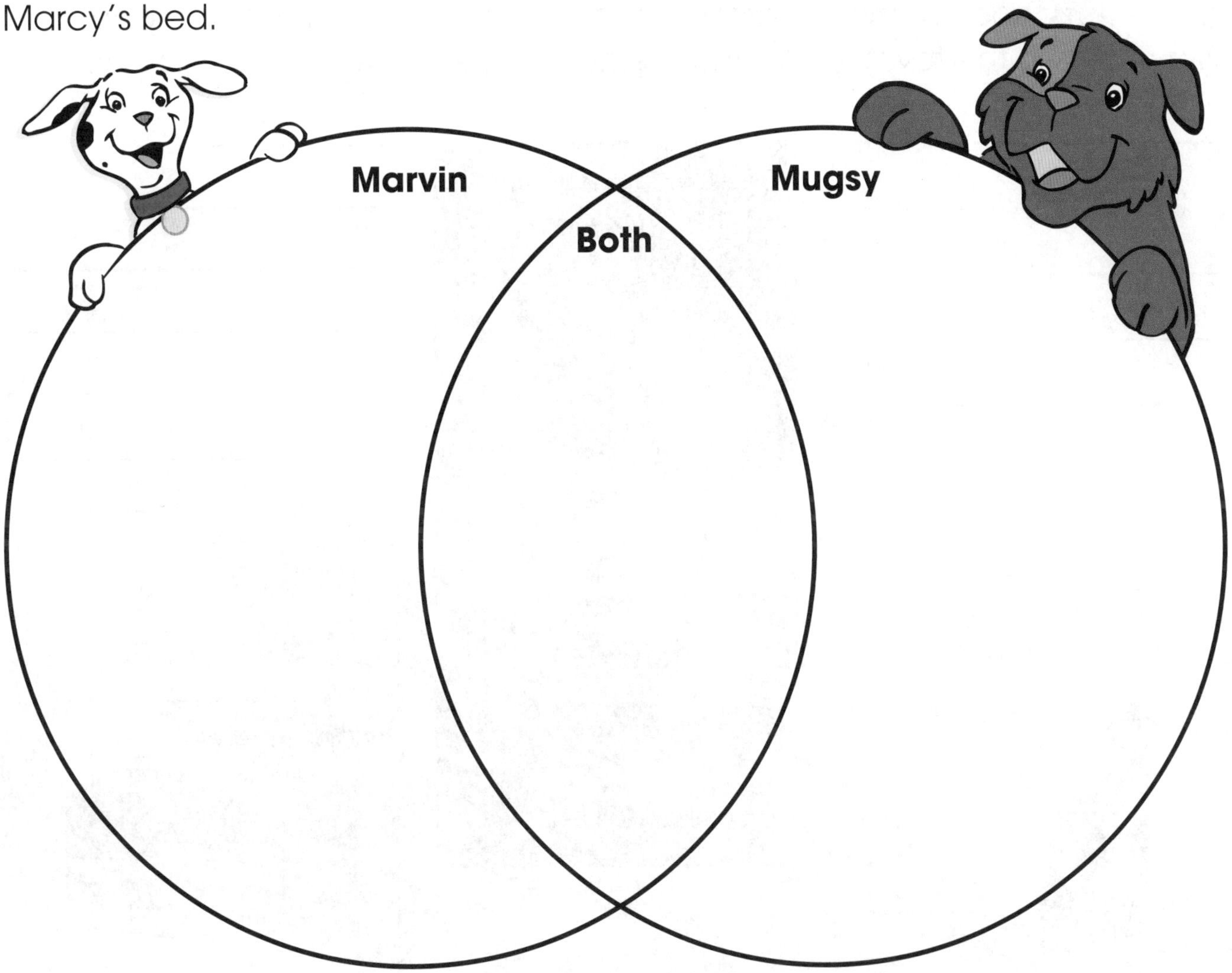

Marvin | **Both** | **Mugsy**

Name ______________________________

Classifying

Sometimes, you want to put things in groups. One way to put things in groups is to sort them by how they are alike. When you put things together that are alike in some way, you classify them.

You can classify the things in your room. In one group, you can put toys and fun things. In the other group, you can put things that you wear.

Directions: Look at the words on the bedroom door. Put the toys and playthings in the toy box. Put the things you wear in the dresser drawers.

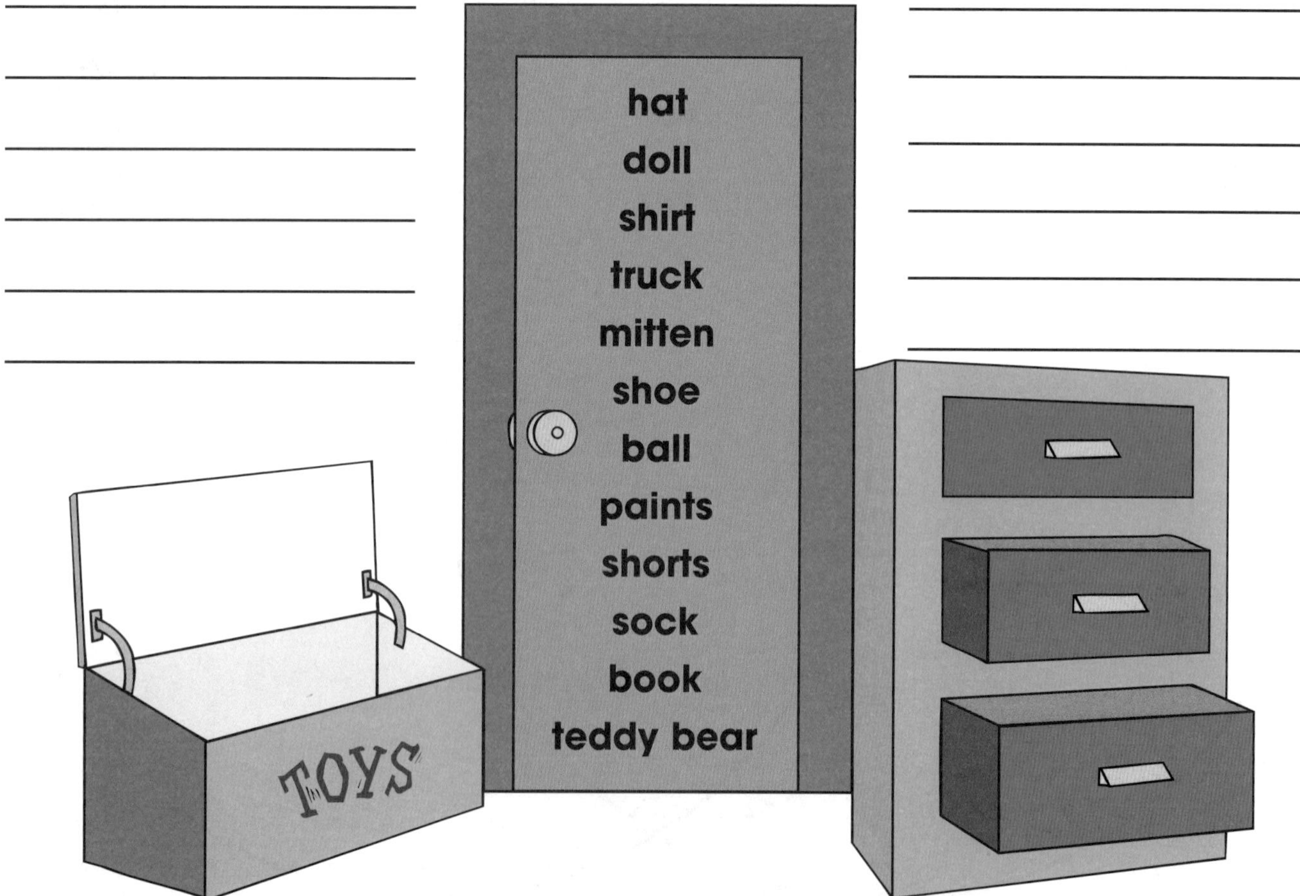

hat
doll
shirt
truck
mitten
shoe
ball
paints
shorts
sock
book
teddy bear
TOYS

Name ______________________

Running! Jumping! Throwing!

To be a strong athlete in track and field events you must be good at running, jumping, and throwing. Many track and field words are listed below.

Directions: Write the words under the correct track and field event.

Running	Jumping	Throwing
______	______	______
______	______	______
______	______	______
______	______	______
______	______	______
______	______	______
______	______	______

lap javelin high jump baton relay long jump
discus cross country broad jump shot put
track pole vault hurdles triple jump hammer

Name ____________________

All Animals

There are many kinds of animals. Three kinds of animals are mammals, birds, and reptiles.

Mammals have fur or hair. Baby mammals drink milk from their mothers' bodies. A whale is a mammal.

Birds are the only animals that have feathers. A robin is a bird.

Reptiles have scaly skin. Most reptiles lay eggs on the land. An alligator is a reptile.

Directions: Read the sentences below. Is the animal in the sentence a mammal, bird, or reptile? Put an **M** on the line if it is a mammal, a **B** if it is a bird, or an **R** if it is a reptile.

___ **1.** Maggie brushes her horse's coat.

___ **2.** The turtle lays its eggs in the sand.

___ **3.** Adam cleans the feathers from his pet's cage.

___ **4.** The baby penguin hides in its father's feathers to stay warm.

___ **5.** The piglets drink their mother's milk.

___ **6.** The scaly skin on the snake is dry.

___ **7.** A blue jay has blue feathers.

___ **8.** The bunny pulls fur from her body to build a nest.

Name ______________________

Baby Animal Names

Many animals are called special names when they are young. A baby deer is called a fawn. A baby cat is called a kitten.

Some young animals have the same name as other kinds of baby animals. A baby elephant is a calf. A baby whale is a calf. A baby giraffe is a calf. A baby cow is a calf.

Some baby animals are called cubs. A baby lion, a baby bear, a baby tiger, and a baby fox are all called cubs.

Some baby animals are called colts. A young horse is a colt. A baby zebra is a colt. A baby donkey is a colt.

Directions: Use the story about baby animal names to complete the chart below. Write the kind of animal that belongs with each special baby name.

calf	cub	colt

Name ____________________

Winter Sleepers

Directions: Read about hibernation. Then, complete page 95.

As days grow shorter and it gets colder, some animals get ready for their winter's sleep. This winter's sleep is called hibernation. Scientists do not know all the secrets of hibernating animals. They do know enough to put hibernating animals into two groups. One group is called "true hibernators." The other group is called "light sleepers."

True hibernators go into a very deep sleep. To get ready for this long winter's sleep, true hibernators will eat and eat so they become fat. As these animals sleep, their body temperature drops below normal. If the animal gets too cold, it will shiver to warm itself. The breathing of true hibernators slows so much that they hardly seem to breathe at all.

True hibernators are animals such as woodchucks, some ground squirrels, the jumping mouse, brown bat, frogs, and snapping turtles.

Light sleepers include skunks, raccoons, the eastern chipmunk, and the grizzly bear.

Some light sleepers will store up food to have during winter while others will eat and become fat. A big difference between light sleepers and true hibernators is that the light sleeper's body temperature drops only a little, and its breathing only slows. These animals are easy to wake and may even get up if the temperature warms. They then go back to sleep when it becomes colder again.

Name ________________________________

Winter Sleepers, cont.

Directions: Read all of the word groups. Then, place them under the correct hibernation type. Use the story on page 94.

will shiver to warm itself
body temperature drops a little
hardly breathes at all
seems more dead than alive
moves about and then goes back to sleep
breathing only slows
easily awakens
body temperature drops far below normal

True Hibernator

____

____

____

____

Light Sleeper

____

____

____

____

Name ______________________

Use the Clues

Context clues can help you figure out words you do not know. Read the words around the new word. Think of a word that makes sense.

Kate swam in a ______?______.

Did Kate swim in a cake or a lake? The word **swim** is a context clue.

Directions: Kate wrote this letter from camp. Read the letter. Use context clues to write the missing words from the word box. What clues did you use?

lake	six
pancakes	forest

Dear Mom and Dad,

I woke up at ______________ o'clock and got dressed. My friends and I ate ______________ for breakfast. We went hiking in the ______________. Then, we went swimming in the ______________. Camp is fun!

Love,
Kate

Context Clues in Action

Directions: Read the story. Use context clues to figure out the meanings of the **boldfaced** words. Draw a line from the word to its meaning. The first one is done for you.

Jack has a plan. He wants to take his parents out to lunch to show that he **appreciates** all the nice things they do for him. His sister Jessica will go, too, so she won't feel left out. Jack is **thrifty**. He saves the **allowance** he earns for doing **chores** around the house. So far, Jack has saved ten dollars. He needs only five dollars more. He is excited about paying the check himself. He will feel like an **adult**.

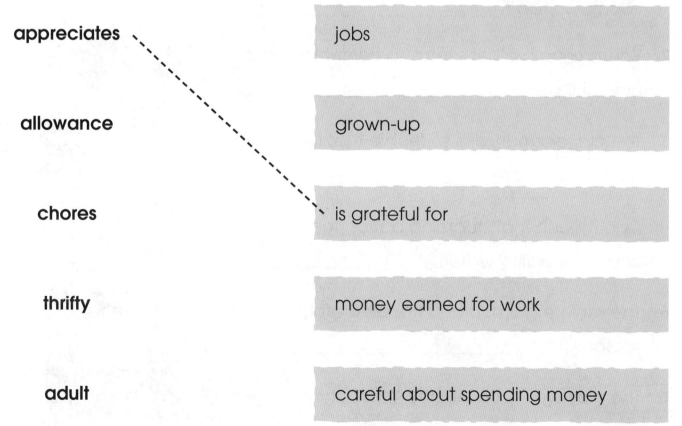

appreciates	jobs
allowance	grown-up
chores	is grateful for
thrifty	money earned for work
adult	careful about spending money

Name ______________________

Chris's Context Clues

Context clues can help you figure out the meaning of a word just by looking at the **other words** in the sentence.

Directions: Read each sentence below. Circle the context clues. Choose a word from the word list to replace each word in **bold**. Write it on the line.

Word List

long	extra	happy
weak	hot	limped

1. I have lost my pen. Do you have a **spare** one I could borrow? ______________

2. Your smiling brother seems so **content** with his new birthday toy. ______________

3. The old, old man was so **feeble** that he looked like he would break! ______________

4. Don't touch that steaming pot on the stove! It is full of **scalding** water! ______________

5. The athlete got hurt and **hobbled** off the football field. ______________

6. The play was quite **lengthy**. I thought it would never end! ______________

Chris's Context Clues, cont.

Context clues can help you figure out the meaning of a word just by looking at the **other words** in the sentence.

Directions: Read each sentence below. Circle the context clues. Choose a word from the word list to replace each word in **bold**. Write it on the line.

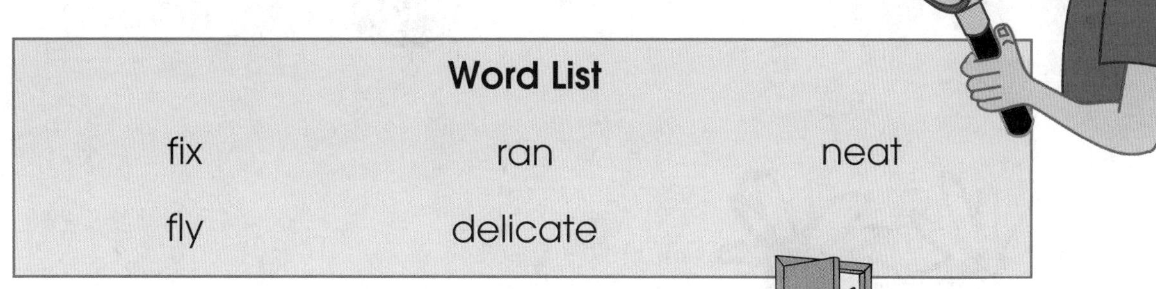

Word List		
fix	ran	neat
fly	delicate	

1. The boy is very **tidy**. He always puts away his toys. ______________________

2. The athletes were like cheetahs. They **sprinted** to the finish line! ______________________

3. A hawk can **soar** very high. ______________

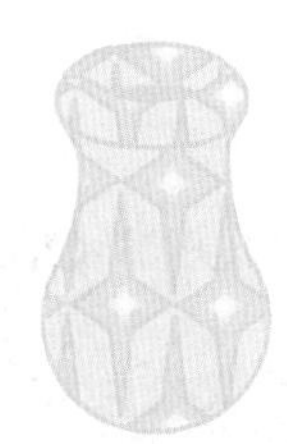

4. I didn't even want to touch the **fragile** crystal vase. ________________

5. If you broke it, you need to **repair** it.

____

Name ______________________

Comprehension: Ladybugs

Directions: Read about ladybugs. Then, answer the questions.

Have you ever seen a ladybug? Ladybugs are red. They have black spots. They have six legs. Ladybugs are pretty!

1. What color are ladybugs? ______________

2. What color are their spots? ______________

3. How many legs do ladybugs have? ______________

Comprehension: Singing Whales

Directions: Read about singing whales. Then, follow the instructions.

Some whales can sing! We cannot understand the words. But we can hear the tune of the humpback whale. Each season, humpback whales sing a different song.

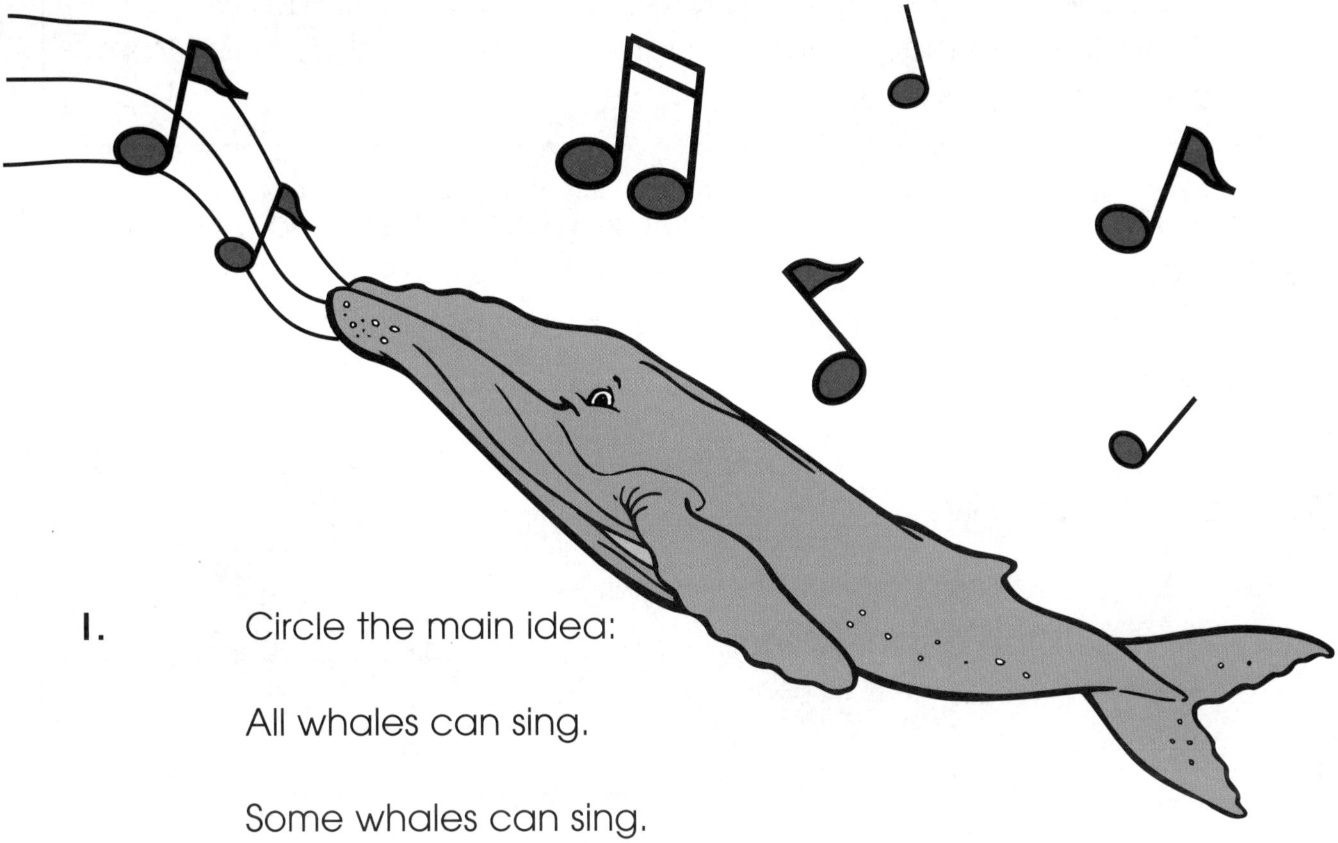

1. Circle the main idea:

   All whales can sing.

   Some whales can sing.

2. Name the kind of whale that sings.

   ____

3. How many different songs does the humpback whale sing each year?

   1　　2　　3　　4

Name ______________________

Hermit Crabs

The hermit crab lives in a shell in or near the ocean. It does not make its own shell. It moves into a shell left by another sea animal. As the hermit crab grows, it gets too big for its shell. It will hunt for a new shell. It will feel the new shell with its claw. If the shell feels just right, the crab will leave its old shell and move into the bigger one. It might even take a shell away from another hermit crab.

Directions: Read about hermit crabs. Use what you learn to finish the sentences.

1. This story is mostly about the ______________________.

2. The hermit crab lives ______________________.

3. When it gets too big for its shell, it will ______________________.

4. The crab will feel the shell with its ______________________.

5. It might take a shell away from ______________________.

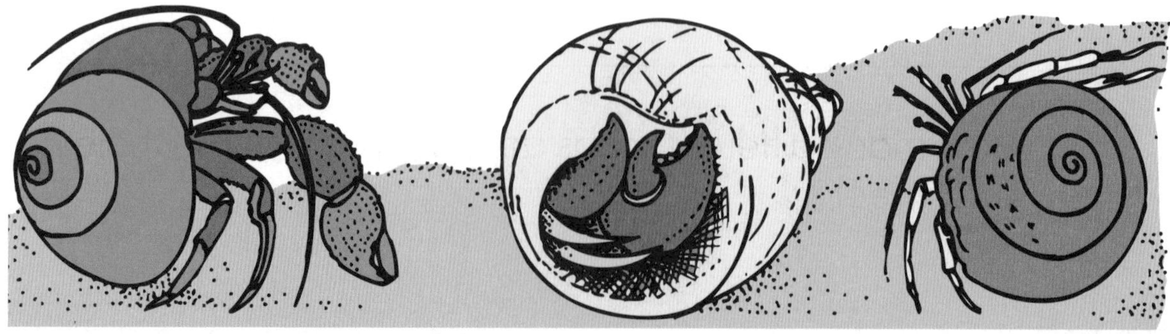

Name ______________________________

The Statue of Liberty

The Statue of Liberty is a symbol of the United States. It stands for freedom. It is the tallest statue in the United States.

The statue is of a woman wearing a robe. She is holding a torch in her right hand. She is holding a book in her left hand. She is wearing a crown. The Statue of Liberty was a gift from the country of France.

Each year, people come from all over the world to visit the statue. Not only do they look at it, they can also go inside the statue. At one time, visitors could go all the way up into the arm. In 1916, the arm was closed to visitors because it was too dangerous. The Statue of Liberty is located on an island in New York Harbor.

Directions: Read the facts above. Then, read each sentence below. If it is true, put a **T** on the line. If it is false, put an **F** on the line.

_____ **1.** The Statue of Liberty is a symbol of the United States.

_____ **2.** People cannot go inside the statue.

_____ **3.** The statue was a gift from Mexico.

_____ **4.** People used to be able to climb up into the statue's arm.

_____ **5.** It is a very short statue.

_____ **6.** The woman statue has a torch in her right hand.

_____ **7.** People come from all over to see the statue.

Name ____________________

Venus Flytraps

Many insects eat plants. There is one kind of plant that eats insects. It is the Venus flytrap. The Venus flytrap works like a trap. Each leaf is shaped like a circle. The circle is in two parts. When the leaf closes, the two parts fold together. The leaf has little spikes all the way around it. Inside the leaf, there are little hairs. If an insect touches the little hairs, the two sides of the Venus flytrap leaf will clap together. The spikes will trap the insect inside. The Venus flytrap will then eat the insect.

Directions: Read about the Venus flytrap. Then, read each sentence below. If it is true, circle the sentence. If it is **not** true, draw an **X** on the sentence.

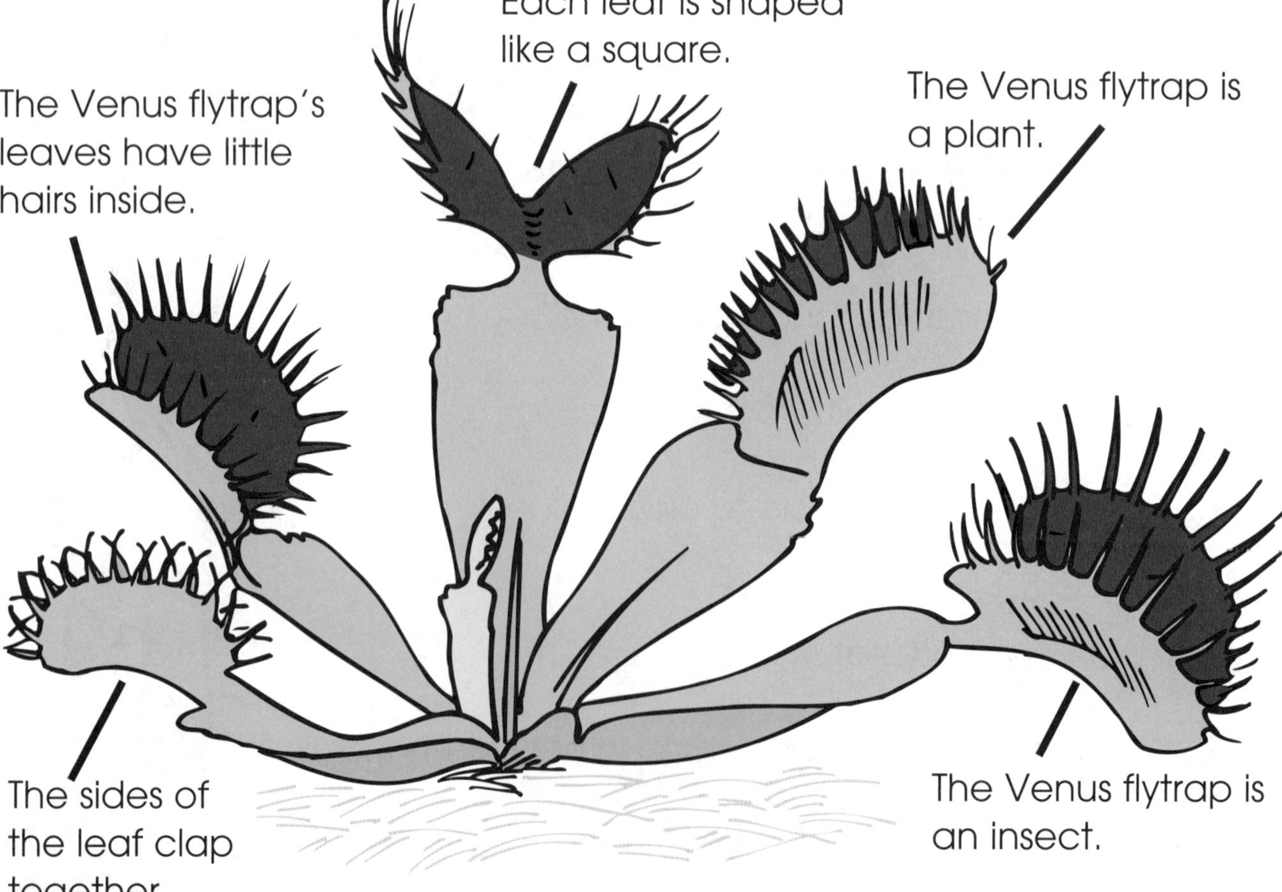

Each leaf is shaped like a square.
The Venus flytrap's leaves have little hairs inside.
The Venus flytrap is a plant.
The sides of the leaf clap together.
The Venus flytrap is an insect.

Name ____________________

Sticklebacks

Sticklebacks are small fish. They have small spines along their backs. The spines keep other fish from trying to swallow them.

Stickleback fish are odd because the male builds the nest for the eggs. He makes the nest out of water plants and sticks. He makes it in the shape of a barrel and glues it together. He uses a thread-like material from his body to glue the nest together.

When the nest is ready, the mother fish comes. She lays her eggs and goes away. The father stays by the nest and guards the eggs. After the eggs hatch, he stays with the baby fish for a few days. If other sea animals try to eat the baby sticklebacks, he will fight them. He keeps the baby fish safe until they can care for themselves.

Directions: Read about the stickleback fish. Use the story to help pick the correct answers to fill in the blanks. Circle the correct answer.

1. The story is mostly about ____.

   spines   enemy sea animals   stickleback fish

2. The stickleback is unusual because ____.

   the female lays eggs   the male builds a nest   the eggs are in the nest

3. The nest is made of ____.

   mud and grass   water plants and sticks   string and glue

4. If an animal tries to eat the baby fish, the stickleback father will ____.

   fight it off   swim away   jump out of the water

Name ______________________________

Eagles

Eagles are large birds. They eat small animals such as mice and rabbits. Eagles make their nests in high places such as the tops of trees. Their nests are made of sticks, weeds, and dirt. Eagles can live in the same nest for many years.

The mother eagle lays one or two eggs each year. When she sits on the eggs, the father eagle brings her food. Baby eagles are called *eaglets*.

Directions: Read about eagles. Then, circle the correct ending to each sentence below.

1. Eagles are

   large dogs.   large birds.

2. Eagles eat

   small animals.

   plants and trees.

3. Eagles

   build a nest each year.

   live in the same nest for many years.

4. The mother eagle lays

   one or two eggs.

   three or four eggs.

5. Baby eagles are called

   igloos.   eaglets.

Name ______________________

Seals

Seals live in the oceans and on land. They eat different kinds of sea animals, such as fish, shrimp, squid, and krill. They are very good swimmers. They use their flippers to help them move in the water and on the land. They talk to each other by making barking sounds.

Directions: Read the facts above. Then, answer each question using complete sentences.

1. What do seals eat? ______________________

____

2. For what do seals use their flippers? ______________________

____

3. Where do seals live? ______________________

____

4. How do seals talk? ______________________

____

Name ______________________

Main Idea

The **main idea** tells about the **whole picture**.

Directions: Which sentence tells the main idea of the picture? Fill in the circle next to the correct answer.

○ The dog is happy.

○ The dog is hot.

○ The garden was in bloom.

○ The garden was messy.

○ I have a new sister.

○ I want to be a babysitter.

○ I met my new teacher.

○ This is the last day of school.

○ The juggler needed practice.

○ The juggler likes scrambled eggs.

Main Idea

The **main idea** tells about the **whole picture**.

Directions: Which sentence tells the main idea of the picture? Fill in the circle next to the correct answer.

○ She saw a shooting star.

○ She likes to climb hills.

○ She likes to stay up late.

○ Skateboarding can be done anywhere.

○ Skateboarding is easy.

○ Skateboarders should wear helmets.

○ Grandpa is a great storyteller.

○ Grandpa is boring.

○ Grandpa is funny.

○ Mom made me a birthday cake.

○ We ate ice cream.

○ I opened presents.

Name ________________

What's the Idea?

Directions: Look at the pictures. Read the sentences in the speech balloons. Fill in the circle beside the sentence that tells the main idea.

My tummy hurts.

○ The mouse wants more to eat.

○ The mouse ate too much cheese.

My hat is blowing away.

○ It is a very windy day.

○ He doesn't want a hat.

I am seven years old today.

○ The cake is very big.

○ Today is her birthday.

I can't find my home.

○ The cat is lost.

○ The cat has a new home.

Read All About It

Directions: Read each part of the paper. Fill in the circle beside the sentence that tells the main idea.

Hundreds Enjoy Town Carnival

○ Many people had fun at the carnival.

○ The carnival was not a success.

Bank Robbers

Caught

○ Five bank robbers got away.

○ Two bank robbers were caught.

CLASSIFIEDS

For Sale

3 black kittens
2 brown puppies

Call
555-4109

○ Someone wants to buy kittens and puppies.

○ Someone wants to sell kittens and puppies.

Garden Club to Meet

Wednesday and Thursday This Week

○ The Garden Club will not meet this week.

○ The Garden Club will meet two times this week.

Name ________________

What's the Main Idea?

The **main idea** tells about the **whole story**.

Directions: Read the story below.

Visiting the city zoo with my class was a lot of fun. Everyone in my class got to pet the llamas. Next, we were given a bag of peanuts to feed the elephants. Finally, we were allowed to take pictures in front of the monkeys' cage. Then, my teacher made a joke. She said she had never seen so much monkeying around!

Read each sentence below and decide whether it tells the main idea. Write **yes** or **no**.

Finally, we were allowed to take pictures in front of the monkeys' cage. ________________

Then, my teacher made a joke. ________________

Next, we were given a bag of peanuts to feed the elephants. ________________

Visiting the city zoo with my class was a lot of fun. ________________

Write the one sentence that tells the main idea:

____

____

The Marvelous Miss Madison!

Miss Madison loves to cook with chocolate chips. She puts chocolate chips in everything she makes! She doesn't make just pancakes, she makes chocolate chip pancakes! When she makes peanut butter sandwiches, she adds chocolate chips. When she heats up hot chocolate (you guessed it!), she adds chocolate chips! Miss Madison could not imagine cooking without chocolate chips!

Directions: What is the main idea of this story? Fill in the circle next to the correct answer.

- ◯ Miss Madison likes to eat.
- ◯ Miss Madison loves to cook with chocolate chips.
- ◯ Miss Madison makes pancakes with chocolate chips.

What is one thing Miss Madison makes with chocolate chips?

- ◯ sandwiches
- ◯ hamburgers
- ◯ muffins

Name ____________________

What Doesn't Belong?

Directions: Read the sentences under each title. Cross out the sentence that does not tell about the main idea.

Fun at the Playground

He runs to the slide.

She plays on the swings.

I clean my room.

They climb the monkey bars.

We sit on the seesaw.

Doing My Homework

I open my book.

I take a bath.

I read the book.

I write the words.

I add the numbers.

Going to the Zoo

The monkeys climb the trees.

The seals eat fish.

The snakes move slowly.

The kitten plays with yarn.

The zebra runs fast.

Eating Dinner

Mother cuts the meat.

Father chews the corn.

Sister drinks the milk.

Brother eats his peas.

Grandmother has a big house.

Name ______________________________

Main Ideas About Meals

Directions: Read each story to find the main idea. Fill in the circle beside the phrase that tells the main idea.

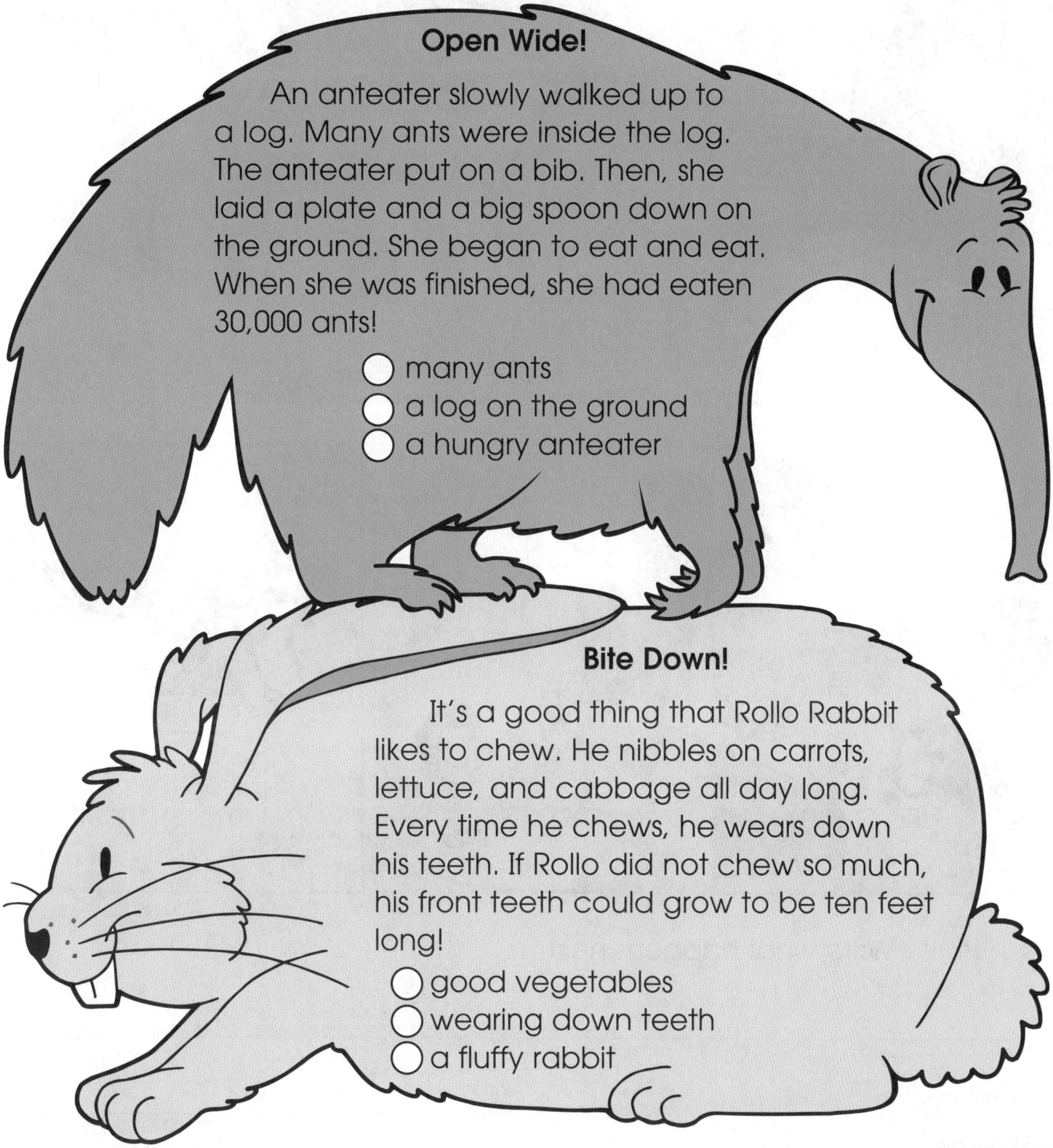

Open Wide!

An anteater slowly walked up to a log. Many ants were inside the log. The anteater put on a bib. Then, she laid a plate and a big spoon down on the ground. She began to eat and eat. When she was finished, she had eaten 30,000 ants!

- ◯ many ants
- ◯ a log on the ground
- ◯ a hungry anteater

Bite Down!

It's a good thing that Rollo Rabbit likes to chew. He nibbles on carrots, lettuce, and cabbage all day long. Every time he chews, he wears down his teeth. If Rollo did not chew so much, his front teeth could grow to be ten feet long!

- ◯ good vegetables
- ◯ wearing down teeth
- ◯ a fluffy rabbit

Name ______________________

What Will Happen Next?

Directions: Write what happens next:

____

____

Name ______________________

What's Next?

Directions: Draw a picture of what will happen next in the boxes below:

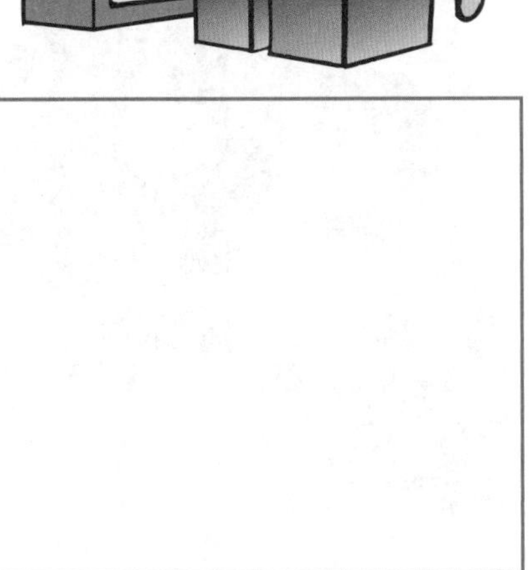

Name ____________________

What Happens Next?

Directions: Read each paragraph. Predict what will happen next by placing an **X** in front of the best answer.

1. Robin went hiking with her friend. It was very hot outside. In the distance, they saw a blue glimmering lake.

____ They turned around and went home.

____ They yelled for help.

____ They waded into the cool water.

2. Jack and Tina are brother and sister. They love to watch basketball games. They also like to practice basketball in their driveway. Their grandma wants to get them the best birthday present ever. What should she get them?

____ Four pairs of shoes.

____ Season tickets to see the Los Angeles Lakers.

____ A new video game.

Name ______________________

What Will They Do?

Directions: Read each sentence. Fill in the circle beside the best prediction. Then, circle the picture that matches your answer.

The boy is putting on his skates.

◯ He will go swimming.

◯ He will go skating.

The girl fills her glass with milk.

◯ She will drink the milk.

◯ She will drink water.

The woman wrote a letter to her friend.

◯ She will call her friend on the phone.

◯ She will put the letter in the mailbox.

The kids gave Sally a birthday gift.

◯ She will open the gift.

◯ She will throw the gift away.

Name ____________________

How Will It End?

Directions: Read each story. Fill in the circle beside the sentence that tells what will happen next.

It is a snowy winter night. The lights flicker once, twice, and then they go out. It is cold and dark. Dad finds the flashlight and matches. He brings logs in from outside. What will Dad do?

- ◯ Dad will make a fire.
- ◯ Dad will cook dinner.
- ◯ Dad will clean the fireplace.

Maggie has a garden. She likes fresh, homegrown vegetables. She says they make salads taste better. Maggie is going to make a salad for a picnic. What will Maggie do?

- ◯ Maggie will buy the salad at the store.
- ◯ Maggie will buy the vegetables at the store.
- ◯ Maggie will use vegetables from her garden.

The big white goose wakes up. It stands and stretches its wings. It looks all around. It feels very hungry. What will the goose do?

- ◯ The goose will go swimming.
- ◯ The goose will look for food.
- ◯ The goose will go back to sleep.

Name ______________________________

Boa Constrictors

Boa constrictors are very big. They may grow up to 14 feet (4.3 meters) long. A boa kills its prey by squeezing it. Then, the prey is swallowed.

Boas do not eat cows or other large animals. They do eat animals that are larger than their own heads. The bones in their jaws stretch so they can swallow small animals such as rodents and birds.

Boa constrictors hunt while hanging from trees. They watch for their prey. Then, they attack. After eating, they may sleep for a week. Boas do not need to eat often. They can live without food for many months.

Boas are not poisonous. They defend themselves by striking and biting with their sharp teeth.

Boa constrictors give birth to live baby snakes. They do not lay eggs. They may have up to fifty baby snakes at one time.

Directions: Use facts from the story to help predict what will happen. Fill in the circle next the correct answer.

1. A boa is hanging from a tree. Suddenly, a bird hops under it. The boa will ____.

   ○ strike and bite it ○ poison it, then eat it

   ○ squeeze it, then swallow it ○ sleep for a week

2. The boa is hungry and hunting for food. Which type of prey will the snake most likely eat?

   ○ cow ○ panther ○ horse ○ mouse

3. A boa constrictor is slithering through the grass. Out of the grass comes a hunter walking toward it. The boa will probably ____.

   ○ strike the hunter ○ squeeze and kill the hunter

   ○ slither up a tree to sleep ○ poison the hunter

Name ________________________

Fact or Opinion?

In sports, there are many facts and opinions. A **fact** is something that is true. An **opinion** is a belief someone has about something.

Directions: Read the sports sentences below. Next to each sentence, write **F** if it is a fact and **O** if it is an opinion.

1. _______ In bowling, a poodle is a ball that rolls down the gutter.
2. _______ I think poodles are cute.
3. _______ Julio is my favorite football player.
4. _______ A football player is a person who plays in a football game.
5. _______ A catcher's mask protects the catcher's face.
6. _______ My catcher's mask is too tight.
7. _______ I had a great putt!
8. _______ A putt is when a golfer hits the ball into the hole on a green.
9. _______ A referee is a person who enforces the rules in a game.
10. _______ Josh thought the referee did a good job.
11. _______ This silly javelin is really hard to throw!
12. _______ A metal spear that is thrown for a distance is called a javelin.
13. _______ Jake said, "The defense tried its best to block the ball."

Name ___________________________

Fact and Opinion: Games!

A **fact** is something that can be proven. An **opinion** is a feeling or belief about something and cannot be proven.

Directions: Read these sentences about different games. Then, write **F** next to each fact and **O** next to each opinion.

_____ 1. Tennis is cool!

_____ 2. There are red and black markers in a Checkers game.

_____ 3. In football, a touchdown is worth six points.

_____ 4. Being a goalie in soccer is easy.

_____ 5. A yo-yo moves on a string.

_____ 6. June's sister looks like the queen on the card.

_____ 7. The six kids need three more players for a baseball team.

_____ 8. Table tennis is more fun than court tennis.

_____ 9. Hide-and-Seek is a game that can be played outdoors or indoors.

_____ 10. Play money is used in many board games.

Name ____________________

Fact and Opinion: A Bounty of Birds

Directions: Read the story. Then, follow the instructions.

Tashi's family likes to go to the zoo. Her favorite animals are all the different kinds of birds. Tashi likes birds because they can fly, they have colorful feathers, and they make funny noises.

Write **F** next to each fact and **O** next to each opinion.

_____ **1.** Birds have two feet.

_____ **2.** All birds lay eggs.

_____ **3.** Parrots are too noisy.

_____ **4.** All birds have feathers and wings.

_____ **5.** It would be great to be a bird and fly south for the winter.

_____ **6.** Birds have hard beaks or bills instead of teeth.

_____ **7.** Pigeons are fun to watch.

_____ **8.** Some birds cannot fly.

_____ **9.** Parakeets make good pets.

_____ **10.** A penguin is a bird.

Name ____________________

Fact and Opinion: Henrietta the Humpback

Directions: Read the story. Then, follow the instructions.

My name is Henrietta, and I am a humpback whale. I live in cold seas in the summer and warm seas in the winter. My long flippers are used to move forward and backward. I like to eat fish. Sometimes, I show off by leaping out of the water. Would you like to be a humpback whale?

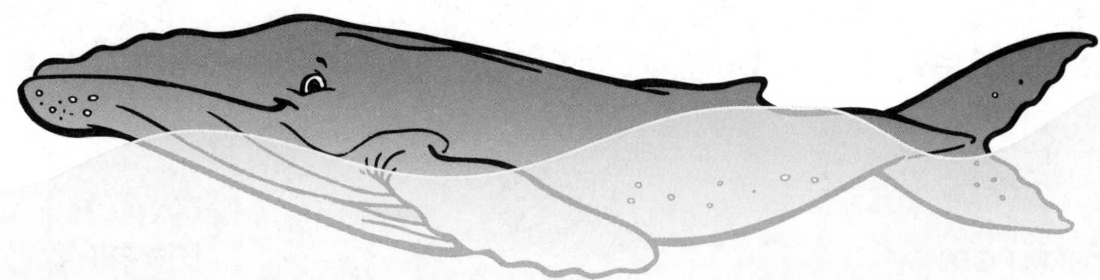

Write **F** next to each fact and **O** next to each opinion.

_____ **1.** Being a humpback whale is fun.

_____ **2.** Humpback whales live in cold seas during the summer.

_____ **3.** Whales are fun to watch.

_____ **4.** Humpback whales use their flippers to move forward and backward.

_____ **5.** Henrietta is a great name for a whale.

_____ **6.** Leaping out of water would be hard.

_____ **7.** Humpback whales like to eat fish.

_____ **8.** Humpback whales show off by leaping out of the water.

Name ______________________________

Strings Attached!

Directions: Draw a line to connect each string of words on the left with a string of words on the right to make a complete sentence. Make sure that each sentence you form makes sense.

Hint: There are several ways to connect the groups of words. Try out different combinations to find the ones you like best.

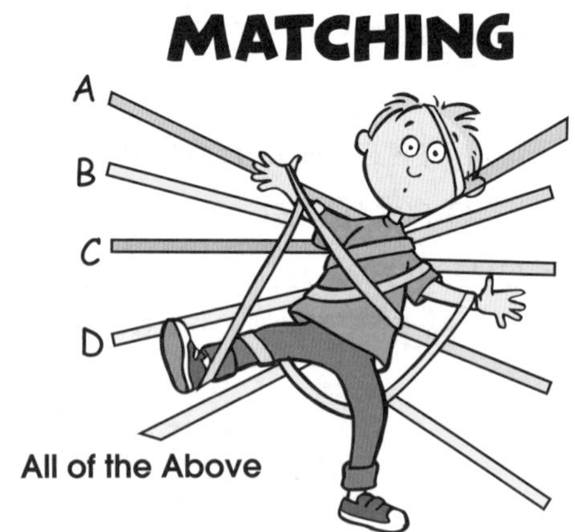

The tired mom	the stinky garbage.
We picked apples	had a shaky voice.
I threw out	smelled bad.
The nervous man	and made a pie!
I love to eat	rocked her baby.
The wet cat	vanilla ice cream.

Name ____________________

Best Guess!

Directions: Read each sentence below. Using the information in the first sentence, decide which answer best completes each question. Fill in the circle next to your answer choice.

"Is it cold in here?" asked my grandma as she shivered.

What do you think your grandma would like you to do?

- ○ Open a window.
- ○ Turn on the heat.
- ○ Give her a hug.

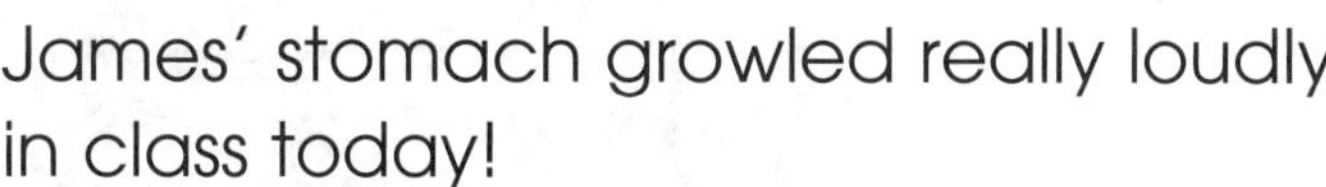

James' stomach growled really loudly in class today!

What would help James?

- ○ medicine
- ○ a new toy
- ○ food

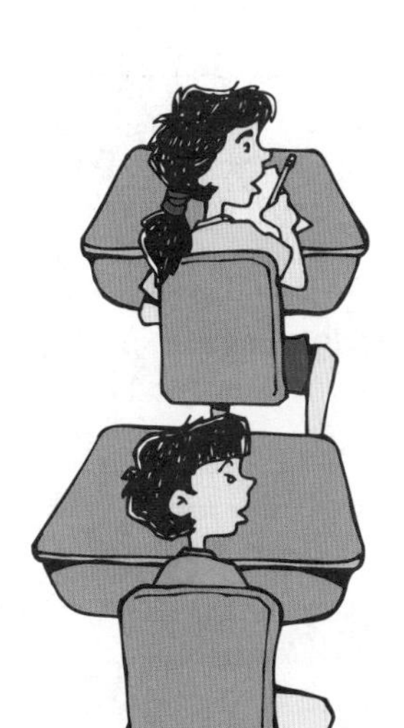

Name ____________________

It Isn't!

Directions: Finish the sentences about the stories.

Something is inside the kitchen cabinet. It isn't a

____________________.

can vase crocodile

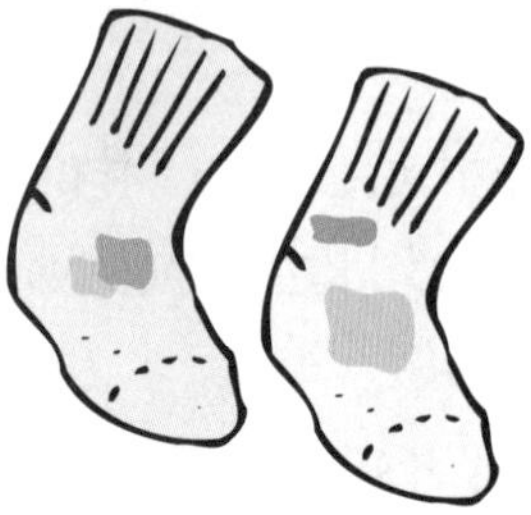

I smell something delicious in the kitchen. It isn't

____________________.

a cherry pie dirty socks a plate of brownies

I touch something soft and fluffy. It isn't

____________________.

sand paper a kitten a bath towel

I taste something sour. It isn't a

____________________.

lemon chocolate bar

I hear something making noise. It isn't

____________________.

a dog a squirrel a book

Making Inferences

Not every story tells you all the facts. Sometimes, you need to put together details to understand what is happening in a story. When you put details together, you **make inferences**.

Directions: Read each story. Fill in the circle beside the inference you can make from the details you have.

Everyone on the Pine School baseball team wears a blue shirt on Mondays. It is Monday and Brenda is wearing a blue shirt.

- ◯ Brenda always wears blue clothes.
- ◯ Brenda cannot find her red shirt.
- ◯ Brenda is on the baseball team.

My cat has brown and white stripes. It meows when it wants to be fed. My cat is meowing now.

- ◯ The cat wants to go outside.
- ◯ The cat is hungry.
- ◯ The cat doesn't like brown and white stripes.

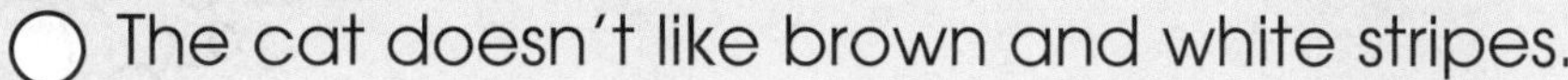

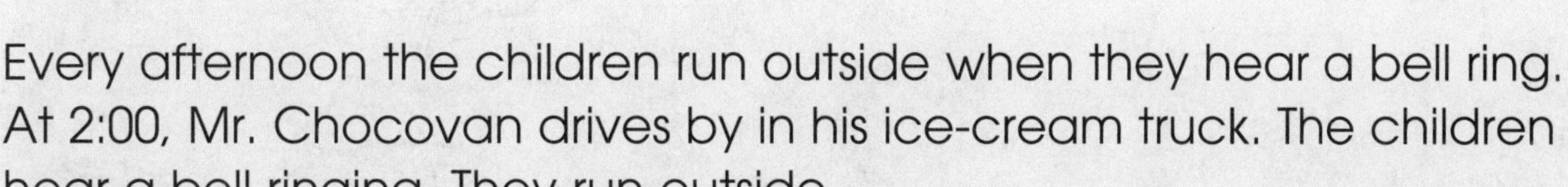

Every afternoon the children run outside when they hear a bell ring. At 2:00, Mr. Chocovan drives by in his ice-cream truck. The children hear a bell ringing. They run outside.

- ◯ It is time for ice cream.
- ◯ It is time for the children to go home.
- ◯ It is time for a fire drill.

Name ______________________________

Inferences About Characters

Directions: Read this story. Look for clues about Tom. Then, follow the directions below the story.

"You can't get me!" Goldie teased Tom when she saw him looking at her.

"I never said that I wanted to get you, anyway," answered Tom, knowing that Goldie was right. He walked away, waving his fluffy tail proudly.

Although Goldie had once been afraid of Tom, she now liked to tease him.

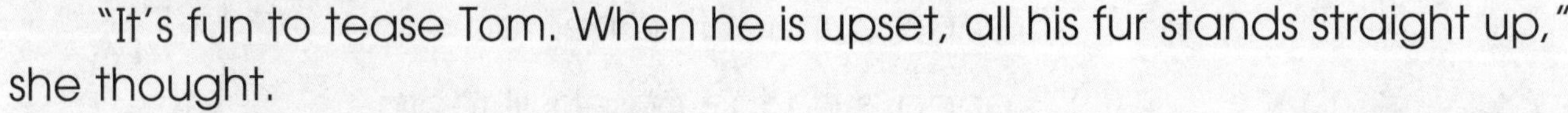

"It's fun to tease Tom. When he is upset, all his fur stands straight up," she thought.

Soon Goldie heard noises. Someone else was home. "It is almost time for dinner," thought Goldie. "I'm really glad to be a goldfish. I'm safe and sound and very well fed."

What does Tom look like? Draw a picture of Tom.

Circle the picture that tells how Goldie feels.

Mind-Reading Tricks

Samantha thought of a good joke. She bragged that she could read Maria's mind. She put her hand on Maria's head, closed her eyes, and said, "You had red punch with your lunch!"

"Wow! You're right!" replied Maria, not realizing that she had a little red ring around her lips.

"That was easy. But I bet you can't tell me what I just ate," said Thomas.

"That's a bunch of baloney," answered Samantha.

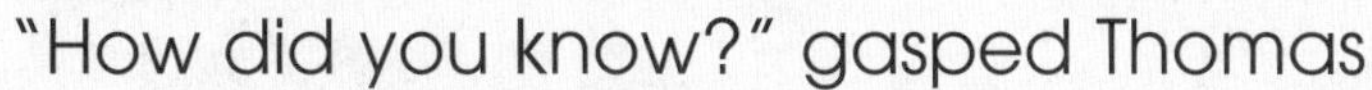

"How did you know?" gasped Thomas.

"It's my little secret," said Samantha, with a sigh of relief.

"Here comes your mom," said Maria. "Can you read her mind, too?"

Samantha looked down at her watch. She should have been home half an hour ago. As she ran to meet her mother, she yelled back, "Yes, I know exactly what she's thinking!"

Directions: Make inferences about Samantha's mind-reading tricks. Fill in the circle beside the correct inference.

1. Was Samantha sure that Thomas had eaten bologna for lunch?
   - ○ No, she was just lucky.
   - ○ Yes, she saw him eat his bologna sandwich.

2. What was Samantha's mother probably thinking?
   - ○ Samantha was a great mind reader.
   - ○ Samantha was late.

Name ___________________________

What Is It?

When you don't get the whole picture, you may need to **draw conclusions** for yourself. To draw a conclusion, think about what you see or read. Think about what you already know. Then, make a good guess.

Directions: Look at each picture. Use what you know and what you see to draw a conclusion. Draw a line to the sentence that tells about each picture.

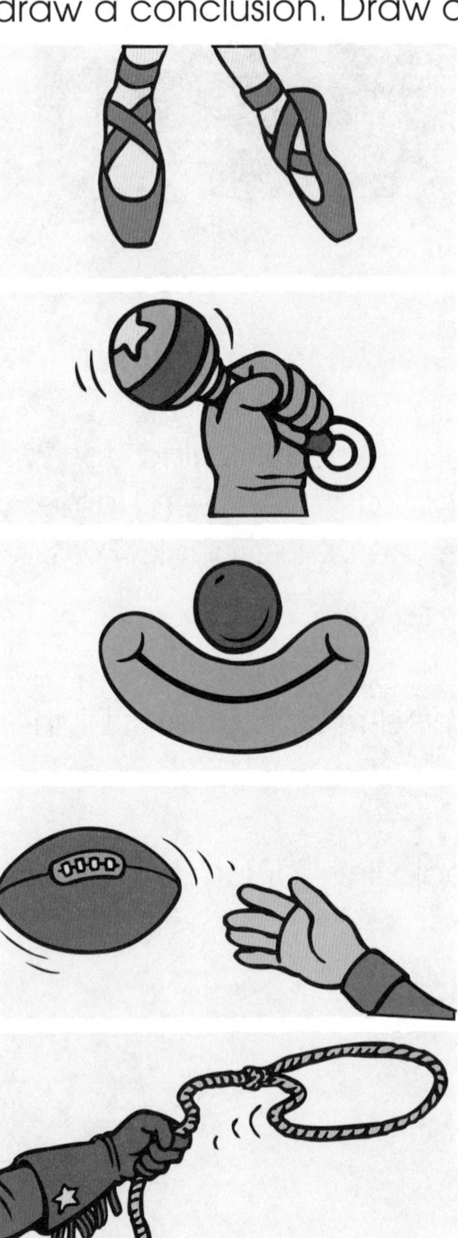

It must be a clown.

It must be a cowhand.

It must be a baby.

It must be a ballet dancer.

It must be a football player.

Name ____________________

Who Said It?

Directions: Use what you see, what you read, and what you know to draw conclusions. Draw a line from the animal to what it might say.

"I save lots of bones and bury them in the yard."

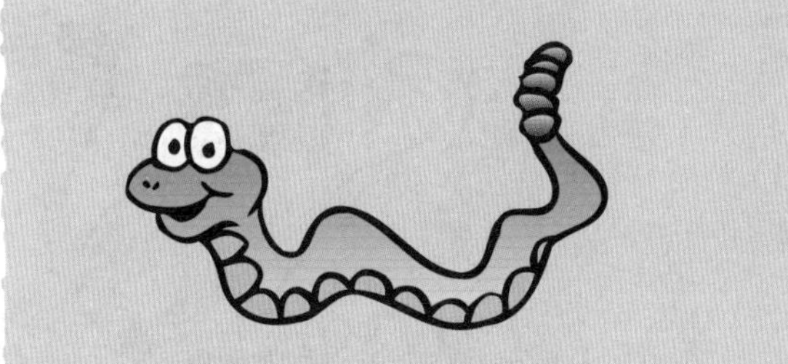

"I live in the ocean and have sharp teeth."

"I love to walk in the snow and slide on the ice."

"I hop on lily pads in a pond with my webbed feet."

"I slither on the ground because I have no arms or legs."

Name ____________________

I Conclude!

Directions: Read each story. Fill in the circle beside the answer that completes the last sentence.

The little house is in the backyard. Inside is a bowl of water. Next to the bowl is a big bone. This house belongs to . . .

○ some birds. ○ a family of elves. ○ a puppy.

The yellow cat is fluffy. The black cat is thin. The tan and white cat acts friendly. The little gray cat is shy. Cats are all . . .

○ different. ○ angry. ○ silly.

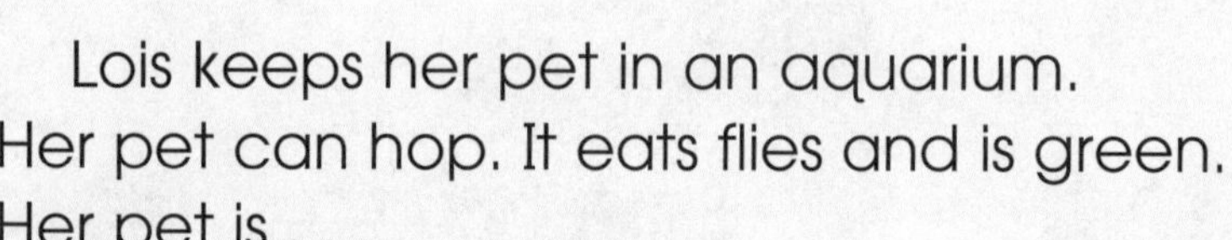

Lois keeps her pet in an aquarium. Her pet can hop. It eats flies and is green. Her pet is . . .

○ a bunny. ○ a frog. ○ very tall.

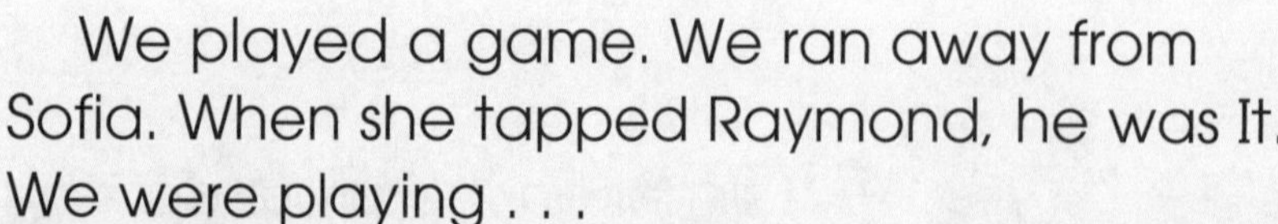

We played a game. We ran away from Sofia. When she tapped Raymond, he was It. We were playing . . .

○ soccer. ○ basketball. ○ tag.

Clues to Conclusions

Directions: Read each story. Fill in the circle beside the correct conclusion.

Joe tried to read the book. He pulled it closer to his face and squinted. What is wrong?

◯ The book isn't very interesting.

◯ Joe needs glasses.

◯ The book is closed.

"My shoes are too tight," said Eddie, "and my pants are too short!" What has happened?

◯ Eddie has put on his older brother's clothes.

◯ Eddie has become shorter.

◯ Eddie has grown.

Patsy went to the beach. She stayed outside for hours. When she came home, she looked in the mirror. Her face was very red. Why did she look different?

◯ Patsy had gotten a bad sunburn.

◯ Patsy got red paint all over herself.

◯ Patsy was very cold.

Name ____________________

Cause and Effect

Cause: An action or act that makes something happen.

Effect: Something that happens because of an action or cause.

Look at the following example of cause and effect.

We forgot to put the lid on the trash can.

The raccoons ate the trash.

Directions: Now, draw a line connecting each cause on the left side of the page to its effect on the right side of the page.

How Did It Happen?

Directions: Read the stories below. Then, write the missing cause or effect.

Audrey left her bike outside in the rain for weeks. When she finally put it back inside the garage, it had rusted.

Cause: Audrey left her bike outside in the rain.

What was the **effect**? ______________________

I dropped a heavy box on my foot by accident. Yoweeeee! That hurt! My mom took me to the doctor.

Cause: ______________________

Effect: ______________________

Noah Webster loved words so much that he decided to write a dictionary!

Cause: ______________________

Effect: ______________________

Name ______________________

Do You Know Why?

Directions: Write the cause from the answer box for each sentence.

Answer Box

The bathtub overflowed.

I studied all the spelling words.

Gill tried to grab the cat.

I didn't water my plants.

A tornado hit our town.

1. ______________________
The cat ran away.

2. ______________________
The floor got wet.

3. ______________________
There was a lot of damage.

4. ______________________
My plants died.

5. ______________________
I won the school spelling bee!

Why Did It Happen?

Directions: Read the effects. Fill in the circle beside the sentence that tells what caused the effect.

The soccer coach is cheering.

- ◯ Her team lost the game.
- ◯ Her team won the game.

Patty found only one cookie in the cookie jar

- ◯ Someone ate all the other cookies.
- ◯ It was a brand new cookie jar.

Fred has a new pair of glasses.

- ◯ Fred was having trouble seeing the chalkboard.
- ◯ There was a sale on glasses.

Lynn turned the fan to high.

- ◯ It was a very cold day.
- ◯ It was a very hot day.

Jason took his umbrella to school.

- ◯ The sky was cloudy.
- ◯ The sun was shining.

Name ______________________

Chain of Effects

Directions: Read the story.

At night, Tran set his alarm clock for seven o'clock. When it rang the next morning, he was so tired he turned the alarm off. Then, he went back to sleep. Tran finally woke up at eight o'clock. Tran had missed the school bus. He had to walk to school. It was a long walk. Tran was very late!

Directions: Draw a line to match a cause to an effect.

Because he was tired,	Tran missed the school bus.
Because Tran turned off the alarm,	he had to walk to school.
Because he woke up at eight o'clock,	Tran turned off the alarm.
Because Tran missed the bus,	Tran was late for school.
Because he had a long walk,	he overslept.

A Cause-and-Effect Fable

Directions: Read the story.

Four animals caught a talking fish. "If you let me go, I will grant each of you one wish," announced the fish.

"Make my trunk smaller!" demanded the vain elephant. "I wish to be the most beautiful elephant that ever lived."

"Make my legs longer!" commanded the alligator. "I want to be taller than all my alligator friends."

"Make my neck shorter!" ordered the giraffe. "I am tired of always staring at the tops of trees."

"Dear Fish, please make me be satisfied with who-o-o-o-o I am," whispered the wise old owl.

Poof! Kazaam! Their wishes were granted. However, soon after, only one of these animals was happy. Can you guess who-o-o-o-o?

Directions: Draw a line to match a cause to an effect.

Cause	Effect
Because of its short trunk,	the giraffe could no longer eat leaves from treetops.
Because of its long legs,	the elephant could no longer spray water on its back.
Because of its short neck,	the owl was happy about his wish.
Because he could still do all the things he needed,	the alligator could no longer hide in shallow water.

Name ______________________________

Fiction or Nonfiction?

Some stories are made up and some are true. **Fiction** stories are made up, and **nonfiction** stories are true.

Directions: Read the passages below. Then, write if they are **fiction** or **nonfiction**.

Following a balanced diet is important for good health. Your body needs many kinds of vitamins and minerals found in different types of food. For example, oranges provide vitamin C, and bananas are a good source of the mineral potassium.

____

We call my dog the alphabet dog. Why? Because my dog can sing the alphabet! That's right! My dog, Smarty Pants, is a dog genius! Smarty Pants can sing the entire alphabet! "S.P.," as we sometimes call her, is also starting her own dog academy to teach other dogs how to sing the alphabet. You should sign up your dog for classes with Smarty Pants today!

____

Name ______________________

Nonfiction: Tornado Tips

Directions: Read about tornadoes. Then, follow the instructions.

A tornado begins over land with strong winds and thunderstorms. The spinning air becomes a funnel. It can cause damage. If you are inside, go to the lowest floor of the building. A basement is a safe place. A bathroom or closet in the middle of a building can be a safe place, too. If you are outside, lie in a ditch. Remember, tornadoes are dangerous.

Write five facts about tornadoes.

1. ______________________________

____

2. ______________________________

____

3. ______________________________

____

4. ______________________________

____

5. ______________________________

____

Name ______________________________

Fiction: Hercules

The **setting** is where a story takes place. The **characters** are the people in a story or play.

Directions: Read about Hercules. Then, answer the questions.

Hercules was born in the warm Atlantic Ocean. He was a very small and weak baby. He wanted to be the strongest hurricane in the world. But he had one problem. He couldn't blow 75-mile-per-hour winds. Hercules blew and blew in the ocean, until one day, his sister, Hola, told him it would be more fun to be a breeze than a hurricane. Hercules agreed. It was a breeze to be a breeze!

1. What is the setting of the story? ______________________________

2. Who are the characters? ______________________________

3. What is the problem? ______________________________

4. How does Hercules solve his problem? ______________________________

____

Name ______________________________

Fiction and Nonfiction: Which Is It?

Directions: Read about fiction and nonfiction books. Then, follow the instructions.

There are many kinds of books. Some books have make-believe stories about princesses and dragons. Some books contain poetry and rhymes, like Mother Goose. These are fiction.

Some books contain facts about space and plants. And still other books have stories about famous people in history like Abraham Lincoln. These are nonfiction.

Write **F** for **fiction** and **NF** for **nonfiction**.

_______ **1.** nursery rhyme

_______ **2.** fairy tale

_______ **3.** true life story of a famous athlete

_______ **4.** Aesop's fables

_______ **5.** dictionary entry about foxes

_______ **6.** weather report

_______ **7.** story about a talking tree

_______ **8.** story about how a tadpole becomes a frog

_______ **9.** story about animal habitats

_______ **10.** riddles and jokes

Name ______________________________

What Is a Character?

A **character** is the person, animal, or object that a story is about. You cannot have a story without a character.

Characters are usually people, but sometimes they can be animals, aliens (!), or even objects that come to life. You can have many characters in a story.

Directions: Read the story below, and then answer the questions about character on the next page.

Adventurous Alenna!

Alenna was seven years old and lived on a tropical island. She had long, blond hair and sea-green eyes. Alenna was very adventurous and was always exploring new things. She started an Adventure Club at her school and led her friends on long bike rides. She also was the youngest person in her family to learn to water-ski!

When her dad asked, "Who wants to go snorkeling to see some fish?" Alenna answered, "I want to go snorkeling!" Alenna was very adventurous.

The End

Character, cont.

First, authors must decide who their main character is going to be. Next, they decide what their main character looks like. Then, they reveal the character's personality by:

what the character does

what the character says

Directions: Answer the questions about the story you just read.

Who is the main character in "Adventurous Alenna!"?

____

What does Alenna look like? Describe her appearance on the line below:

____

Give two examples of what Alenna **does** that shows that she is adventurous:

1. ___________________________

2. ___________________________

Give an example of what Alenna **says** that reveals she is adventurous.

____

____

Name ____________________

Setting—Place

Every story has a **setting**. The setting is the **place** where the story happens. Think of a place that you know well. It could be your room, your kitchen, your backyard, your classroom, or an imaginary place.

Directions: Brainstorm some words and ideas about that place. Think about what you see, hear, smell, taste, or feel in that place. Brainstorm your ideas for a setting below:

see hear smell

taste touch

Where are we? ____________________

Name ______________________________

Setting—Time

The **setting** is the **place** where the story happens. The setting is also the **time** in which the story happens. A reader needs to know **when** the story is happening. Does it take place at night? On a sunny day? In the future? During the winter?

Time can be:

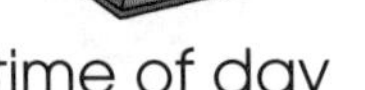

time of day

a holiday

a season of the year

a time in the future

a time in history

Directions: Read the following story. Then, answer the questions below.

Knock, Knock!

One windy fall night there was a knock at the door. "Who is it?" I asked.

"It's your dog, Max. Please let me in," Max said.

"Oh, good. I was getting worried about you!" I said. Then, I let Max inside.

I thought to myself how glad I was that scientists had invented voice boxes for dogs. How did people in the olden days ever know when to let their dogs inside if their dogs couldn't talk? The Doggie Voice Box is such a wonderful invention. I'm so happy that I live in the year 2090!

What time of day is it?______________________________

What season is it?______________________________

What year does this story take place?______________________________

Name ______________________

Extra! Extra! Read All About It!

Newspaper reporters have very important jobs. They have to catch a reader's attention and, at the same time, **tell the facts**.

Newspaper reporters write their stories by answering **who**, **what**, **where**, **when**, **why**, and **how**.

Directions: Think about a book you just read and answer the questions below.

Who: **Who** is the story about?

____

What: **What** happened to the main character?

____

Where: **Where** does the story take place?

____

When: **When** does the story take place?

____

Why: **Why** do these story events happen?

____

How: **How** do these events happen?

____

Extra! Extra! Read All About It!

Directions: Use your answers on page 150 to write a newspaper article about the book you read.

BIG CITY TIMES

Title

____

(Write a catchy title for your article.)

____

____

____

____

____

____

____

____

____

____

Name ____________________

Common Nouns

A **common noun** names a person, place, or thing.

Example: The **boy** had several **chores** to do.

Directions: Fill in the circle below each common noun.

1. First, the boy had to feed his puppy.
2. He got fresh water for his pet.
3. Next, the boy poured some dry food into a bowl.
4. He set the dish on the floor in the kitchen.
5. Then, he called his dog to come to dinner.
6. The boy and his dad worked in the garden.
7. The father turned the dirt with a shovel.
8. The boy carefully dropped seeds into little holes.
9. Soon, tiny plants would sprout from the soil.
10. Sunshine and showers would help the radishes grow.

Name ______________________

Proper Nouns

A **proper noun** names a specific or certain person, place, or thing. A proper noun always begins with a capital letter.

Example: Becky flew to **St. Louis** in a **Boeing 747**.

Directions: Put a ✓ in front of each proper noun.

_______ 1. uncle

_______ 2. Aunt Retta

_______ 3. Forest Park

_______ 4. Gateway Arch

_______ 5. Missouri

_______ 6. school

_______ 7. Miss Hunter

_______ 8. Northwest Plaza

_______ 9. New York Science Center

_______ 10. Ms. Small

_______ 11. Doctor Chang

_______ 12. Union Station

_______ 13. Henry Shaw

_______ 14. museum

_______ 15. librarian

_______ 16. shopping mall

Directions: Underline the proper nouns.

1. Becky went to visit Uncle Harry.
2. He took her to see the Cardinals play baseball.
3. The game was at Busch Stadium.
4. The St. Louis Cardinals played the Chicago Cubs.
5. Mark McGwire hit a home run.

Name ________________________

Singular Nouns

A **singular noun** names one person, place, or thing.

Example: My **mother** unlocked the old **trunk** in the **attic**.

Directions: If the noun is singular, draw a line from it to the trunk. If the noun is **not** singular, draw an **X** on the word.

teddy bear	**hammer**	**picture**	**sweater**
bonnet	**letters**	**seashells**	**fiddle**
kite	**ring**	**feather**	**books**
postcard	**crayon**	**doll**	**dishes**
blocks	**hats**	**bicycle**	**blanket**

Name ________________________________

Plural Nouns

A **plural noun** names more than one person, place, or thing.

Example: Some **dinosaurs** ate **plants** in **swamps**.

Directions: Underline each plural noun.

1. Large animals lived millions of years ago.
2. Dinosaurs roamed many parts of the Earth.
3. Scientists look for fossils.
4. The bones can tell a scientist many things.
5. These bones help tell what the creatures were like.
6. Some had curved claws and whip-like tails.
7. Others had beaks and plates of armor.
8. Some dinosaurs lived on the plains, and others lived in forests.
9. You can see the skeletons of dinosaurs at some museums.
10. We often read about these animals in books.

Name ____________________

Action Verbs

A **verb** is a word that can show action.

Example: I **jump**. He **kicks**. He **walked**.

Directions: Underline the verb in each sentence. Write it on the line.

1. Our school plays games on Field Day. ____________________
2. Juan runs 50 yards. ____________________
3. Carmen hops in a sack race. ____________________
4. Paula tosses a ball through a hoop. ____________________
5. One girl carries a jellybean on a spoon. ____________________
6. Lola bounces the ball. ____________________
7. Some boys chase after balloons. ____________________
8. Mark chooses me for his team. ____________________
9. The children cheer for the winners. ____________________
10. Everyone enjoys Field Day. ____________________

Name ___________________________

Ready for Action!

Directions: Draw a line to match each action word to the picture that shows it.

kick

catch

slide

run

jump

Name ____________________

Irregular Verbs

Verbs that do not add **ed** to show what happened in the past are called **irregular verbs**.

Example: **Present** **Past**

run, runs ran

fall, falls fell

Jim **ran** past our house yesterday.
He **fell** over a wagon on the sidewalk.

Directions: Fill in the verbs that tell what happened in the past in the chart. The first one is done for you.

Present	Past
hear, hears	heard
draw, draws	
do, does	
give, gives	
sell, sells	
come, comes	
fly, flies	
build, builds	
know, knows	
bring, brings	

Linking Verbs

A **linking verb** does not show action. Instead, it links the subject with a word in the predicate. **Am**, **is**, **are**, **was**, and **were** are **linking verbs**.

Example: Many people **are** collectors.
(**Are** connects **people** and **collectors**.)
The collection **was** large.
(**Was** connects **collection** and **large**.)

Directions: Underline the linking verb in each sentence.

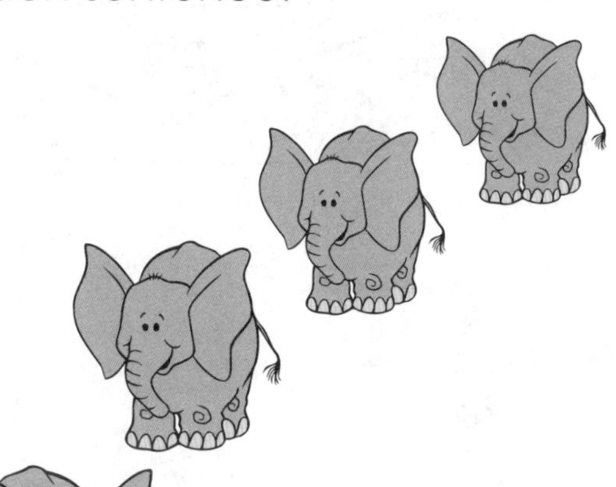

1. I am happy.
2. Toy collecting is a nice hobby.
3. Mom and Dad are helpful.
4. The rabbit is beautiful.
5. Itsy and Bitsy are stuffed mice.
6. Monday was special.
7. I was excited.
8. The class was impressed.
9. The elephants were gray.
10. My friends were a good audience.

Name ______________________

Adjectives

An **adjective** is a word that describes a noun.
It tells **how many**, **what kind**, or **which one**.

Example: Yolanda has a **tasty** lunch.

Directions: Color each space that has an adjective. Do not color the other spaces.

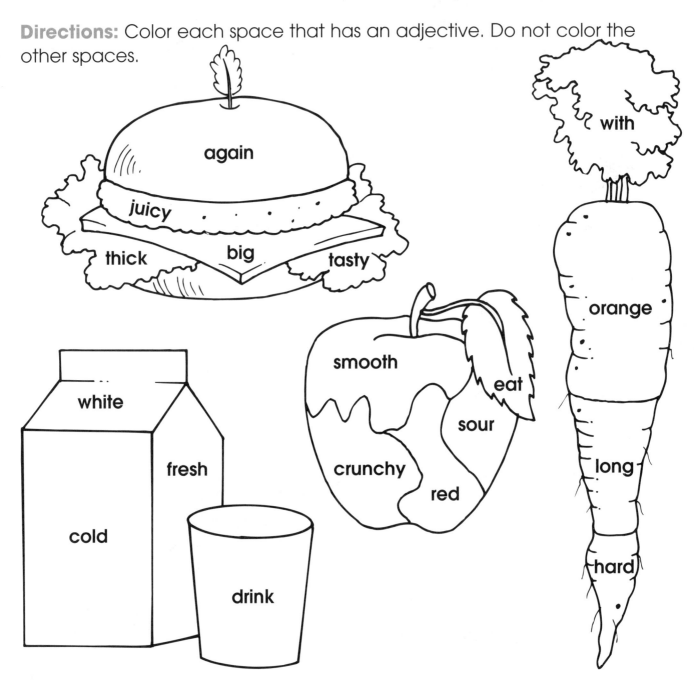

again
juicy
thick
big
tasty

with
orange
long
hard

smooth
eat
sour
crunchy
red

white
fresh
cold
drink

Add the Adjectives

Directions: Write a describing word on each line. Draw a picture to match each sentence.

high mountain

The ________ flag waved over the ________ building.

A ________ lion searched for food in the ________ jungle.

We saw ________ fish in the ________ aquarium.

Her ________ car was parked by the ________ van.

The ________ dog barked and chased the ________ truck.

The ________ building was filled with ________ packages.

Name ______________________

Better Sentences

Directions: Describing words like adjectives can make a better sentence. Write a word on each line to make the sentences more interesting. Draw pictures of your sentences.

1. The skater won a medal.

   The ______________ skater won a ______________ medal.

2. The jewels were in the safe.

   The ______________ jewels were in the ______________ safe.

3. The airplane flew through the storm.

   The ______________ airplane flew through the ______________ storm.

4. A fireman rushed into the house.

   A ______________ fireman rushed into the ______________ house.

5. The detective hid behind the tree.

   The ______________ detective hid behind the ______________ tree.

1.	2.

3.	4.	5.

Name ______________________________

Describing People

Directions: Choose two words from the box that describe each character. Then, complete each sentence to tell why you chose those words.

understanding	spoiled	responsible	lazy	helpful	upset	happy
busy	caring	kind	mean	confused	unhappy	patient	nice

The girl is ________________ and ________________

because she ________________________________

____

____

____

Mother is ________________ and ________________

because she ________________________________

____

____

____

Father is ________________ and ________________

because he ________________________________

____

____

____

Name ______________________________

Using Exact Adjectives

Use an **adjective** that best describes the noun or pronoun. Be specific.

Example: David had a nice birthday.
David had a **fun** birthday.

Directions: Rewrite each sentence, replacing **nice** or **good** with a better adjective from the box or one of your own.

sturdy	**new**	**great**	**chocolate**	**delicious**	**special**

1. David bought a nice pair of in-line skates.

____

2. He received a nice helmet.

____

3. He got nice knee pads.

____

4. Father baked a good cake.

____

5. David made a good wish.

____

6. Mom served good ice cream.

____

Subjects of Sentences

The **subject** of a sentence tells **who** or **what** does something.

Example: Some people eat foods that may seem strange to you.

Directions: Underline the subject of each sentence.

1. Some people like crocodile steak.
2. The meat tastes like fish.
3. Australians eat kangaroo meat.
4. Kangaroo meat tastes like beef.
5. People in the Southwest eat rattlesnake meat.
6. Snails make a delicious treat for some people.
7. Some Africans think roasted termites are tasty.
8. Bird's-nest soup is a famous Chinese dish.
9. People in Florida serve alligator meat.
10. Almost everyone treats themselves with ice cream.

Name ______________________

Predicates of Sentences

The **predicate** of a sentence tells what the subject is or does. It is the verb part of the sentence.

Examples: Sally Ride **flew in a space shuttle**.

She **was an astronaut**.

Directions: Underline the predicate in each sentence.

1. She was the first American woman astronaut in space.
2. Sally worked hard for many years to become an astronaut.
3. She studied math and science in college.
4. Ms. Ride passed many tests.
5. She learned things quickly.
6. Sally trained to become a jet pilot.
7. This astronaut practiced using a robot arm.
8. Ms. Ride used the robot arm on two space missions.
9. She conducted experiments with it.
10. The robot arm is called a remote manipulator.

Wheelies

Build sentences using a subject part and a predicate part.

You will need: disk patterns below (may be enlarged), tagboard, rubber cement, scissors, a fastener, writing paper, pencils

Directions: With an adult, cut out the two disks below. Cut out two more from tagboard. Using rubber cement, glue the tagboard disks to the disks with the words. Let them dry and laminate them. Place the smaller disk on top and secure it in the center with the brad.

Then, turn the top disk to match a subject part (large circle) and a predicate part (smaller circle). Then, write the two parts to form a sentence. Keep the circles in the same position and write the other sentences formed.

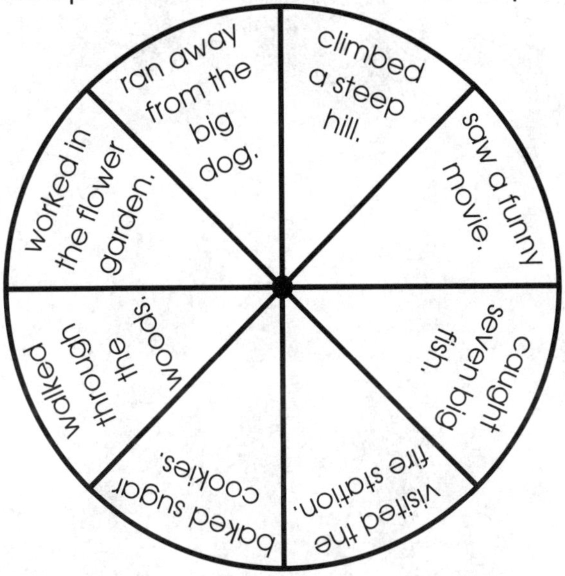

climbed a steep hill.

saw a funny movie.

caught seven big fish.

visited the fire station.

baked sugar cookies.

walked through the woods.

worked in the flower garden.

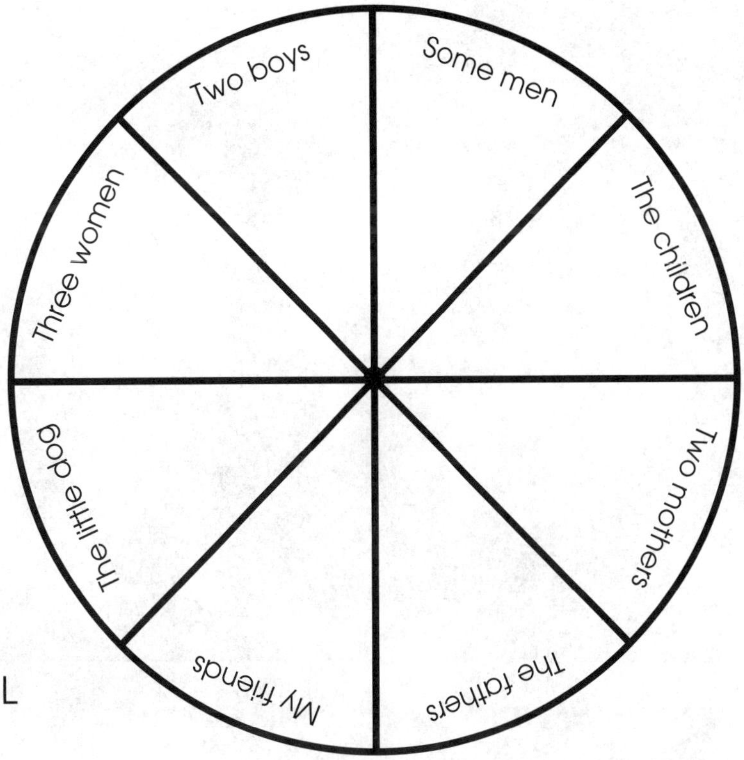

ran away from the big dog.

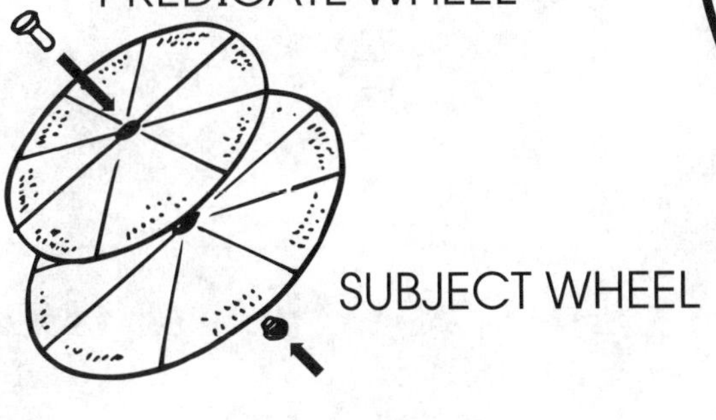

PREDICATE WHEEL

SUBJECT WHEEL

Some men

The children

Two mothers

The fathers

My friends

The little dog

Three women

Two boys

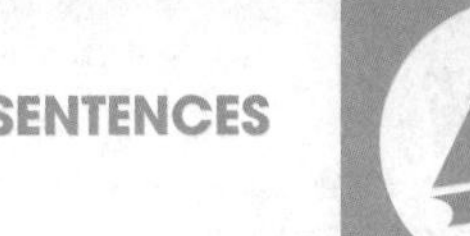

Name ______________________________

Compound Subjects

A **compound subject** has two or more subjects joined by the word **and**.

Example: **Owls** are predators. **Wolves** are predators.
Owls and wolves are predators. (compound subject)

Directions: If the sentence has a compound subject, write **CS**. If it does not, write **No**.

_______ **1.** A predator is an animal that eats other animals.

_______ **2.** Prey is eaten by predators.

_______ **3.** Robins and bluejays are predators.

_______ **4.** Some predators eat only meat.

_______ **5.** Crocodiles and hawks eat meat only.

_______ **6.** Raccoons and foxes eat both meat and plants.

Directions: Combine the subjects of the two sentences to make a compound subject. Write the new sentence on the line.

1. Snakes are predators. Spiders are predators.

____

2. Frogs prey on insects. Chameleons prey on insects.

____

Name ______________________

Compound Predicates

A **compound predicate** has two or more predicates joined by the word **and**.

Example: Abe Lincoln was born in Kentucky. Abe Lincoln lived in a log cabin there.
Abe Lincoln **was born in Kentucky and lived in a log cabin there**.

Directions: If the sentence has a compound predicate, write **CP**. If it does not, write **No**.

_______ **1.** Abe Lincoln cut trees and chopped wood.

_______ **2.** Abe and his sister walked to a spring for water.

_______ **3.** Abe's family packed up and left Kentucky.

_______ **4.** They crossed the Ohio River to Indiana.

_______ **5.** Abe's father built a new home.

_______ **6.** Abe's mother became sick and died.

_______ **7.** Mr. Lincoln married again.

_______ **8.** Abe's new mother loved Abe and his sister and cared for them.

Complete Sentences

A **sentence** is a group of words that tells a whole idea. It has a subject and a predicate.

Examples: Some animals have stripes.
(sentence)
Help to protect.
(not a sentence)

Directions: Write **S** in front of each sentence. Write **No** if it is **not** a sentence.

_______ 1. There are different kinds of chipmunks.

_______ 2. They all have.

_______ 3. They all have stripes to help protect them.

_______ 4. The stripes make them hard to see in the forest.

_______ 5. Zebras have stripes, too.

_______ 6. Some caterpillars also.

_______ 7. Other animals have spots.

_______ 8. Some dogs have spots.

_______ 9. Beautiful, little fawns.

_______ 10. Their spots help to hide them in the woods.

Name ______________________

Summer Camp

A **statement** is a telling sentence. It begins with a capital letter and ends with a period.

Directions: Write each statement correctly on the lines.

1. everyone goes to breakfast at 6:30 each morning

____

2. only three people can ride in one canoe

____

3. each person must help clean the cabins

____

4. older campers should help younger campers

____

5. all lights are out by 9:00 each night

____

6. everyone should write home at least once a week

____

Questions

A **question** is an asking sentence. It begins with a capital letter and ends with a question mark.

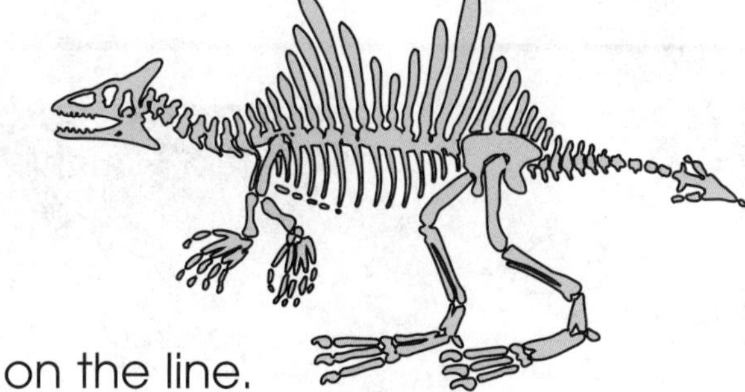

Directions: Write each question correctly on the line.

1. is our class going to the science museum

____

2. will we get to spend the whole day there

____

3. will a guide take us through the museum

____

4. do you think we will see dinosaur bones

____

5. is it true that the museum has a mummy

____

6. can we take lots of pictures at the museum

____

7. will you spend the whole day at the museum

____

Name ______________________

More Questions

Directions: Write five questions about the picture.

____

____

____

____

____

Name ______________________

Kinds of Sentences

A **statement** ends with a period. **.** A **question** ends with a question mark. **?**

Directions: Write the correct mark in each box.

1. Would you like to help me make an aquarium ☐
2. We can use my brother's big fish tank ☐
3. Will you put this colored sand in the bottom ☐
4. I have three shells to put on the sand ☐
5. Can we use your little toy boat, too ☐
6. Let's go buy some fish for our aquarium ☐
7. Will twelve fish be enough ☐
8. Look, they seem to like their new home ☐
9. How often do we give them fish food ☐
10. Let's tell our friends about our new aquarium ☐

Name ______________________________

Writing Sentences

Every sentence begins with a capital letter.

Come to the Fourth of July Picnic.
Town Park—All Day

Directions: Write three statements about the picture.

____

____

____

Directions: Write three questions about the picture.

____

____

____

Four Kinds of Sentences

A **statement** tells something. A **question** asks something. An **exclamation** shows surprise or strong feeling. A **command** tells someone to do something.

Example: The shuttle is ready for takeoff. (statement)
Are all systems go? (question)
What a sight! (exclamation)
Take a picture of this. (command)

Directions: Use the code to color the spaces.

Code
statement—**yellow**
question—**red**
exclamation—**blue**
command—**gray**

That's incredible!

There it goes!

How exciting!

This is a thrill!

Are there any animals on board?

How high does it fly?

Will they land soon?

There are five astronauts.

Can the astronauts see the Moon?

Way to go!

How brave they are!

The shuttle goes fast.

They do experiments.

One uses the robot arm.

What a view!

What a sight!

It orbits the Earth.

Look up there.

Stay out of the way.

Take the picture now.

Watch the liftoff.

Name ______________________________

Review of Sentences

Directions: Underline the sentence that is written correctly in each group.

1. Do Penguins live in antarctica?
   do penguins live in Antarctica.
   Do penguins live in Antarctica?

2. penguins cannot fly?
   Penguins cannot fly.
   penguins cannot fly.

Directions: Write **S** for **statement**, **Q** for **question**, **E** for **exclamation**, or **C** for **command** on the line.

_______ 1. Two different kinds of penguins live in Antarctica.

_______ 2. Do emperor penguins have black and white bodies?

_______ 3. Look at their webbed feet.

_______ 4. They're amazing!

Directions: Underline the **subject** of the sentence with **one** line. Underline the **predicate** with **two** lines.

1. Penguins eat fish, squid, and shrimp.
2. Leopard seals and killer whales hunt penguins.
3. A female penguin lays one egg.

Name ____________________

My Bag's Ready!

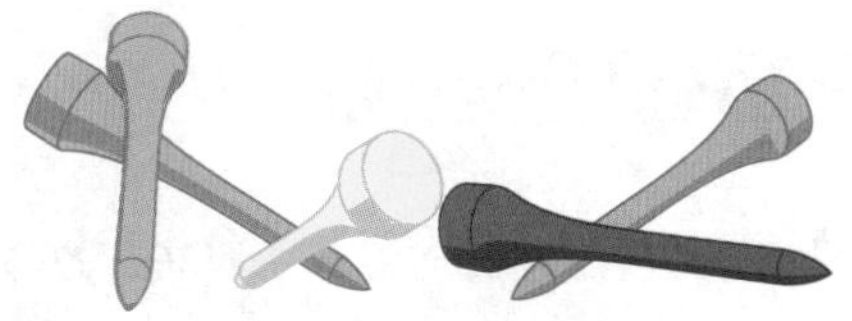

The first letter of a word is used to put words in alphabetical (ABC) order.

Directions: Write the golf words below in ABC order. If two or more words begin with the same letter, go to the next letter to put them in ABC order.

club tee bag ball scorecard cart towel

1. ____________________
2. ____________________
3. ____________________
4. ____________________
5. ____________________
6. ____________________
7. ____________________

Name ____________________

Drop In!

Drop in means to start at the top of a ramp.

Directions: Write the words in ABC order. "Drop in" from the top of the ramp.

Name ______________________

Slam Dunk!

HOME VISITOR 12 18 10:00

Directions: Put the words in the box in ABC order.

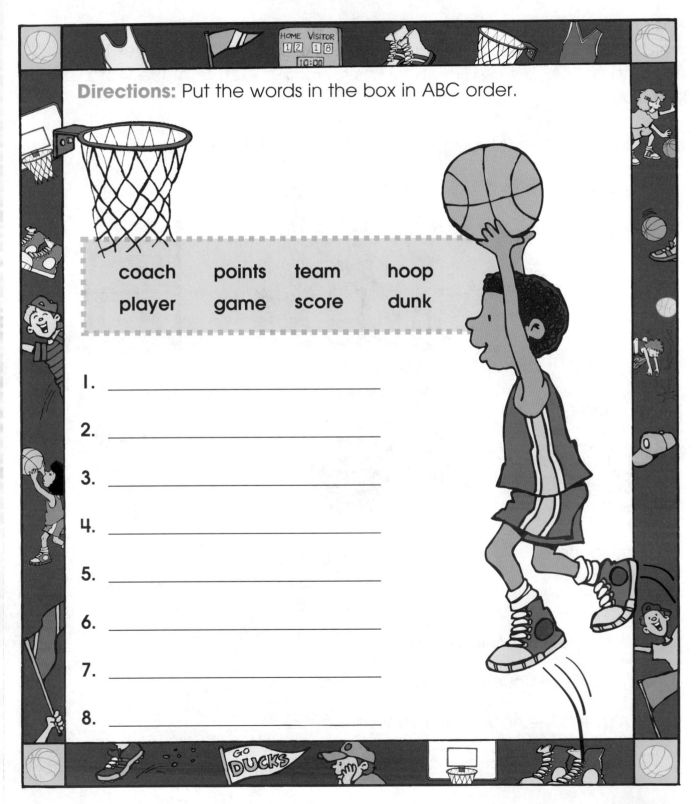

coach	points	team	hoop
player	game	score	dunk

1. ______________________
2. ______________________
3. ______________________
4. ______________________
5. ______________________
6. ______________________
7. ______________________
8. ______________________

GO DUCKS

Name ____________________

Learning Dictionary Skills

A **dictionary** is a book that gives the meaning of words. It also tells how words sound. Words in a dictionary are in ABC order. That makes them easier to find. A picture dictionary lists a word, a picture of the word, and its meaning.

Directions: Look at this page from a picture dictionary. Then, answer the questions.

baby

A very young child.

band

A group of people who play music.

bank

A place where money is kept.

bark

The sound a dog makes.

berry

A small, juicy fruit.

board

A flat piece of wood.

1. What is a small, juicy fruit? ____________________

2. What is a group of people who play music? ____________________

3. What is the name for a very young child? ____________________

4. What is a flat piece of wood called? ____________________

Learning Dictionary Skills

Directions: Look at this page from a picture dictionary. Then, answer the questions.

safe

A metal box.

sea

A body of water.

seed

The beginning of a plant.

---

sheep

An animal that has wool.

skate

A shoe with wheels or a blade on it.

snowstorm

A time when much snow falls.

---

squirrel

A small animal with a bushy tail.

stone

A small rock.

store

A place where items are sold.

1. What kind of animal has wool? ______________________
2. What do you call a shoe with wheels on it? ______________________
3. When a lot of snow falls, what is it called? ______________________
4. What is a small animal with a bushy tail? ______________________
5. What is a place where items are sold? ______________________
6. When a plant starts, what is it called? ______________________

Name ____________________

Learning Dictionary Skills

Directions: Look at this page from a picture dictionary. Then, answer the questions.

table

Furniture with legs and a flat top.

tail

A slender part that is on the back of an animal.

teacher

A person who teaches lessons.

telephone

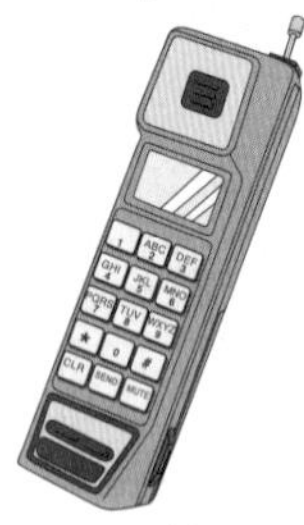

A machine that sends and receives sounds.

ticket

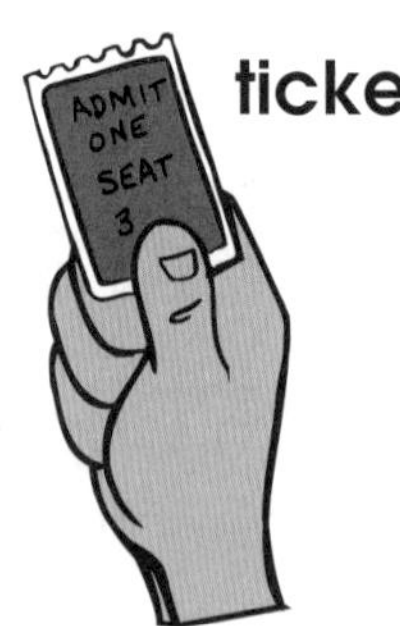

A paper slip or card.

tiger

An animal with stripes.

1. Who is a person who teaches lessons? ____________________
2. What is the name of an animal with stripes? ____________________
3. What is a piece of furniture with legs and a flat top? ____________________
4. What is the definition of a ticket?

____

5. What is a machine that sends and receives sounds?

____

Name ________________________

Learning Dictionary Skills

The **guide words** at the top of a page in a dictionary tell you what the first and last words on the page will be. Only words that come in ABC order between those two words will be on that page. Guide words help you find the page you need to look up a word.

Directions: Write each word from the box in ABC order between each pair of guide words.

faint	fence	farmer	feet	family
far	feed	fan	farm	face

face **fence**

________________________ ________________________

________________________ ________________________

________________________ ________________________

________________________ ________________________

________________________ ________________________

How to Help Your Child Prepare for Standardized Testing

Preparing All Year Round

Perhaps the most valuable way you can help your child prepare for standardized achievement tests is by providing enriching experiences. Keep in mind also that test results for younger children are not as reliable as for older students. If a child is hungry, tired, or upset, this may result in a poor test score. Here are some tips on how you can help your child do his or her best on standardized tests.

Read aloud with your child. Reading aloud helps develop vocabulary and fosters a positive attitude toward reading. Reading together is one of the most effective ways you can help your child succeed in school.

Share experiences. Baking cookies together, planting a garden, or making a map of your neighborhood are examples of activities that help build skills that are measured on the tests, such as sequencing and following directions.

Become informed about your state's testing procedures. Ask about or watch for announcements of meetings that explain about standardized tests and statewide assessments in your school district. Talk to your child's teacher about your child's individual performance on these state tests during a parent-teacher conference.

Help your child know what to expect. Read and discuss with your child the test-taking tips in this book. Your child can prepare by working through a couple of strategies a day so that no practice session takes too long.

Help your child with his or her regular school assignments. Set up a quiet study area for homework. Supply this area with pencils, paper, markers, a calculator, a ruler, a dictionary, scissors, glue, and so on. Check your child's homework and offer to help if he or she gets stuck. But remember, it's your child's homework, not yours. If you help too much, your child will not benefit from the activity.

Keep in regular contact with your child's teacher. Attend parent-teacher conferences, school functions, PTA or PTO meetings, and school board meetings. This will help you get to know the educators in your district and the families of your child's classmates.

Learn to use computers as an educational resource. If you do not have a computer and Internet access at home, try your local library.

Remember—simply getting your child comfortable with testing procedures and helping him or her know what to expect can improve test scores!

Getting Ready for the Big Day

There are lots of things you can do on or immediately before test day to improve your child's chances of testing success. What's more, these strategies will help your child prepare him- or herself for school tests, too, and promote general study skills that can last a lifetime.

Provide a good breakfast on test day. Instead of sugar cereal, which provides immediate but not long-term energy, have your child eat a breakfast with protein or complex carbohydrates, such as an egg, whole grain cereal or toast, or a banana-yogurt shake.

Promote a good night's sleep. A good night's sleep before the test is essential. Try not to overstress the importance of the test. This may cause your child to lose sleep because of anxiety. Doing some exercise after school and having a quiet evening routine will help your child sleep well the night before the test.

Assure your child that he or she is not expected to know all of the answers on the test. Explain that other children in higher grades may take the same test, and that the test may measure things your child has not yet learned in school. Help your child understand that you expect him or her to put forth a good effort—and that this is enough. Your child should not try to cram for these tests. Also avoid threats or bribes; these put undue pressure on children and may interfere with their best performance.

Keep the mood light and offer encouragement. To provide a break on test days, do something fun and special after school—take a walk around the neighborhood, play a game, read a favorite book, or prepare a special snack together. These activities keep your child's mood light—even if the testing sessions have been difficult—and show how much you appreciate your child's effort.

READING: WORD ANALYSIS

Lesson 1: Word Sounds

Directions: Choose the best answer to each question.

Example

A. Which word has the same beginning sound as sheep?

- Ⓐ chin
- Ⓑ shake
- Ⓒ seven
- Ⓓ sleep

Practice

Read all the answer choices before choosing the one you think is correct.

1. Which word has the same beginning sound as blue?

- Ⓐ blast
- Ⓑ boy
- Ⓒ brush
- Ⓓ few

2. Which word has the same vowel sound as join?

- Ⓕ tool
- Ⓖ joke
- Ⓗ spoil
- Ⓙ cold

3. Which word has the same ending sound as from?

- Ⓐ float
- Ⓑ barn
- Ⓒ come
- Ⓓ fry

4. Which word has the same vowel sound as found?

- Ⓕ down
- Ⓖ flood
- Ⓗ road
- Ⓙ could

5. Which word has the same ending sound as spend?

- Ⓐ seen
- Ⓑ pound
- Ⓒ pain
- Ⓓ spot

6. Which word has the same beginning sound as another?

- Ⓕ about
- Ⓖ arm
- Ⓗ clue
- Ⓙ ace

READING: WORD ANALYSIS

Lesson 2: Rhyming Words

Directions: Choose the best answer to each question.

Example

A. Which picture rhymes with the word fun?

Ⓐ 

Ⓑ 

Ⓒ 

If you are not sure which answer is correct, take your best guess.

Practice

1. Which picture rhymes with the word seal?

Ⓐ 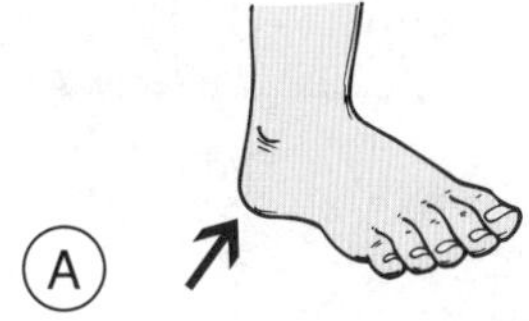

Ⓑ 

Ⓒ 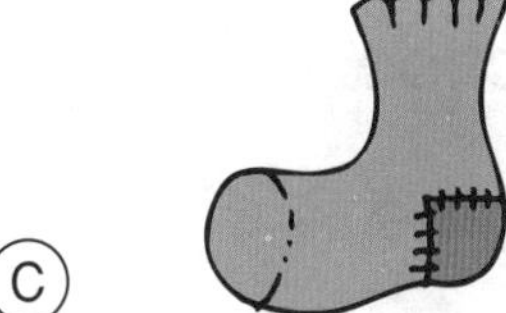

2. Which picture rhymes with the word bag?

Ⓕ 

Ⓖ 

Ⓗ 

3. Which picture rhymes with the word five?

Ⓐ 

Ⓑ 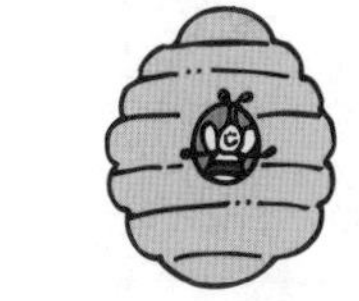

Ⓒ 

4. Which picture rhymes with the word honey?

Ⓕ 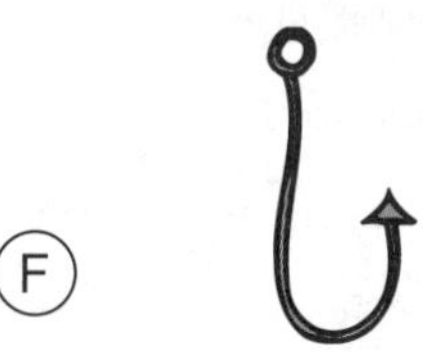

Ⓖ 

Ⓗ 

STOP

READING: WORD ANALYSIS

Lesson 3: Word Sounds

Directions: Choose the word that has the same sound as the underlined part of the word.

Examples

A. This one has been done for you.

umbrella

- (A) use
- (B) cube
- (C) skunk
- (D) four

B. Practice this one with your teacher.

growl

- (F) food
- (G) couch
- (H) home
- (J) grow

Match the sound of the underlined letter or letters. Look at each answer choice and say each answer choice quietly to yourself.

Practice

1. came

- (A) rain
- (B) hand
- (C) black
- (D) swam

2. her

- (F) fire
- (G) real
- (H) here
- (J) turn

3. easy

- (A) child
- (B) keep
- (C) here
- (D) head

4. good

- (F) sound
- (G) but
- (H) could
- (J) hold

5. this

- (A) their
- (B) still
- (C) kind
- (D) mine

6. coat

- (F) know
- (G) out
- (H) people
- (J) school

READING: WORD ANALYSIS

Lesson 4: Word Study

Directions: Choose the word that completes each sentence.

Example

A. The girls were ______________ at the joke.

Ⓐ surprise
Ⓑ surprises
Ⓒ surprised

Clue When deciding which answer is best, try each answer choice in the blank.

Practice

1. She ______ cake and candy to the party.

Ⓐ taken
Ⓑ bring
Ⓒ brought
Ⓓ buy

2. The boys love to ______ pictures.

Ⓕ painting
Ⓖ painted
Ⓗ paint
Ⓙ paints

3. Jack's room was the ______ in the house.

Ⓐ clean
Ⓑ cleaner
Ⓒ cleans
Ⓓ cleanest

4. She saw the ______ star in the sky.

Ⓕ brightest
Ⓖ brighted
Ⓗ brightly
Ⓙ brights

5. My ______ loves to read.

Ⓐ teach
Ⓑ learn
Ⓒ taught
Ⓓ teacher

6. The baby ______ through the storm.

Ⓕ slept
Ⓖ sleeping
Ⓗ sleeped
Ⓙ sleepiest

STOP

Name ______________________

READING: WORD ANALYSIS

Lesson 5: Contractions and Compound Words

Directions: Choose the best answer to each question.

Examples

A. Which word is a compound word, a word that is made up of two smaller words?

- (A) footprint
- (B) remember
- (C) narrow
- (D) explain

B. Look at the word. Find the answer that tells what the contraction means.

aren't

- (F) are not
- (G) are late
- (H) are most
- (J) are then

If a question is too difficult, skip it and come back to it later.

Practice

1. Which word is a compound word?

- (A) repeat
- (B) follow
- (C) shopping
- (D) outside

2. Which word is a compound word?

- (F) introduce
- (G) overpass
- (H) describe
- (J) unnecessary

3. Which word is a compound word?

- (A) being
- (B) enough
- (C) family
- (D) everyone

4. don't

- (F) did it
- (G) drive in
- (H) do think
- (J) do not

5. they're

- (A) they rest
- (B) they are
- (C) they run
- (D) they care

6. she'll

- (F) she falls
- (G) she all
- (H) she will
- (J) she likes

Name ______________________

READING: WORD ANALYSIS

Lesson 6: Root Words and Suffixes

Directions: Choose the best answer to each question.

Examples

A. Which word is the root or base word for the word mostly?

- (A) cost
- (B) tly
- (C) ly
- (D) most

B. Which word is the ending or suffix for the word helpless?

- (F) elp
- (G) help
- (H) less
- (J) ess

Stay with your first answer. Change it only if you are sure it is wrong and another answer is better.

Practice

1. Which word is the root word for kindness?

- (A) in
- (B) ness
- (C) kind
- (D) ind

2. Which word is the root word for trying?

- (F) try
- (G) ing
- (H) rying
- (J) tri

3. Which word is the root word for faster?

- (A) fas
- (B) fast
- (C) aster
- (D) ter

4. Which word is the suffix for rested?

- (F) ted
- (G) rest
- (H) ed
- (J) sted

5. Which word is the suffix for softly?

- (A) ftly
- (B) soft
- (C) sof
- (D) ly

6. Which word is the suffix for treatment?

- (F) treat
- (G) eat
- (H) ment
- (J) nt

Name ______________________________

READING: VOCABULARY

Lesson 7: Picture Vocabulary

Directions: Choose the word that matches the picture.

Examples

A. This one has been done for you.

- (A) bottle
- (B) pour
- (C) glass
- (D) spill

B. Practice this one with your teacher.

- (F) sleep
- (G) baby
- (H) blanket
- (J) awake

Look at the picture carefully and then read the choices.

Practice

1.

- (A) clean
- (B) sing
- (C) blow
- (D) eat

2.

- (F) crying
- (G) happy
- (H) smiling
- (J) talking

3.

- (A) baby
- (B) stand
- (C) come
- (D) crib

4.

- (F) out
- (G) whisper
- (H) shout
- (J) laugh

Name ___________________________

READING: VOCABULARY

Lesson 8: Word Meaning

Directions: Look at the underlined words in each sentence. Which word means the same thing?

Example

A. Which word is <u>part of your hand</u>?

Ⓐ toe
Ⓑ tooth
Ⓒ ring
Ⓓ finger

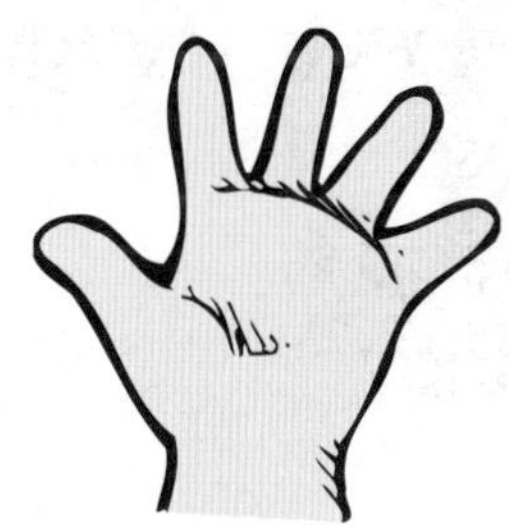

Key words in the question will help you find the answer.

Practice

1. Which word is <u>something that flies</u>?

Ⓐ bird
Ⓑ cat
Ⓒ worm
Ⓓ dog

2. Which word means <u>to leave</u>?

Ⓕ enter
Ⓖ grow
Ⓗ exit
Ⓙ stay

3. Which word means <u>to finish</u>?

Ⓐ finally
Ⓑ different
Ⓒ start
Ⓓ complete

4. Which word means <u>to start</u>?

Ⓕ read
Ⓖ begin
Ⓗ end
Ⓙ done

5. Which word is <u>something you drive on</u>?

Ⓐ shoes
Ⓑ road
Ⓒ stop
Ⓓ door

6. Which word is <u>where a worm lives</u>?

Ⓕ ground
Ⓖ nest
Ⓗ house
Ⓙ car

Name ______________________

READING: VOCABULARY

Lesson 9: Synonyms

Directions: Look at the underlined word in each sentence. Which word is a synonym for that word?

Example

A. His clothes were muddy.

- Ⓐ loose
- Ⓑ cheap
- Ⓒ baggy
- Ⓓ dirty

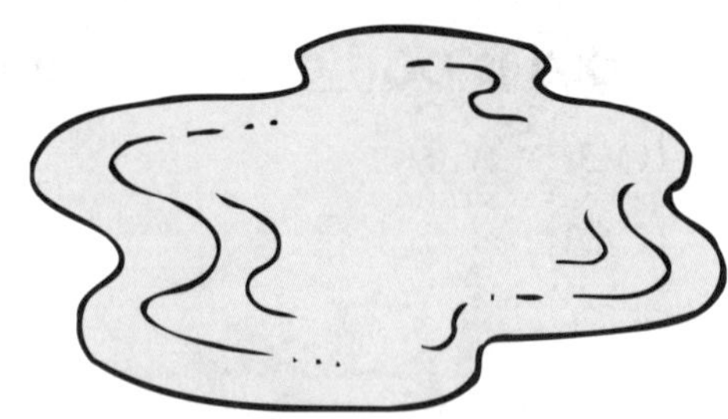

Use other words in the sentence to help you find the meaning of the word.

Practice

1. Jesse wanted to solve the hard riddle.

- Ⓐ job
- Ⓑ race
- Ⓒ puzzle
- Ⓓ portion

2. Carl thought it was a strange day.

- Ⓕ nice
- Ⓖ long
- Ⓗ short
- Ⓙ different

3. Alyson was always smiling.

- Ⓐ never
- Ⓑ forever
- Ⓒ usually
- Ⓓ sometimes

4. They like to create jokes.

- Ⓕ make
- Ⓖ bake
- Ⓗ hear
- Ⓙ doing

5. He likes to eat small apples.

- Ⓐ little
- Ⓑ rain
- Ⓒ ready
- Ⓓ leave

6. She watched as the sun came up.

- Ⓕ licked
- Ⓖ heard
- Ⓗ felt
- Ⓙ looked

READING: VOCABULARY

Lesson 10: Antonyms

Directions: Look at the underlined word in each sentence. Choose the word that is the antonym of the underlined word.

Example

A. His room was large.

(A) pretty
(B) big
(C) small
(D) noisy

Look for the answer that means the opposite of the underlined word. Skip difficult questions and come back to them later.

Practice

1. Her brother was young.

(A) busy
(B) new
(C) tired
(D) old

2. The family took a trip to the city.

(F) zoo
(G) park
(H) country
(J) building

3. The bedroom was always messy.

(A) lost
(B) neat
(C) sand
(D) dirty

4. She was the best at spelling.

(F) worst
(G) simple
(H) good
(J) rest

5. They had real money to go shopping.

(A) need
(B) less
(C) fake
(D) his

6. My sister likes ice cream.

(F) mother
(G) father
(H) brother
(J) uncle

Name ______________________

READING: VOCABULARY

Lesson 11: Words in Context

Directions: Choose the word that best fits in the blank.

Examples

The ___(A)___ was easy to enter. All you had to do was go to the park. To win, you had to ___(B)___ how many jelly beans were in the jar.

A.
- (A) door
- (B) contest
- (C) tunnel

B.
- (F) guess
- (G) read
- (H) count

When deciding which answer is best, try each answer choice in the blank.

Practice

Each house on the block had a ___(1)___ backyard. Each had small patches of lawn and flowers. Some even had ___(2)___ gardens.

1.
- (A) unlikely
- (B) neat
- (C) lost

2.
- (F) sand
- (G) problem
- (H) vegetable

One morning Chris couldn't ___(3)___ his homework. He looked on his ___(4)___, but it wasn't there. He wondered, "Where could it be?"

3.
- (A) find
- (B) hidden
- (C) hear

4.
- (F) lamp
- (G) dog
- (H) desk

Name ______________________________

READING: VOCABULARY

Lesson 12: Multiple Meaning Words

Directions: Some words have more than one meaning. Choose the word that will make sense in both blanks.

Example

A. I ________ for the door.
She bumped her ________ when she fell.

Ⓐ went Ⓒ self
Ⓑ leg Ⓓ head

Clue: **Remember, the correct answer must make sense in both blanks.**

Practice

1. _____ the light over here.
The _____ on this pencil broke.

Ⓐ point
Ⓑ eraser
Ⓒ shine
Ⓓ top

2. The boat began to _____. Dad washed the dishes in the _____.

Ⓕ wait
Ⓖ tub
Ⓗ sink
Ⓙ pan

3. Hit the _____ with the hammer.
The _____ on my little finger is broken.

Ⓐ tack
Ⓑ nail
Ⓒ skin
Ⓓ wood

4. Did you _____ your visitor well?
My dog loves to get a _____ from me.

Ⓕ feed
Ⓖ snack
Ⓗ enjoy
Ⓙ treat

5. The brown _____ was sleeping in the cave.
She could not ____ to hear any more scary stories.

Ⓐ hear
Ⓑ fox
Ⓒ bear
Ⓓ take

STOP

Name ______________________

READING: COMPREHENSION

Lesson 13: Picture Comprehension

Directions: Look at the picture. Then, choose the word that best fits in the blank.

Example

A. The train is ________ in a few minutes.

- (A) whistled
- (B) arriving
- (C) hours
- (D) floating

Look back at the picture when you choose an answer to fit in the blank.

Practice

1. The line for the movie ________ around the corner.

- (A) went
- (B) ran
- (C) skipped
- (D) sang

2. This was a film that everyone wanted to ________.

- (F) like
- (G) hear
- (H) see
- (J) drink

3. Jenna caught small fish on her new fishing ________.

- (A) bait
- (B) camp
- (C) box
- (D) rod

4. Her ________ helped her take it off the hook.

- (F) mom
- (G) dad
- (H) baby
- (J) brother

Name ______________________

READING: COMPREHENSION

Lesson 14: Critical Reading

Directions: Read each sentence. Choose the sentence that describes something that could **not** happen.

Example

A. (A) The wind was blowing hard and it was snowing.

(B) Because of the storm, school was closed.

(C) Pedro and Juanita dressed in warm clothing to play outside.

(D) Their dog, Barney, dressed himself in a hat and gloves too.

Read the sentences carefully. Think about what could and could not happen.

Practice

1. (A) Mr. and Mrs. Jennings heard a noise outside and realized their kitten was missing.

(B) Mrs. Jennings flapped her arms fast and flew out the door.

(C) They looked under the bushes and all around the house.

(D) They weren't sure where the kitten was hiding but they kept looking.

2. (F) Uncle Paul and Jeff were sailing their boat.

(G) It was windy and they were having a good day.

(H) It was almost time for lunch.

(J) Out of the clouds dropped a picnic basket filled with food.

STOP

Name ____________________

READING: COMPREHENSION

Lesson 15: Fiction

Directions: Read or listen to the story below and answer the questions that follow.

Example

Camels are strong, sturdy animals that live in the desert. Camels are able to live in the desert because their bodies are designed for it.

A. What is the main idea?

- (A) camels are strong animals
- (B) living in the desert
- (C) bodies
- (D) animals in the desert

Practice

Read or listen to the paragraph below. It tells about a girl who thinks it would be great if no one could see her. Then, answer the questions.

If Cassie Were Invisible

Cassie kicked at the dirty clothes on her floor. She was upset. Her dad told her to clean her room. Cassie wished she was invisible. Then she wouldn't have to clean anything! If she were invisible, she would go to school and not do any work. She would stay up late. She would never have to take baths. Best of all, her brother couldn't pick on her. But, wait! If she were invisible, she wouldn't get any apple pie. And no one would ask her to play. Cassie would never get to hug her grandparents. Maybe being invisible wouldn't be so much fun after all.

1. In the beginning, why does Cassie want to be invisible?

- (A) Because she wants to play.
- (B) Because she loves apple pie.
- (C) Because she didn't like dad.
- (D) Because she didn't want to clean her room.

2. Why does Cassie decide she doesn't want to be invisible?

- (F) She loves to clean.
- (G) Her mom misses her.
- (H) She wouldn't get to hug her grandparents.
- (J) She wants to be smart.

3. Who is the main character in the story?

- (A) the dad
- (B) Cassie
- (C) the grandparents
- (D) the teacher

4. Where does the story take place?

- (F) at school
- (G) at Cassie's grandparents
- (H) at the park
- (J) at Cassie's house

READING: COMPREHENSION

Lesson 15: Fiction (cont.)

Directions: Read or listen to the story below. It tells about Sam being the oldest child in his family. Then, answer the questions.

The Oldest

Sometimes, Sam likes being the oldest. He can stay up one hour later. He can go places by himself. He also gets a bigger allowance for helping around the house. When his friend Brennan asks him to spend the night, Sam's mom says yes. He even gets to stay at his friend's house to eat dinner sometimes. Sam thinks it's great that he can read, ride a bike, and spell better than his brother. Sam's sister loves when he reads stories to her. Sam likes it too. When his mom needs help cooking, she asks Sam because he is the oldest.

Sometimes, Sam doesn't like being the oldest. He has to babysit his sister. She likes to go where he does. He also has to act more like a grown-up. Sam always has more jobs to do around the house. He has to help wash the dishes and take out the trash. His brother and sister get help when they have to clean their rooms. Sam doesn't get help. Sam doesn't like to be the oldest when his brother and sister want him to play with them all the time.

5. What can Sam do better than his brother?

- (A) play soccer
- (B) eat candy
- (C) ride a bike
- (D) watch movies

6. What does Sam think about having to act more like a grown up?

- (F) He likes it.
- (G) He thinks his brother should act more grown-up.
- (H) It is one reason why he doesn't like to be the oldest.
- (J) He wants his parents to treat his brother like they treat him.

7. Who is the main character in the story?

- (A) Brennan
- (B) the sister
- (C) the brother
- (D) Sam

8. What is the main idea of the story?

- (F) washing dishes
- (G) eating dinner
- (H) playing outside
- (J) being the oldest

Name ______________________

READING: COMPREHENSION

Lesson 16: Nonfiction

Directions: Read or listen to the paragraph below that tells how to make a peanut butter and jelly sandwich. Then, answer the questions.

How to Make a Peanut Butter and Jelly Sandwich

You will need peanut butter, jelly, and two pieces of bread. First, spread peanut butter on one piece of bread. Next, spread jelly on the other piece. Then, put the two pieces of bread together. Next, cut the sandwich in half. Last, eat your sandwich and enjoy!

1. What is the paragraph explaining?

- (A) how to make peanut butter
- (B) how to cut sandwiches
- (C) how to make peanut butter and jelly sandwiches
- (D) how to put bread together

2. Which of these is an opinion?

- (F) Peanut butter and jelly sandwiches have jelly in them.
- (G) The paragraph says to cut the sandwich.
- (H) You can use two pieces of bread.
- (J) Peanut butter and jelly sandwiches are great.

3. What does the paragraph say to do after you spread peanut butter on one piece of bread?

- (A) cut the sandwich
- (B) spread jelly on the other piece of bread
- (C) put the two pieces together
- (D) eat your sandwich and enjoy eating it

4. What don't you need to make a peanut butter and jelly sandwich?

- (F) bread
- (G) peanut butter
- (H) milk
- (J) jelly

READING: COMPREHENSION

Lesson 16: Nonfiction (cont.)

Directions: Read or listen to the paragraph below that tells about dolphins and sharks. Then, answer the questions.

Dolphins and Sharks

Dolphins and sharks both live in the ocean, but they are very different. Dolphins are mammals. Sharks are fish. Both animals swim underwater. Sharks breathe through gills, and dolphins have lungs. Dolphins breathe through a blowhole on their heads. Dolphins have smooth, slippery skin, but sharks have scales. Dolphins give birth to live young. Sharks lay eggs. When the eggs hatch, young sharks come out. Sharks and dolphins live in water, but they have many differences.

5. Which animal has smooth, slippery skin?

- Ⓐ dolphins
- Ⓑ sharks
- Ⓒ eggs
- Ⓓ fish

6. Why did the author write about dolphins and sharks?

- Ⓕ to feel the smooth skin of the dolphins
- Ⓖ to learn how to swim
- Ⓗ to tell others about dolphins and sharks
- Ⓙ to breathe through the gills

7. What do you know about dolphins and sharks?

- Ⓐ They are mostly alike.
- Ⓑ They both have blowholes.
- Ⓒ There are many different things about them.
- Ⓓ They live in rivers and streams.

8. What do sharks need to breathe?

- Ⓕ lungs
- Ⓖ blowholes
- Ⓗ noses
- Ⓙ gills

TEST PRACTICE

Name ____________________

READING PRACTICE TEST ANSWER SHEET

STUDENT'S NAME																	
LAST											FIRST						MI
A	A	A	A	A	A	A	A	A	A	A	A	A	A	A	A	A	A
B	B	B	B	B	B	B	B	B	B	B	B	B	B	B	B	B	B
C	C	C	C	C	C	C	C	C	C	C	C	C	C	C	C	C	C
D	D	D	D	D	D	D	D	D	D	D	D	D	D	D	D	D	D
E	E	E	E	E	E	E	E	E	E	E	E	E	E	E	E	E	E
F	F	F	F	F	F	F	F	F	F	F	F	F	F	F	F	F	F
G	G	G	G	G	G	G	G	G	G	G	G	G	G	G	G	G	G
H	H	H	H	H	H	H	H	H	H	H	H	H	H	H	H	H	H
I	I	I	I	I	I	I	I	I	I	I	I	I	I	I	I	I	I
J	J	J	J	J	J	J	J	J	J	J	J	J	J	J	J	J	J
K	K	K	K	K	K	K	K	K	K	K	K	K	K	K	K	K	K
L	L	L	L	L	L	L	L	L	L	L	L	L	L	L	L	L	L
M	M	M	M	M	M	M	M	M	M	M	M	M	M	M	M	M	M
N	N	N	N	N	N	N	N	N	N	N	N	N	N	N	N	N	N
O	O	O	O	O	O	O	O	O	O	O	O	O	O	O	O	O	O
P	P	P	P	P	P	P	P	P	P	P	P	P	P	P	P	P	P
Q	Q	Q	Q	Q	Q	Q	Q	Q	Q	Q	Q	Q	Q	Q	Q	Q	Q
R	R	R	R	R	R	R	R	R	R	R	R	R	R	R	R	R	R
S	S	S	S	S	S	S	S	S	S	S	S	S	S	S	S	S	S
T	T	T	T	T	T	T	T	T	T	T	T	T	T	T	T	T	T
U	U	U	U	U	U	U	U	U	U	U	U	U	U	U	U	U	U
V	V	V	V	V	V	V	V	V	V	V	V	V	V	V	V	V	V
W	W	W	W	W	W	W	W	W	W	W	W	W	W	W	W	W	W
X	X	X	X	X	X	X	X	X	X	X	X	X	X	X	X	X	X
Y	Y	Y	Y	Y	Y	Y	Y	Y	Y	Y	Y	Y	Y	Y	Y	Y	Y
Z	Z	Z	Z	Z	Z	Z	Z	Z	Z	Z	Z	Z	Z	Z	Z	Z	Z

SCHOOL

TEACHER

FEMALE ○ MALE ○

BIRTHDATE				
MONTH	DAY		YEAR	
JAN ○	0	0	0	0
FEB ○	1	1	1	1
MAR ○	2	2	2	2
APR ○	3	3		3
MAY ○		4		4
JUN ○		5		5
JUL ○		6		6
AUG ○		7		7
SEP ○		8		8
OCT ○		9		9
NOV ○				
DEC ○				

GRADE ① ② ③

Part 1: WORD ANALYSIS

A Ⓐ Ⓑ Ⓒ Ⓓ	5 Ⓐ Ⓑ Ⓒ Ⓓ	8 Ⓕ Ⓖ Ⓗ Ⓙ	D Ⓕ Ⓖ Ⓗ	16 Ⓕ Ⓖ Ⓗ	19 Ⓐ Ⓑ Ⓒ Ⓓ
1 Ⓐ Ⓑ Ⓒ Ⓓ	6 Ⓕ Ⓖ Ⓗ Ⓙ	9 Ⓐ Ⓑ Ⓒ Ⓓ	E Ⓐ Ⓑ Ⓒ	F Ⓕ Ⓖ Ⓗ Ⓙ	20 Ⓕ Ⓖ Ⓗ Ⓙ
2 Ⓕ Ⓖ Ⓗ Ⓙ	B Ⓕ Ⓖ Ⓗ Ⓙ	10 Ⓕ Ⓖ Ⓗ Ⓙ	13 Ⓐ Ⓑ Ⓒ	G Ⓐ Ⓑ Ⓒ Ⓓ	21 Ⓐ Ⓑ Ⓒ Ⓓ
3 Ⓐ Ⓑ Ⓒ Ⓓ	C Ⓐ Ⓑ Ⓒ Ⓓ	11 Ⓐ Ⓑ Ⓒ Ⓓ	14 Ⓕ Ⓖ Ⓗ	17 Ⓐ Ⓑ Ⓒ Ⓓ	22 Ⓕ Ⓖ Ⓗ Ⓙ
4 Ⓕ Ⓖ Ⓗ Ⓙ	7 Ⓐ Ⓑ Ⓒ Ⓓ	12 Ⓕ Ⓖ Ⓗ Ⓙ	15 Ⓐ Ⓑ Ⓒ	18 Ⓕ Ⓖ Ⓗ Ⓙ	

Part 2: VOCABULARY

A Ⓐ Ⓑ Ⓒ Ⓓ	6 Ⓕ Ⓖ Ⓗ Ⓙ	12 Ⓕ Ⓖ Ⓗ Ⓙ	18 Ⓕ Ⓖ Ⓗ Ⓙ	23 Ⓐ Ⓑ Ⓒ Ⓓ	29 Ⓐ Ⓑ Ⓒ Ⓓ
1 Ⓐ Ⓑ Ⓒ Ⓓ	7 Ⓐ Ⓑ Ⓒ Ⓓ	13 Ⓐ Ⓑ Ⓒ Ⓓ	19 Ⓐ Ⓑ Ⓒ Ⓓ	24 Ⓕ Ⓖ Ⓗ Ⓙ	30 Ⓕ Ⓖ Ⓗ Ⓙ
2 Ⓕ Ⓖ Ⓗ Ⓙ	8 Ⓕ Ⓖ Ⓗ Ⓙ	14 Ⓕ Ⓖ Ⓗ Ⓙ	20 Ⓕ Ⓖ Ⓗ Ⓙ	25 Ⓐ Ⓑ Ⓒ Ⓓ	31 Ⓐ Ⓑ Ⓒ Ⓓ
3 Ⓐ Ⓑ Ⓒ Ⓓ	9 Ⓐ Ⓑ Ⓒ Ⓓ	15 Ⓐ Ⓑ Ⓒ Ⓓ	21 Ⓐ Ⓑ Ⓒ Ⓓ	26 Ⓕ Ⓖ Ⓗ Ⓙ	32 Ⓕ Ⓖ Ⓗ Ⓙ
4 Ⓕ Ⓖ Ⓗ Ⓙ	10 Ⓕ Ⓖ Ⓗ Ⓙ	16 Ⓕ Ⓖ Ⓗ Ⓙ	22 Ⓕ Ⓖ Ⓗ Ⓙ	27 Ⓕ Ⓖ Ⓗ Ⓙ	33 Ⓐ Ⓑ Ⓒ Ⓓ
B Ⓕ Ⓖ Ⓗ Ⓙ	C Ⓐ Ⓑ Ⓒ Ⓓ	D Ⓕ Ⓖ Ⓗ Ⓙ	E Ⓐ Ⓑ Ⓒ Ⓓ	28 Ⓐ Ⓑ Ⓒ Ⓓ	34 Ⓐ Ⓑ Ⓒ Ⓓ
5 Ⓐ Ⓑ Ⓒ Ⓓ	11 Ⓐ Ⓑ Ⓒ Ⓓ	17 Ⓐ Ⓑ Ⓒ Ⓓ	F Ⓕ Ⓖ Ⓗ Ⓙ	G Ⓕ Ⓖ Ⓗ Ⓙ	

Part 3: READING COMPREHENSION

A Ⓐ Ⓑ Ⓒ Ⓓ	4 Ⓕ Ⓖ Ⓗ Ⓙ	8 Ⓕ Ⓖ Ⓗ Ⓙ	12 Ⓐ Ⓑ Ⓒ Ⓓ	16 Ⓕ Ⓖ Ⓗ Ⓙ	20 Ⓐ Ⓑ Ⓒ Ⓓ
1 Ⓐ Ⓑ Ⓒ Ⓓ	5 Ⓐ Ⓑ Ⓒ Ⓓ	9 Ⓐ Ⓑ Ⓒ Ⓓ	13 Ⓕ Ⓖ Ⓗ Ⓙ	17 Ⓐ Ⓑ Ⓒ Ⓓ	
2 Ⓕ Ⓖ Ⓗ Ⓙ	6 Ⓕ Ⓖ Ⓗ Ⓙ	10 Ⓕ Ⓖ Ⓗ Ⓙ	14 Ⓐ Ⓑ Ⓒ Ⓓ	18 Ⓕ Ⓖ Ⓗ Ⓙ	
3 Ⓐ Ⓑ Ⓒ Ⓓ	7 Ⓐ Ⓑ Ⓒ Ⓓ	11 Ⓐ Ⓑ Ⓒ Ⓓ	15 Ⓕ Ⓖ Ⓗ Ⓙ	19 Ⓐ Ⓑ Ⓒ Ⓓ	

Name ______________________

READING PRACTICE TEST

Part 1: Word Analysis

Directions: Choose the best answer to each question.

Example

A. Which word has the same beginning sound as small?

- (A) snow
- (B) smooth
- (C) shown
- (D) something

1. Which word has the same vowel sound as catch?

- (A) came
- (B) bad
- (C) eat
- (D) clean

2. Which word has the same beginning sound as block?

- (F) box
- (G) breeze
- (H) blink
- (J) answer

3. Which word has the same ending sound as work?

- (A) yard
- (B) stood
- (C) took
- (D) watch

4. Which word has the same vowel sound as stood?

- (F) two
- (G) those
- (H) road
- (J) could

5. Which word has the same ending sound as with?

- (A) while
- (B) kiss
- (C) bath
- (D) these

6. Which word has the same beginning sound as same?

- (F) ham
- (G) rain
- (H) shall
- (J) sand

Name ______________________

READING PRACTICE TEST

Part 1: Word Analysis (cont.)

Directions: Choose the best answer to each question.

Examples

B. Which word is a compound word, a word that is made up of two smaller words?

- (F) complete
- (G) certain
- (H) became
- (J) sunlight

C. Find the answer that tells what the contraction means.

that'll

- (A) that is
- (B) that will
- (C) that all
- (D) that calls

If an item is too difficult, skip it and come back to it later.

7. Which word is a compound word?

- (A) sidewalk
- (B) building
- (C) darkness
- (D) small

8. Which word is a compound word?

- (F) several
- (G) party
- (H) person
- (J) playground

9. Which word is a compound word?

- (A) nice
- (B) clothes
- (C) snowball
- (D) picture

10. needn't

- (F) need noses
- (G) need not
- (H) need night
- (J) need next

11. could've

- (A) could leave
- (B) could have
- (C) could very
- (D) could has

12. what's

- (F) what is
- (G) what stinks
- (H) what shakes
- (J) what sees

READING PRACTICE TEST

Part I: Word Analysis (cont.)

Directions: Choose the word that best fits in the blanks.

Examples

Jawan ___(D)___ down at the table. He was hungry and the ___(E)___ looked good.

D.
- (F) ate
- (G) look
- (H) sat

E.
- (A) chair
- (B) mom
- (C) food

We usually take our vacation in July. Mom and Dad ___(13)___ a house at the beach. It's not as big as our regular house, but everyone has a place to ___(14)___.

13.
- (A) rent
- (B) park
- (C) read

14.
- (F) sand
- (G) beach
- (H) sleep

It was my birthday! I was ___(15)___ seven years old. My mom made me a pretty cake. I blew out all the candles. My mom and dad gave me a great gift, a ___(16)___ bicycle!

15.
- (A) making
- (B) turning
- (C) looked

16.
- (F) ugly
- (G) new
- (H) even

Name ___________________________

READING PRACTICE TEST

Part 1: Word Analysis (cont.)

Directions: Choose the best answer to each question.

Examples

F. Which word is the root or base word for the word biggest?

- (F) big
- (G) gest
- (H) est
- (J) bigge

G. Which word is the ending or suffix for the word broken?

- (A) en
- (B) broke
- (C) bro
- (D) roke

17. Which word is the root word for certainly?

- (A) ly
- (B) cert
- (C) certain
- (D) change

18. Which word is the root word for fullness?

- (F) falling
- (G) ness
- (H) full
- (J) fur

19. Which word is the root word for slower?

- (A) slip
- (B) er
- (C) low
- (D) slow

20. Which word is the suffix for lighter?

- (F) light
- (G) er
- (H) igh
- (J) lig

21. Which word is the suffix for completely?

- (A) ly
- (B) pete
- (C) complete
- (D) come

22. Which word is the suffix for listing?

- (F) ing
- (G) list
- (H) isti
- (J) licking

READING PRACTICE TEST

Part 2: Vocabulary

Directions: Choose the word that best matches the picture.

Example

A.

Ⓐ hammer
Ⓑ drill
Ⓒ nail
Ⓓ wood

Look at the picture carefully and then read the choices.

1.

Ⓐ smell
Ⓑ feel
Ⓒ hear
Ⓓ see

2.

Ⓕ clap
Ⓖ shake
Ⓗ touch
Ⓙ snap

3.

Ⓐ leaf
Ⓑ wood
Ⓒ branch
Ⓓ tree

4.

Ⓕ watering
Ⓖ smoking
Ⓗ steaming
Ⓙ cooking

Name ____________________

READING PRACTICE TEST

Part 2: Vocabulary (cont.)

Directions: Choose the best answer.

Example

B. Which word means to soar like a bird?

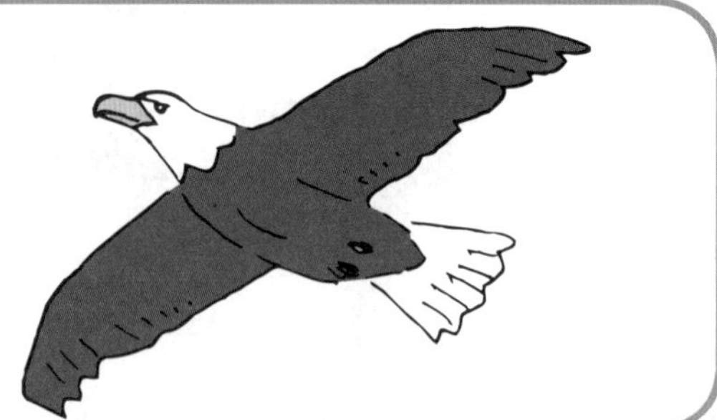

- (F) air
- (G) ride
- (H) run
- (J) fly

Key words in the question will help you find the answer.

5. Which word is something that walks?

- (A) cat
- (B) worm
- (C) snake
- (D) fish

6. Which word means to take air in through your nose?

- (F) cough
- (G) swim
- (H) eat
- (J) breathe

7. Which word means to talk about?

- (A) write
- (B) dream
- (C) enjoy
- (D) discuss

8. Which word means to follow after?

- (F) chase
- (G) begin
- (H) fall
- (J) turn

9. Which word means feeling like you need something to eat?

- (A) full
- (B) hungry
- (C) ate
- (D) food

10. Which word means to bend toward?

- (F) lean
- (G) reach
- (H) sleep
- (J) drop

READING PRACTICE TEST

Part 2: Vocabulary (cont.)

Directions: Look at the underlined word in each sentence. Which word is a synonym for that word?

Example

C. Her mom wrote a <u>note</u> to the teacher.

Ⓐ message
Ⓑ defeat
Ⓒ pencil
Ⓓ ticket

Use the meaning of the sentence to help you find the meaning of the word.

11. Susan was <u>grateful</u> that her dad drove her to school.

Ⓐ thankful
Ⓑ busy
Ⓒ curious
Ⓓ finished

12. The brothers <u>yelled</u> for their dog to come home.

Ⓕ cared
Ⓖ called
Ⓗ heard
Ⓙ whispered

13. Grandma asked me to <u>split</u> the cookies evenly between the children.

Ⓐ use
Ⓑ think
Ⓒ divide
Ⓓ stand

14. I always keep my room very <u>neat</u>.

Ⓕ bad
Ⓖ pretty
Ⓗ tidy
Ⓙ dark

15. She likes to eat <u>big</u> oranges

Ⓐ huge
Ⓑ tiny
Ⓒ ready
Ⓓ round

16. She watched the cat <u>jump</u> off the chair.

Ⓕ leap
Ⓖ lick
Ⓗ break
Ⓙ dream

Name ______________________________

READING PRACTICE TEST

Part 2: Vocabulary (cont.)

Directions: Look at the underlined word in each sentence. Choose the word that is the antonym of the underlined word.

Example

D. He has an <u>unusual</u> voice.

- (F) loud
- (G) regular
- (H) soft
- (J) small

17. They drove down the <u>narrow</u> road.

- (A) long
- (B) new
- (C) bumpy
- (D) wide

18. She picked her <u>fancy</u> dress to wear to the party.

- (F) best
- (G) plain
- (H) small
- (J) little

19. She made sure the knot was good and <u>tight</u>.

- (A) clean
- (B) different
- (C) loose
- (D) last

20. After granting our three wishes, the kind fairy <u>vanished</u> from sight.

- (F) appeared
- (G) asked
- (H) going
- (J) got

21. He thought his bike was <u>fast</u>.

- (A) funny
- (B) food
- (C) last
- (D) slow

22. On Thursday, Daniel was <u>absent</u>.

- (F) giving
- (G) present
- (H) hurt
- (J) gone

READING PRACTICE TEST

Part 2: Vocabulary (cont.)

Directions: Choose the word that best fits in each blank.

Examples

Mr. Jennings went __(E)__ after work. He bought food for dinner and then he went __(F)__.

E.
- (A) shopping
- (B) walking
- (C) driving

F.
- (F) soon
- (G) fast
- (H) home

When deciding which answer is best, try each answer choice in the blank.

Our neighbor is a gardener. One of her __(23)__ trees recently died. She said it was because of a bug that likes to eat __(24)__.

23.
- (A) girl
- (B) half
- (C) small

24.
- (F) each
- (G) leaves
- (H) dirt

One sunny June day, a man __(25)__ too fast down the road. A police officer stopped him and gave him a __(26)__.

25.
- (A) drove
- (B) paced
- (C) ran

26.
- (F) picture
- (G) ticket
- (H) rest

There are many different __(27)__ of bats. One kind is the brown bat.

27.
- (A) only
- (B) paper
- (C) kinds

__(28)__ brown bats eat insects. One bat can eat 600 mosquitoes in just an hour.

28.
- (F) second
- (G) little
- (H) sleep

Name ____________________

READING PRACTICE TEST

Part 2: Vocabulary (cont.)

Directions: Some words have more than one meaning. Choose the word that will make sense in both blanks.

Example

G. My mom gets to take ________ at work.
I get mad when my brother________ my toys.

- Ⓐ misses
- Ⓑ breaks
- Ⓒ picks
- Ⓓ walks

29. He carried his________to the baseball field.
The ________ was hanging in the cave.

- Ⓐ bat
- Ⓑ men
- Ⓒ ball
- Ⓓ sheep

30. In the ________ my mom plants all of her flowers.
The ________ next to the mountain had fresh water.

- Ⓕ picnic
- Ⓖ fall
- Ⓗ spring
- Ⓙ snow

31. Did you go to the _______ with your friends?
Where should I _____ the car?

- Ⓐ party
- Ⓑ school
- Ⓒ park
- Ⓓ drive

32. A bear had a heavy _______.
My mom bought me a new _______ for winter.

- Ⓕ hat
- Ⓖ fur
- Ⓗ enjoy
- Ⓙ coat

33. The river _______ into two seperate streams.
The _______ on the tree swayed in the wind

- Ⓐ leaves
- Ⓑ branches
- Ⓒ wanted
- Ⓓ goes

34. Cinderella was the most beautiful girl at the _______.
Hunter's grandma bought him a red _______ for his birthday.

- Ⓕ party
- Ⓖ gift
- Ⓗ ball
- Ⓙ bike

STOP

Name ______________________

READING PRACTICE TEST

Part 3: Story Comprehension

Example

Bigfoot is a creature that may be real or make-believe. Although many people say they have seen this creature, scientists want more proof. Is there a man-like beast lurking around the woods in countries all over the world?

A. What is Bigfoot?

Ⓐ a huge foot
Ⓑ a giant sock
Ⓒ a creature
Ⓓ a country

Read or listen to the paragraph below that tells about horses. Then, answer the questions.

Horses

Horses are beautiful animals. Most horses have smooth, shiny coats. They have long manes and tails. Their hair may be brown, black, white, yellow, or spotted. Sometimes horses neigh, or make a loud, long cry. Horses need to be brushed every day. This helps keep them clean. Many people keep horses as pets or to work on farms. Some people enjoy riding them for fun. Horses are wonderful animals.

1. What does the word neigh mean?

Ⓐ to smile
Ⓑ to be different colors
Ⓒ to keep clean by brushing
Ⓓ to make a loud, long cry

2. How often should horses be brushed?

Ⓕ every day
Ⓖ every week
Ⓗ every month
Ⓙ every year

3. What do you know about horses?

Ⓐ Horses are the same color.
Ⓑ Horses never make noise.
Ⓒ Some people enjoy riding horses for fun.
Ⓓ Horses have feathers.

4. If you had a horse for a pet, what might happen?

Ⓕ You would have to feed it.
Ⓖ You would have to brush its mane and tail.
Ⓗ You would have to have a place for the horse to stay.
Ⓙ All of the above

Name ______________________

READING PRACTICE TEST

Part 3: Story Comprehension (cont.)

Directions: Read or listen to the paragraphs below that tell about stars. Then, answer the questions.

Stars

(1) When you look up on a clear, dark night, you can see small points of light called stars. Actually, stars are not small at all. Some stars may be 50 million miles across! Stars just look like points of light because they are so far from Earth. Our sun is a star. It looks bigger than other stars in the sky because it is closer to us. A star's brightness depends on its mass and distance from Earth. Bigger stars are brighter than smaller ones. Stars also look brighter when they are closer.

(2) To make it easier to study, people have grouped stars into patterns. The patterns are called constellations. They may be large or small. They may have bright or dim stars. Sometimes in a constellation, the bright stars may be in the shape of a person or animal.

(3) Stars, unlike planets, make their own heat and light. The color of a star's light can tell us how much heat it has. The cooler stars give off a reddish light. The hottest stars look blue or blue-white in color. Stars do not last the same amount of time. They all will eventually burn out.

5. What does the word constellation mean?

- Ⓐ large and in space
- Ⓑ different stars people see from Mars
- Ⓒ different color stars we can see from the earth
- Ⓓ a pattern of stars that are grouped together

6. Which of the following is an opinion?

- Ⓕ Stars are fun to look at every night.
- Ⓖ Our sun is a star.
- Ⓗ Stars look brighter when they are closer.
- Ⓙ Cooler stars give off a reddish light.

7. What is a supporting detail for paragraph 2?

- Ⓐ Colors of stars help us to know how hot they are.
- Ⓑ Our sun is a star.
- Ⓒ It takes imagination to find when different patterns in the sky look like people or animals.
- Ⓓ When stars burn out they turn into new kinds of stars.

8. What would happen if you traveled through space and got closer and closer to a star?

- Ⓕ You would see it get smaller.
- Ⓖ It would look like a rainbow.
- Ⓗ It would get brighter.
- Ⓙ All of the above

GO ON

READING PRACTICE TEST

Part 3: Story Comprehension (cont.)

Directions: Read or listen to the paragraph below. It tells about honey and bees. Then, answer the questions.

Sweet as Honey

Honey is sweet and thick. Honeybees make it. First, they fly from flower to flower. At each flower, they collect nectar. Nectar is watery. It is found inside flower blossoms. The bees sip the nectar from flowers. Next, they store it in their bodies. It is kept in their honey bags. Then, the nectar in the honey bags changes. It changes into two kinds of sugars. The bees fly back to their hives. Finally, they put the nectar into their hives. While it is there, most of the water leaves or evaporates. All that is left is the sweet, thick honey inside the honeycomb. People who collect honey remove the combs. Last, the sweet honey is sold for us to eat.

9. What is nectar?

- (A) a flower
- (B) a watery substance that bees sip from flowers
- (C) another name for honey
- (D) a part of a bee's body that makes honey

10. What would happen if the bees didn't have honey bags?

- (F) They couldn't make honey.
- (G) They would fly in circles.
- (H) They couldn't find flowers.
- (J) They wouldn't be able to see.

11. What happens after the bees put the nectar into their hives?

- (A) They fly from flower to flower.
- (B) They collect the nectar.
- (C) The bees sip the nectar from flowers.
- (D) Most of the water leaves or evaporates.

12. If you were a honey collector, where would you go to find honey?

- (F) in the store
- (G) in the honeybees' hive
- (H) in your house
- (J) in the sand

Name ____________________

READING PRACTICE TEST

Part 3: Story Comprehension (cont.)

Directions: Read or listen to the paragraphs below that tell about a mom who lost her spaghetti. Then, answer the questions.

The Investigation

The bowl sat empty. "Oh, no! My spaghetti is missing!" shrieked Mom. "I was supposed to take it to the school potluck tonight. What am I going to do?"

I decided to help my mom find her lost spaghetti. "Don't panic Mom, I'll look for clues," I said as I started looking around. The spaghetti had been in the bowl, on the counter, near the sink. First, I ran outside to check for footprints. There were none! It must have been an inside job.

Who would be my first suspect? I went to my baby sister Laurie's room. I checked in her crib, in her toy box, and in the closet. There was no sign of the spaghetti.

Next, I went to question my second suspect. I asked Dad if he had seen anything unusual. He had been mowing the lawn and didn't know anything about the case.

My leads seemed to be vanishing. Could a thief have come into our house and helped himself to dinner? Had aliens zapped it aboard their spaceship?

I looked around. Suddenly, I noticed through the open window two birds carrying long, red-and-white worms in their beaks. The Case of the Missing Spaghetti was closed!

13. What is the solution to The Case of the Missing Spaghetti?

- (A) Dad took the spaghetti.
- (B) Laurie ate the spaghetti.
- (C) Birds took the spaghetti.
- (D) Mom had put the spaghetti in the fridge.

14. Who was the second suspect?

- (F) baby Laurie
- (G) Mom
- (H) Dad
- (J) the birds

15. How do you know Dad didn't take the spaghetti?

- (A) He was mowing the lawn.
- (B) He was watching Laurie.
- (C) He liked pizza better.
- (D) Dad didn't like to investigate.

16. Why might the birds have taken the spaghetti?

- (F) They liked Italian food.
- (G) They thought they were worms.
- (H) They wanted to try something different.
- (J) They needed to make a nest.

READING PRACTICE TEST

Part 3: Story Comprehension (cont.)

Directions: Read or listen to the paragraphs below that tell about a boy who builds a robot. Then, answer the questions.

Bert, the Inventor

Every day after school, Bert locked himself in his bedroom. He was working on a secret project. He didn't tell anyone what he was doing. Not even his best friend Larry.

Bert finally finished. He had made a robot that looked exactly like himself. The robot had orange hair, freckles, and glasses. The robot and Bert both talked in a squeaky voice. "Life is going to be easy now!" exclaimed Bert. "I'm going to send my robot to school while I stay home and play."

The next morning the robot ate breakfast. Then, he rode the bus to school. After school the bus dropped the robot back home. The robot knocked on the door.

"Sweetie, I am so glad you're home. I really missed you!" said Mom. Then, she took the robot into the kitchen and gave him a snack before dinner.

"We had lots of fun at school today," said the robot. "We went to the space museum. I got to try on a real space suit. It was too big for me but the teacher took my picture."

Bert was listening outside the kitchen. He was sad. He wanted to be an astronaut someday. He decided this wasn't a good idea. So the next day, Bert went to school himself.

17. What did Bert look like?

Ⓐ He had curly hair and was tall.
Ⓑ He had red hair and wore a cap.
Ⓒ He was short with blonde hair.
Ⓓ He had orange hair, freckles, and glasses.

18. Why did Bert decide to go to school himself?

Ⓕ He missed his mom's smile.
Ⓖ He missed going to the space museum.
Ⓗ He missed his friend Larry.
Ⓙ He missed eating breakfast and going to school.

19. Where does this story take place?

Ⓐ at school
Ⓑ at the grocery store
Ⓒ at Larry's house
Ⓓ at Bert's house

20. Why did Bert create the robot?

Ⓕ He wanted to make life easier and have the robot go to school for him.
Ⓖ His mom was feeling sick and needed help cleaning.
Ⓗ He didn't want to be friends with Larry anymore.
Ⓙ He was sad that he didn't have any brothers.

STOP

Answer Key

4

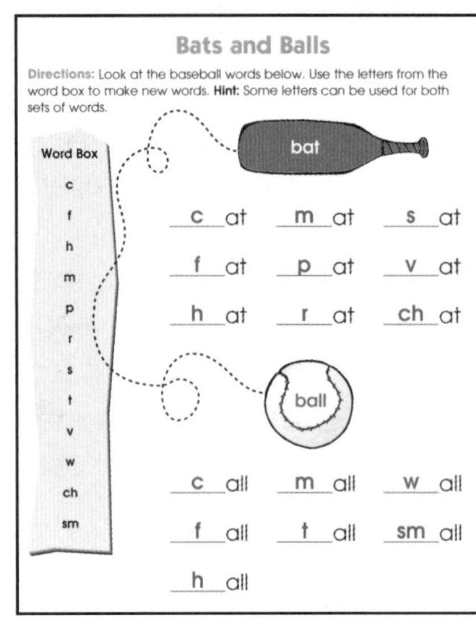

5

6

7

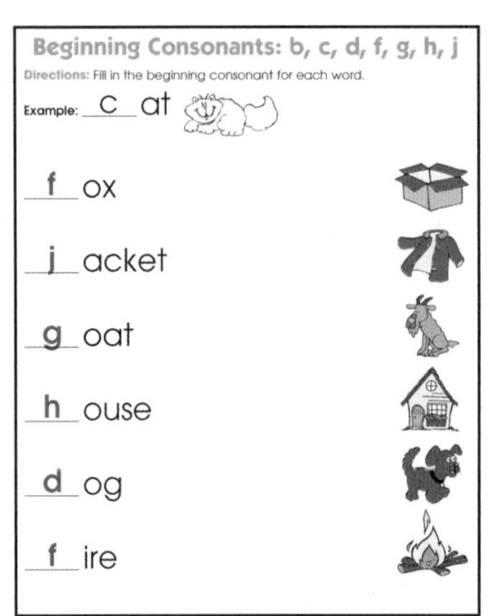

8

9

Answer Key

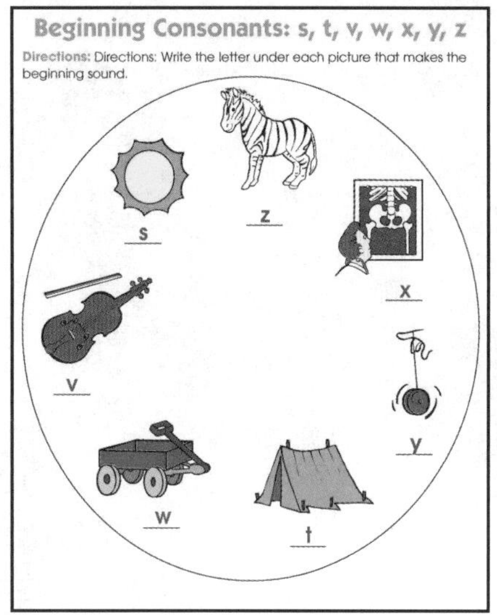
Beginning Consonants: s, t, v, w, x, y, z

Directions: Directions: Write the letter under each picture that makes the beginning sound.

s z x v y w t

10

Ending Consonants: b, d, f, g

Directions: Fill in the ending consonant for each word.

ma d

cu b

roo f

do g

be d

bi b

11

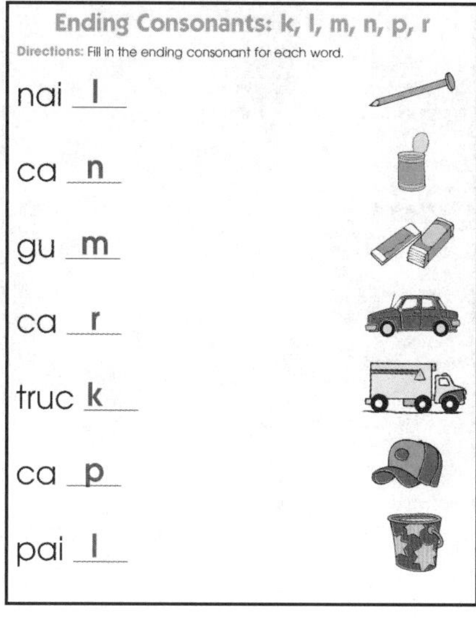
Ending Consonants: k, l, m, n, p, r

Directions: Fill in the ending consonant for each word.

nai l

ca n

gu m

ca r

truc k

ca p

pai l

12

Ending Consonants: s, t, x

Directions: Fill in the ending consonant for each word.

ca t

bo x

bu s

fo x

boa t

ma t

13

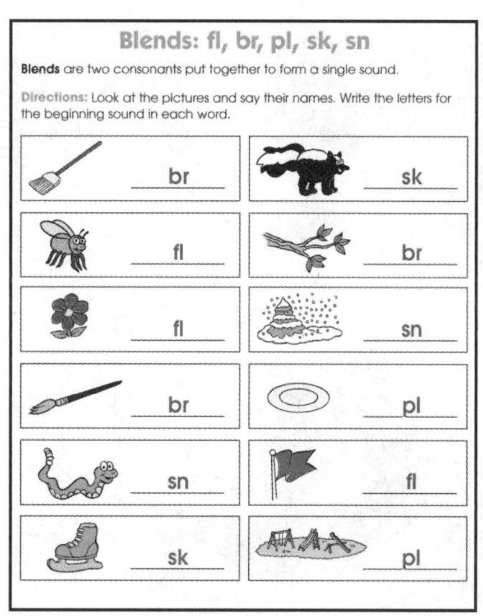
Blends: fl, br, pl, sk, sn

Blends are two consonants put together to form a single sound.

Directions: Look at the pictures and say their names. Write the letters for the beginning sound in each word.

br	sk
fl	br
fl	sn
br	pl
sn	fl
sk	pl

14

Blends: bl, sl, cr, cl

Directions: Look at the pictures and say their names. Write the letters for the beginning sound in each word.

cl own	bl anket	cr ayon
cl ock	sl ide	cl oud
sl ed	cr ab	cr ocodile

15

Answer Key

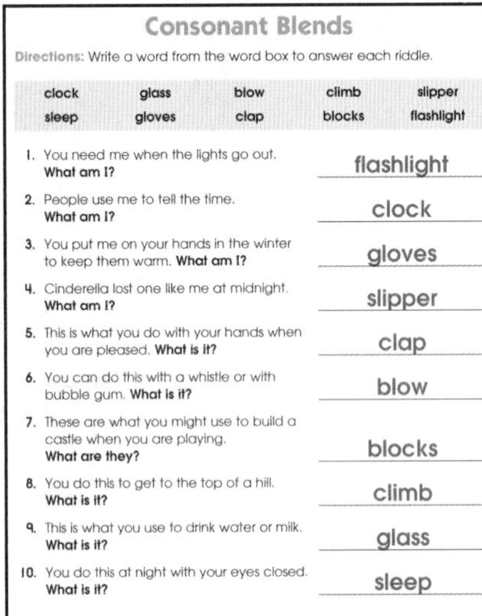

Consonant Blends

Directions: Write a word from the word box to answer each riddle.

clock	glass	blow	climb	slipper
sleep	gloves	clap	blocks	flashlight

1. You need me when the lights go out. **What am I?** flashlight
2. People use me to tell the time. **What am I?** clock
3. You put me on your hands in the winter to keep them warm. **What am I?** gloves
4. Cinderella lost one like me at midnight. **What am I?** slipper
5. This is what you do with your hands when you are pleased. **What is it?** clap
6. You can do this with a whistle or with bubble gum. **What is it?** blow
7. These are what you might use to build a castle when you are playing. **What are they?** blocks
8. You do this to get to the top of a hill. **What is it?** climb
9. This is what you use to drink water or milk. **What is it?** glass
10. You do this at night with your eyes closed. **What is it?** sleep

16

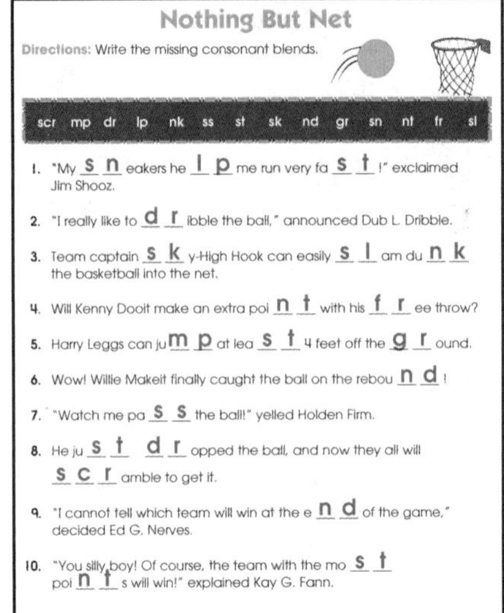

Nothing But Net

Directions: Write the missing consonant blends.

scr mp dr lp nk ss st sk nd gr sn nt fr sl

1. "My **sn**eakers he**lp** me run very fa**st**!" exclaimed Jim Shooz.
2. "I really like to **dr**ibble the ball," announced Dub L. Dribble.
3. Team captain **Sk**y-High Hook can easily **sl**am du**nk** the basketball into the net.
4. Will Kenny Doolt make an extra poi**nt** with his **fr**ee throw?
5. Harry Leggs can ju**mp** at lea**st** 4 feet off the **gr**ound.
6. Wow! Willie Makeit finally caught the ball on the rebou**nd**!
7. "Watch me pa**ss** the ball!" yelled Holden Firm.
8. He ju**st** **dr**opped the ball, and now they all will **scr**amble to get it.
9. "I cannot tell which team will win at the e**nd** of the game," decided Ed G. Nerves.
10. "You silly boy! Of course, the team with the mo**st** poi**nt**s will win!" explained Kay G. Fann.

17

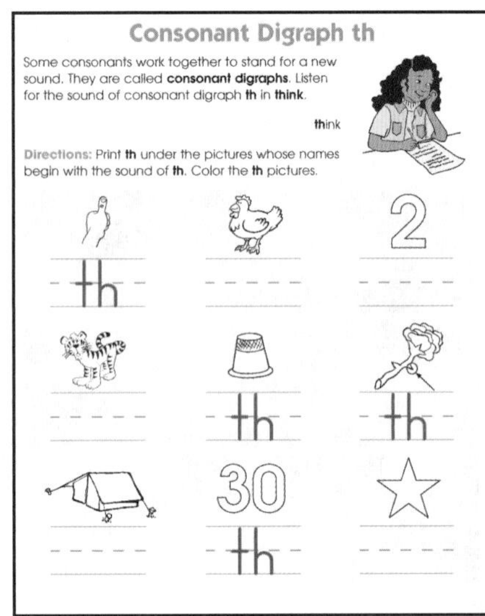

Consonant Digraph th

Some consonants work together to stand for a new sound. They are called **consonant digraphs**. Listen for the sound of consonant digraph **th** in **think**.

think

Directions: Print **th** under the pictures whose names begin with the sound of **th**. Color the **th** pictures.

th		
	th	th
	th	

18

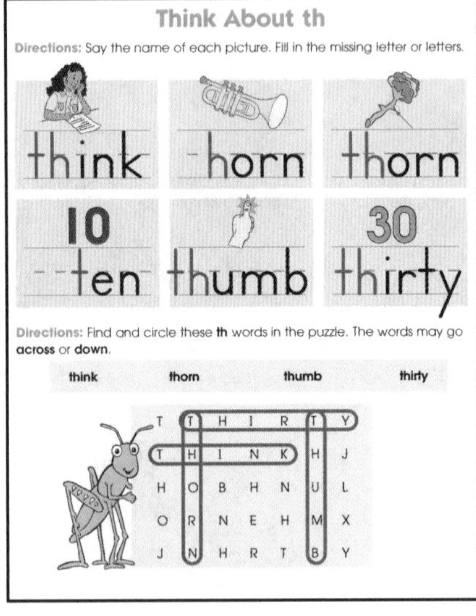

Think About th

Directions: Say the name of each picture. Fill in the missing letter or letters.

think	horn	thorn
10 ten	thumb	30 thirty

Directions: Find and circle these **th** words in the puzzle. The words may go **across** or **down**.

think thorn thumb thirty

T T H I R T Y
T H I N K H J
H O B H N U L
O R N E H M X
J N H R T B Y

19

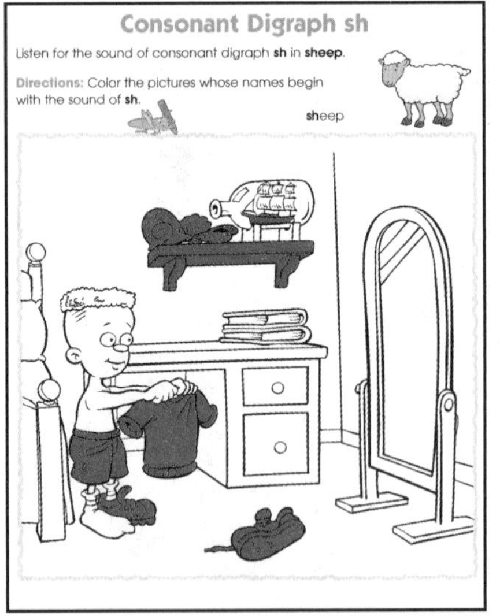

Consonant Digraph sh

Listen for the sound of consonant digraph **sh** in **sheep**.

Directions: Color the pictures whose names begin with the sound of **sh**.

sheep

20

Change a Word

Directions: Make a new word by changing the beginning sound to **sh**. Write the new word on the line.

zip	sell	beep
ship	shell	sheep
tin	line	lift
shin	shine	shift
red	cape	cave
shed	shape	shave
top	bake	feet
shop	shake	sheet

21

Answer Key

Consonant Digraph wh
Directions: Write wh, th, or sh to complete each word.
wheel whale sheep
think wheat thorn
ship thirty white

22

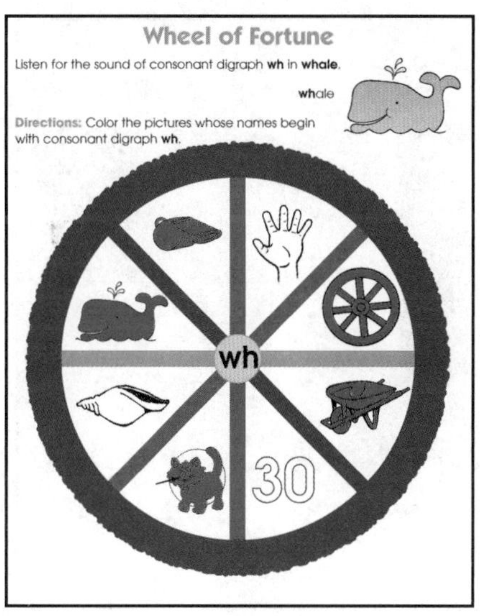

23

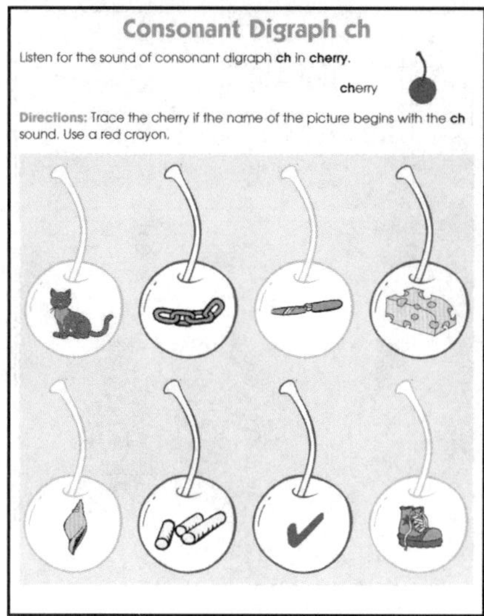

Consonant Digraph ch
Listen for the sound of consonant digraph ch in cherry.
cherry
Directions: Trace the cherry if the name of the picture begins with the ch sound. Use a red crayon.

24

Read and Write Digraphs
Directions: Write a word from the box to label each picture.
chest check sheep
chimp cherry thirty
chain cheese wheel
cherry sheep chain
chest wheel cheese
chimp thirty check
30

25

26

27

Answer Key

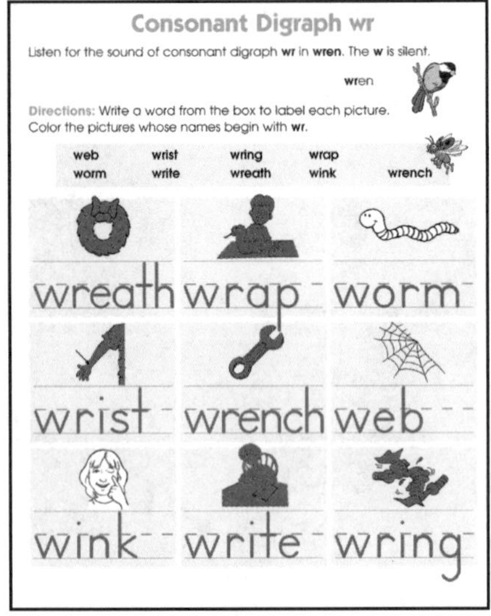

Consonant Digraph wr

Listen for the sound of consonant digraph **wr** in **wren**. The **w** is silent.

wren

Directions: Write a word from the box to label each picture. Color the pictures whose names begin with **wr**.

web	wrist	wring	wrap	
worm	write	wreath	wink	wrench

wreath	wrap	worm
wrist	wrench	web
wink	write	wring

28

At the Pool

Directions: Write the correct letters from the word box to complete the word for each picture.

Word Box: wh, bl, sw, cl, st, ch

wh istle

cl ipboard

starting cl ock

st opwat ch

sw im cap

29

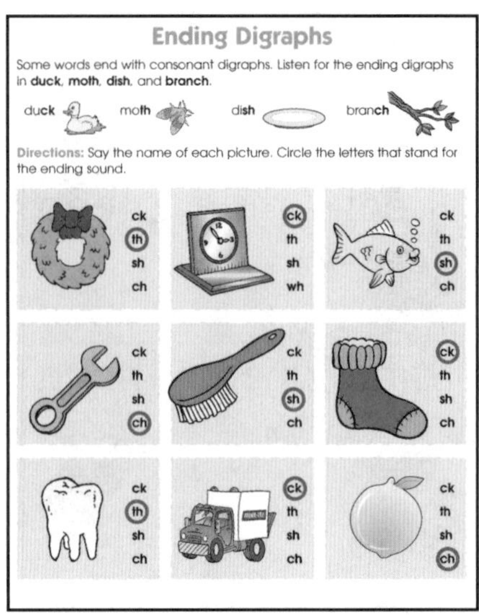

Ending Digraphs

Some words end with consonant digraphs. Listen for the ending digraphs in **duck**, **moth**, **dish**, and **branch**.

duck moth dish branch

Directions: Say the name of each picture. Circle the letters that stand for the ending sound.

(circled answers shown in bold)

ck **th** sh ch	**ck** th sh wh	ck th **sh** ch
ck th sh **ch**	ck th **sh** ch	**ck** th sh ch
ck **th** sh ch	**ck** th sh ch	ck th sh **ch**

30

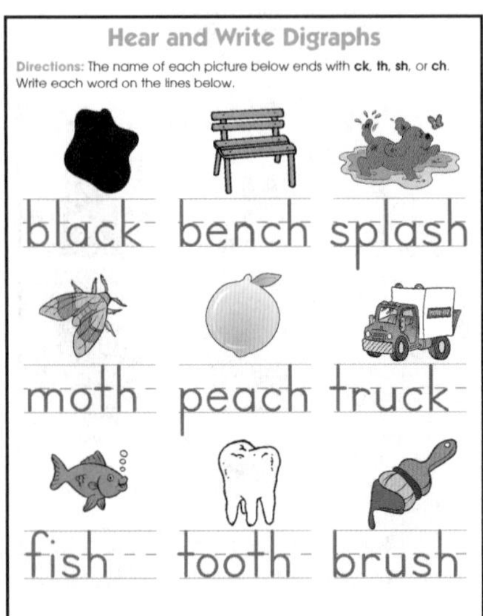

Hear and Write Digraphs

Directions: The name of each picture below ends with **ck**, **th**, **sh**, or **ch**. Write each word on the lines below.

black	bench	splash
moth	peach	truck
fish	tooth	brush

31

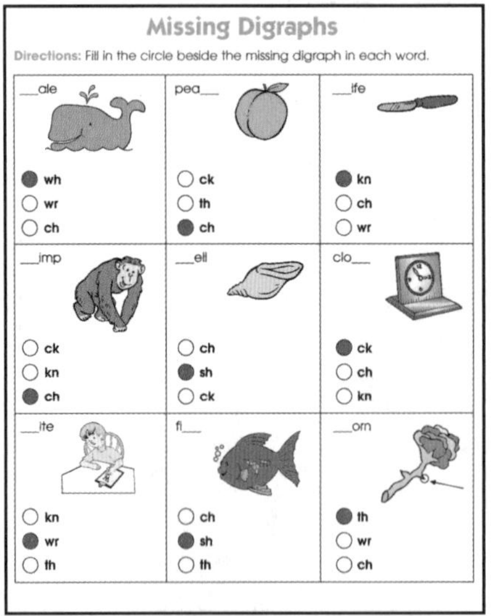

Missing Digraphs

Directions: Fill in the circle beside the missing digraph in each word.

__ale ● wh ○ wr ○ ch	pea__ ○ ck ○ th ● ch	__ife ● kn ○ ch ○ wr
__imp ○ ck ○ kn ● ch	__ell ○ ch ● sh ○ ck	clo__ ● ck ○ ch ○ kn
__ite ○ kn ● wr ○ th	fi__ ○ ch ● sh ○ th	__orn ● th ○ wr ○ ch

32

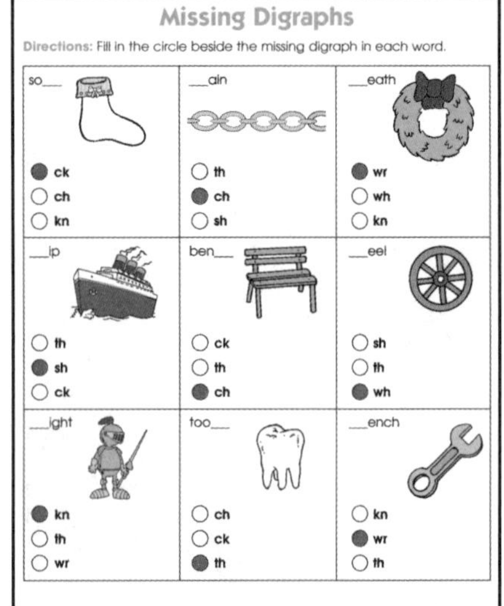

Missing Digraphs

Directions: Fill in the circle beside the missing digraph in each word.

so__ ● ck ○ ch ○ kn	__ain ○ th ● ch ○ sh	__eath ● wr ○ wh ○ kn
__ip ○ th ● sh ○ ck	ben__ ○ ck ○ th ● ch	__eel ○ sh ○ th ● wh
__ight ● kn ○ th ○ wr	too__ ○ ch ○ ck ● th	__ench ○ kn ● wr ○ th

33

Answer Key

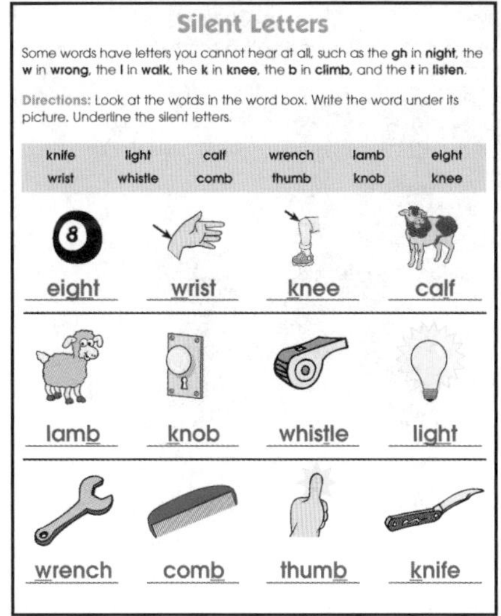

Silent Letters

Some words have letters you cannot hear at all, such as the **gh** in **night**, the **w** in **wrong**, the **l** in **walk**, the **k** in **knee**, the **b** in **climb**, and the **t** in **listen**.

Directions: Look at the words in the word box. Write the word under its picture. Underline the silent letters.

knife	light	calf	wrench	lamb	eight
wrist	whistle	comb	thumb	knob	knee

eight, wrist, knee, calf

lamb, knob, whistle, light

wrench, comb, thumb, knife

34

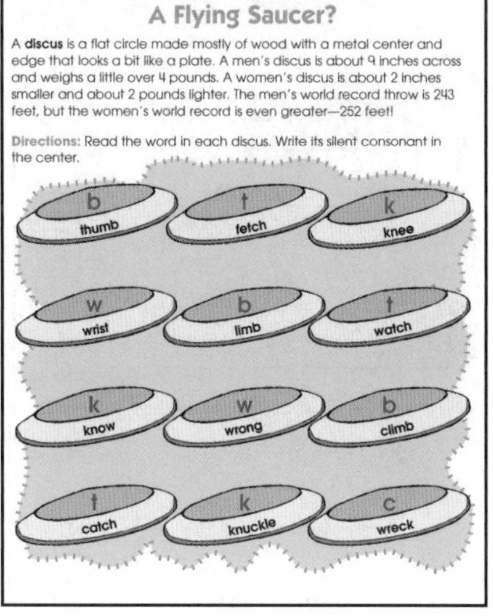

A Flying Saucer?

A **discus** is a flat circle made mostly of wood with a metal center and edge that looks a bit like a plate. A men's discus is about 9 inches across and weighs a little over 4 pounds. A women's discus is about 2 inches smaller and about 2 pounds lighter. The men's world record throw is 243 feet, but the women's world record is even greater—252 feet!

Directions: Read the word in each discus. Write its silent consonant in the center.

35

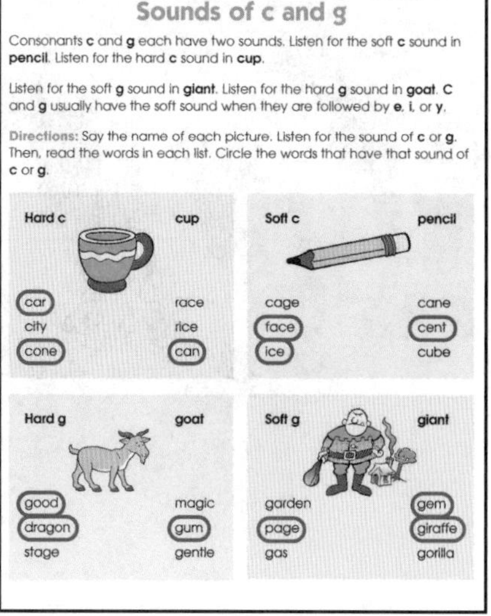

Sounds of c and g

Consonants **c** and **g** each have two sounds. Listen for the soft **c** sound in **pencil**. Listen for the hard **c** sound in **cup**.

Listen for the soft **g** sound in **giant**. Listen for the hard **g** sound in **goat**. **C** and **g** usually have the soft sound when they are followed by **e**, **i**, or **y**.

Directions: Say the name of each picture. Listen for the sound of **c** or **g**. Then, read the words in each list. Circle the words that have that sound of **c** or **g**.

Hard c cup
car race
city rice
cone can
Soft c pencil
cage cane
face cent
ice cube
Hard g goat
good magic
dragon gum
stage gentle
Soft g giant
garden gem
page giraffe
gas gorilla

36

Hard and Soft c and g

Directions: Underline the letter that follows the **c** or **g** in each word. Write **hard** if the word has the hard **c** or hard **g** sound. Write **soft** if the word has the soft **c** or soft **g** sound.

37

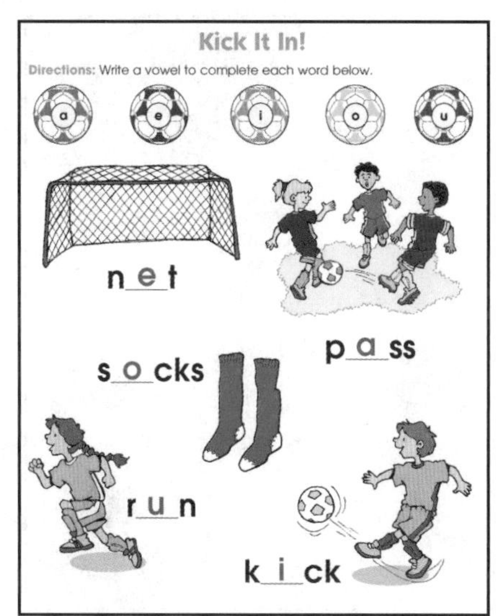

Kick It In!

Directions: Write a vowel to complete each word below.

38

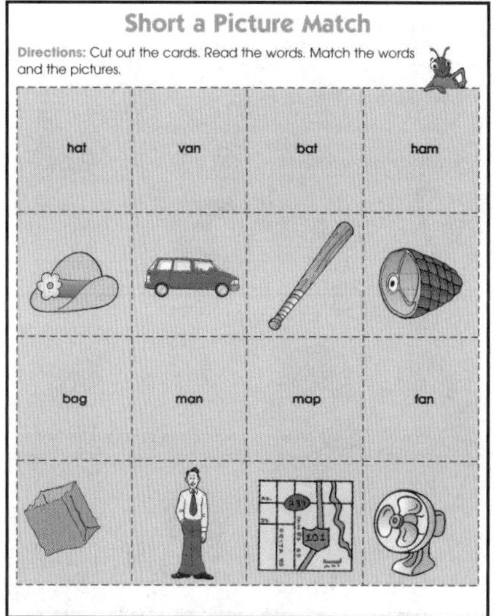

Short a Picture Match

Directions: Cut out the cards. Read the words. Match the words and the pictures.

39

Answer Key

The Donkey's Tail
Directions: Find the donkey tails with pictures whose names have the short **i** sound. Cut them out. Glue those tails onto the donkeys.

41

Feed the Pup
Directions: Cut out the picture cards. Say the name of each picture. If the name has the sound of short **u**, glue the card in the pup's bowl.

43

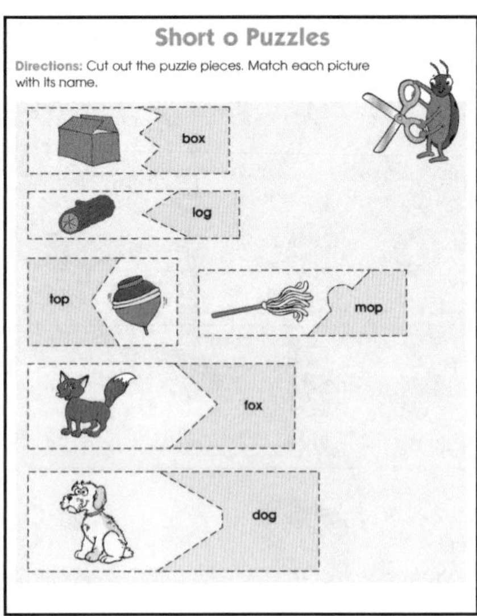
Short o Puzzles
Directions: Cut out the puzzle pieces. Match each picture with its name.

box
log
top
mop
fox
dog

45

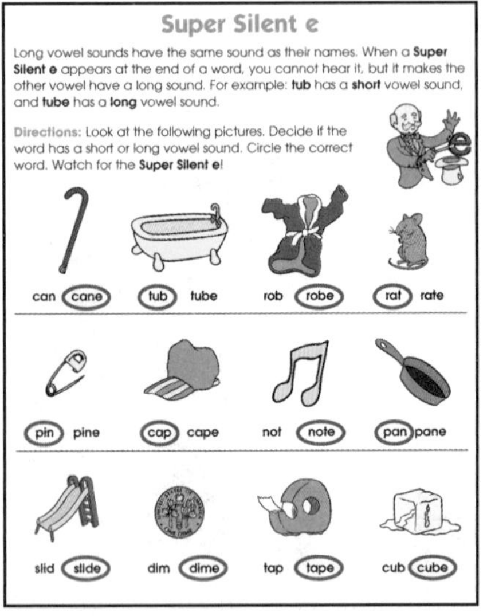
Super Silent e
Long vowel sounds have the same sound as their names. When a **Super Silent e** appears at the end of a word, you cannot hear it, but it makes the other vowel have a long sound. For example: **tub** has a **short** vowel sound, and **tube** has a **long** vowel sound.

Directions: Look at the following pictures. Decide if the word has a short or long vowel sound. Circle the correct word. Watch for the **Super Silent e**!

can (cane) | (tub) tube | rob (robe) | (rat) rate
(pin) pine | (cap) cape | not (note) | (pan) pane
slid (slide) | dim (dime) | tap (tape) | cub (cube)

49

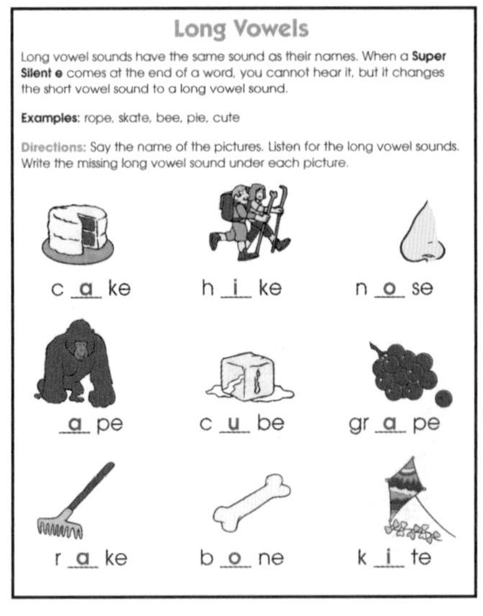
Long Vowels
Long vowel sounds have the same sound as their names. When a **Super Silent e** comes at the end of a word, you cannot hear it, but it changes the short vowel sound to a long vowel sound.

Examples: rope, skate, bee, pie, cute

Directions: Say the name of the pictures. Listen for the long vowel sounds. Write the missing long vowel sound under each picture.

c _a_ ke | h _i_ ke | n _o_ se
_a_ pe | c _u_ be | gr _a_ pe
r _a_ ke | b _o_ ne | k _i_ te

50

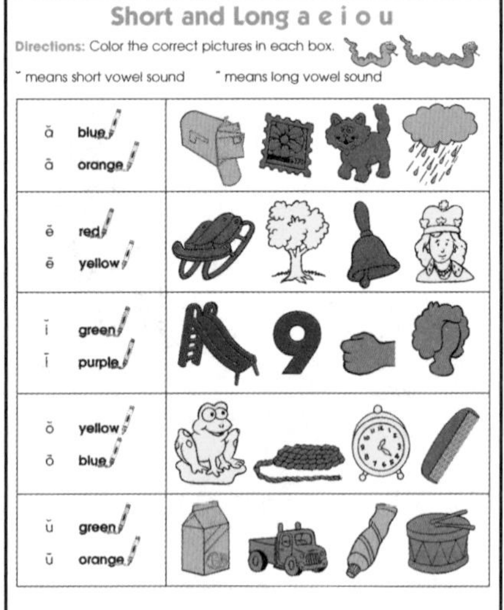
Short and Long a e i o u
Directions: Color the correct pictures in each box.

˘ means short vowel sound ¯ means long vowel sound

ă blue ā orange	
ĕ red ē yellow	
ĭ green ī purple	
ŏ yellow ō blue	
ŭ green ū orange	

51

Answer Key

Tricky ar
When r follows a vowel, it changes the vowel's sound. Listen for the ar sound in star.
Directions: Color the pictures whose names have the ar sound.
star

52

53

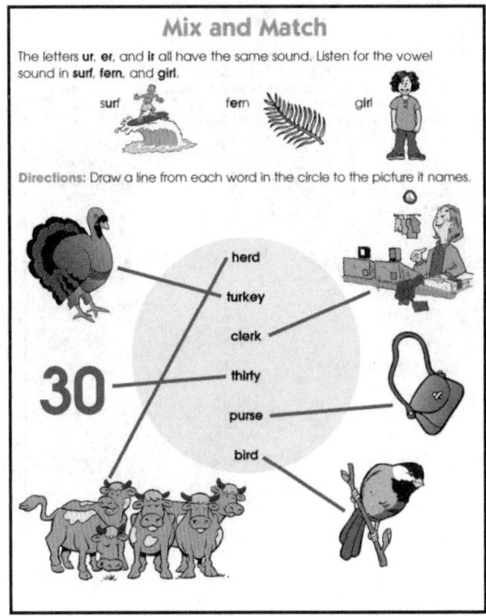

54

55

56

57

Answer Key

58

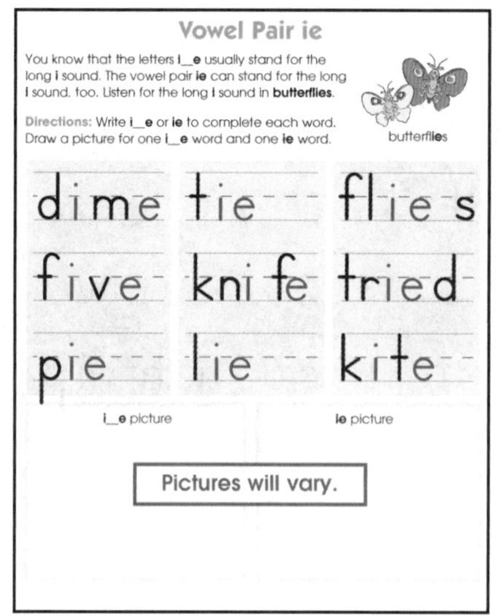

59

60

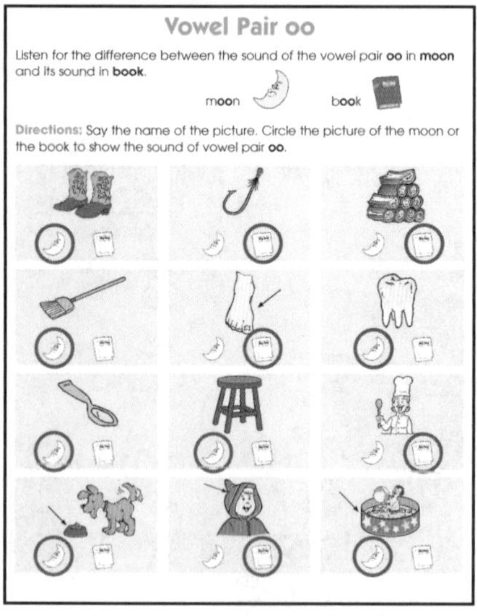

61

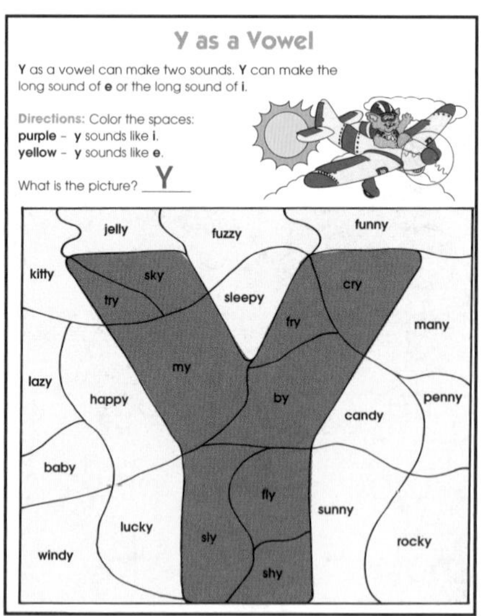

62

63

Answer Key

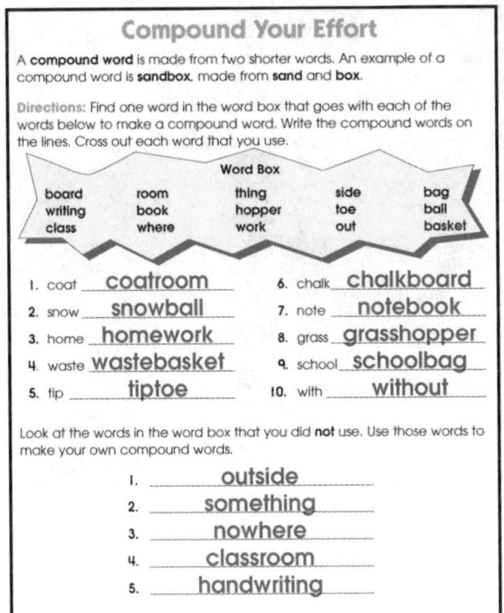

Compound Your Effort

A **compound word** is made from two shorter words. An example of a compound word is **sandbox**, made from **sand** and **box**.

Directions: Find one word in the word box that goes with each of the words below to make a compound word. Write the compound words on the lines. Cross out each word that you use.

Word Box				
board	room	thing	side	bag
writing	book	hopper	toe	ball
class	where	work	out	basket

1. coat coatroom
2. snow snowball
3. home homework
4. waste wastebasket
5. tip tiptoe
6. chalk chalkboard
7. note notebook
8. grass grasshopper
9. school schoolbag
10. with without

Look at the words in the word box that you did **not** use. Use those words to make your own compound words.

1. outside
2. something
3. nowhere
4. classroom
5. handwriting

64

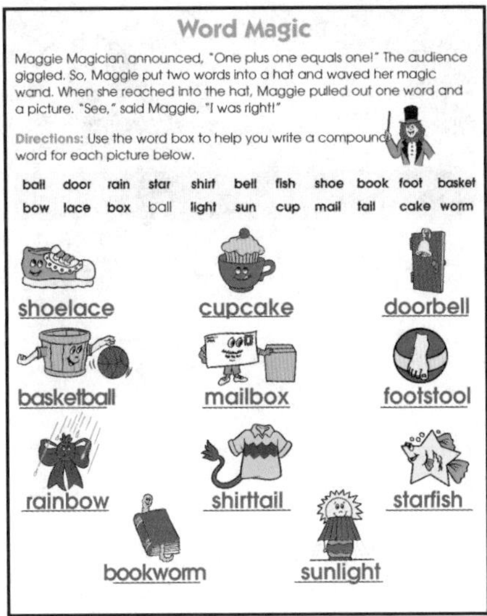

Word Magic

Maggie Magician announced, "One plus one equals one!" The audience giggled. So, Maggie put two words into a hat and waved her magic wand. When she reached into the hat, Maggie pulled out one word and a picture. "See," said Maggie, "I was right!"

Directions: Use the word box to help you write a compound word for each picture below.

ball door rain star shirt bell fish shoe book foot basket
bow lace box ball light sun cup mail tail cake worm

shoelace cupcake doorbell
basketball mailbox footstool
rainbow shirttail starfish
bookworm sunlight

65

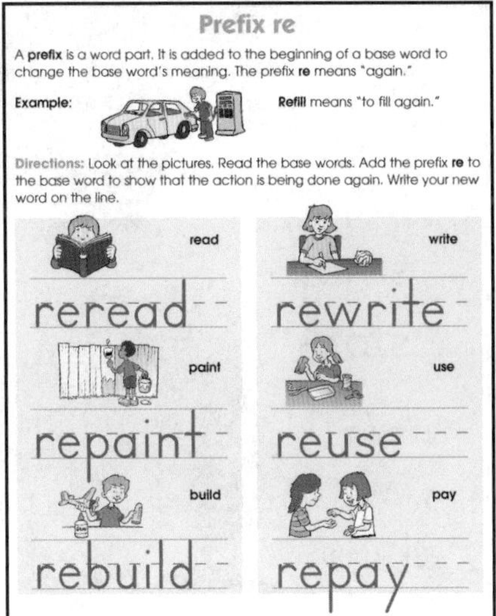

Prefix re

A **prefix** is a word part. It is added to the beginning of a base word to change the base word's meaning. The prefix **re** means "again."

Example: **Refill** means "to fill again."

Directions: Look at the pictures. Read the base words. Add the prefix **re** to the base word to show that the action is being done again. Write your new word on the line.

read — reread
write — rewrite
paint — repaint
use — reuse
build — rebuild
pay — repay

66

Prefixes un and dis

The prefixes **un** and **dis** mean "not" or "the opposite of."

Unlocked means "not locked."

Dismount is the opposite of "mount."

Directions: Look at the pictures. Circle the word that tells about the picture. Then, write the word on the line.

tied / (untied) — untied
like / (dislike) — dislike
(happy) / unhappy — happy
(obey) / disobey — obey
safe / (unsafe) — unsafe
honest / (dishonest) — dishonest

67

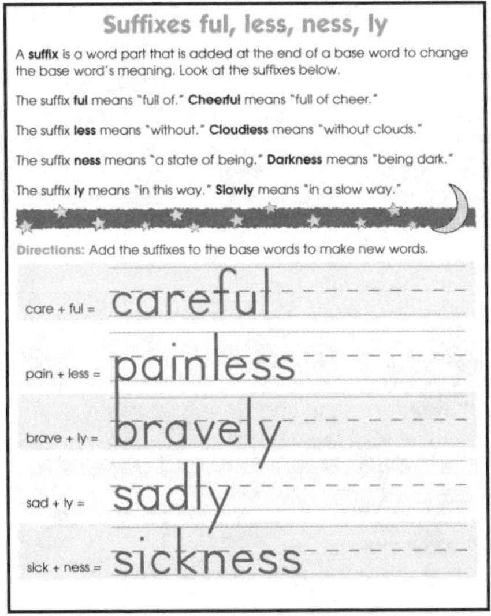

Suffixes ful, less, ness, ly

A **suffix** is a word part that is added at the end of a base word to change the base word's meaning. Look at the suffixes below.

The suffix **ful** means "full of." **Cheerful** means "full of cheer."

The suffix **less** means "without." **Cloudless** means "without clouds."

The suffix **ness** means "a state of being." **Darkness** means "being dark."

The suffix **ly** means "in this way." **Slowly** means "in a slow way."

Directions: Add the suffixes to the base words to make new words.

care + ful = careful
pain + less = painless
brave + ly = bravely
sad + ly = sadly
sick + ness = sickness

68

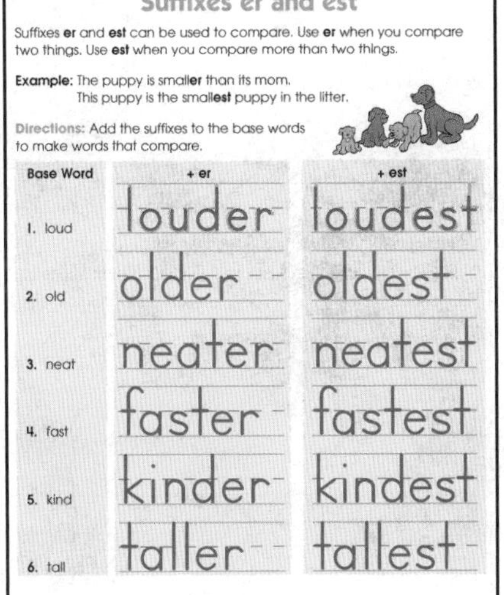

Suffixes er and est

Suffixes **er** and **est** can be used to compare. Use **er** when you compare two things. Use **est** when you compare more than two things.

Example: The puppy is small**er** than its mom.
This puppy is the small**est** puppy in the litter.

Directions: Add the suffixes to the base words to make words that compare.

Base Word	+ er	+ est
1. loud	louder	loudest
2. old	older	oldest
3. neat	neater	neatest
4. fast	faster	fastest
5. kind	kinder	kindest
6. tall	taller	tallest

69

Answer Key

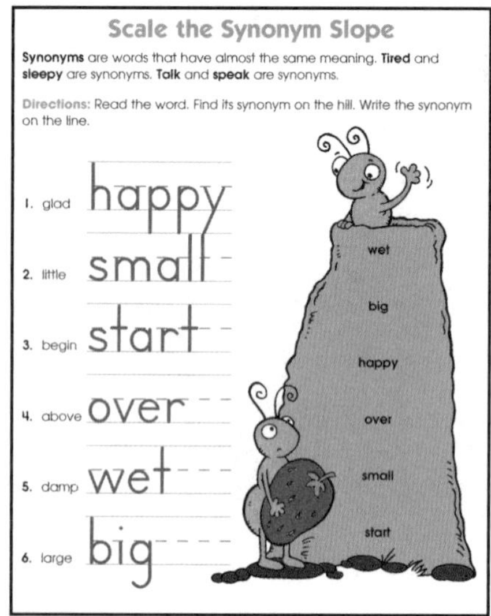

Scale the Synonym Slope

Synonyms are words that have almost the same meaning. **Tired** and **sleepy** are synonyms. **Talk** and **speak** are synonyms.

Directions: Read the word. Find its synonym on the hill. Write the synonym on the line.

1. glad happy
2. little small
3. begin start
4. above over
5. damp wet
6. large big

70

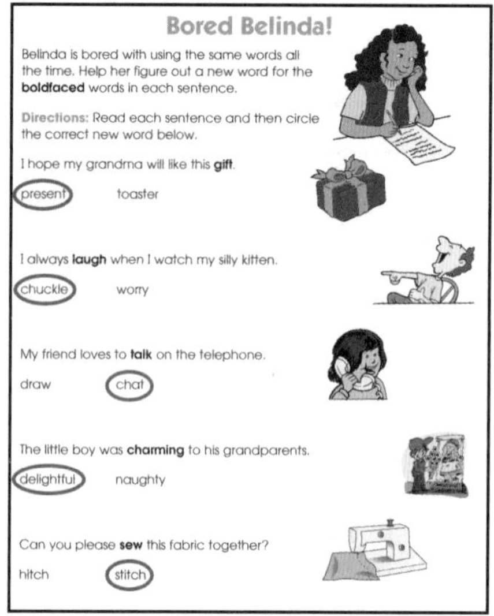

Bored Belinda!

Belinda is bored with using the same words all the time. Help her figure out a new word for the **boldfaced** words in each sentence.

Directions: Read each sentence and then circle the correct new word below.

I hope my grandma will like this **gift**.

(present) toaster

I always **laugh** when I watch my silly kitten.

(chuckle) worry

My friend loves to **talk** on the telephone.

draw (chat)

The little boy was **charming** to his grandparents.

(delightful) naughty

Can you please **sew** this fabric together?

hitch (stitch)

71

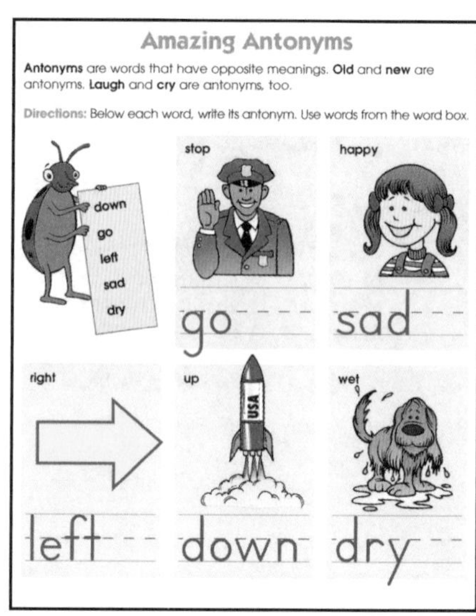

Amazing Antonyms

Antonyms are words that have opposite meanings. **Old** and **new** are antonyms. **Laugh** and **cry** are antonyms, too.

Directions: Below each word, write its antonym. Use words from the word box.

stop — go

happy — sad

right — left

up — down

wet — dry

72

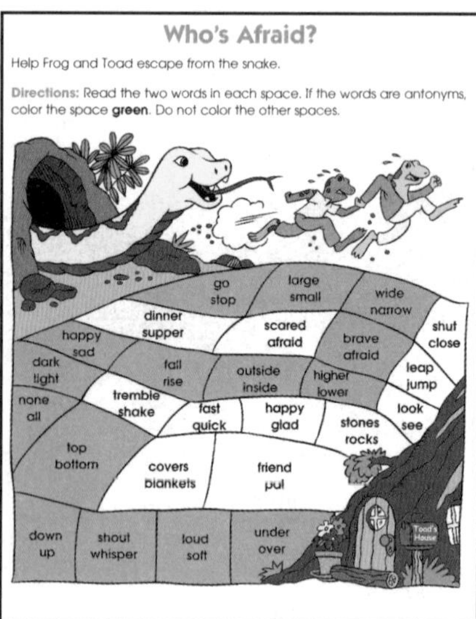

Who's Afraid?

Help Frog and Toad escape from the snake.

Directions: Read the two words in each space. If the words are antonyms, color the space **green**. Do not color the other spaces.

73

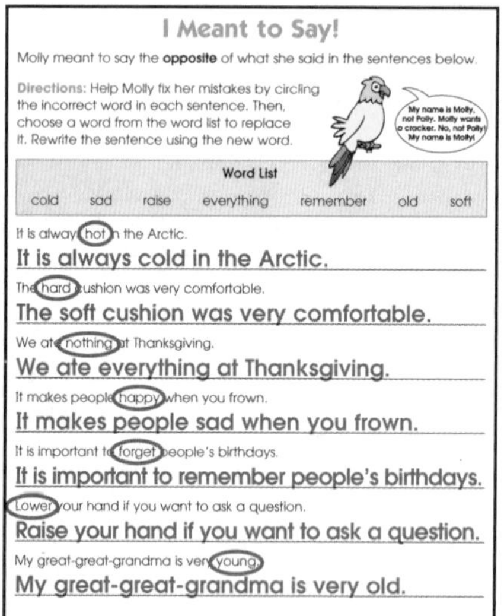

I Meant to Say!

Molly meant to say the **opposite** of what she said in the sentences below.

Directions: Help Molly fix her mistakes by circling the incorrect word in each sentence. Then, choose a word from the word list to replace it. Rewrite the sentence using the new word.

Word List

cold sad raise everything remember old soft

It is always (hot) in the Arctic.

It is always cold in the Arctic.

The (hard) cushion was very comfortable.

The soft cushion was very comfortable.

We ate (nothing) at Thanksgiving.

We ate everything at Thanksgiving.

It makes people (happy) when you frown.

It makes people sad when you frown.

It is important to (forget) people's birthdays.

It is important to remember people's birthdays.

(Lower) your hand if you want to ask a question.

Raise your hand if you want to ask a question.

My great-great-grandma is very (young).

My great-great-grandma is very old.

74

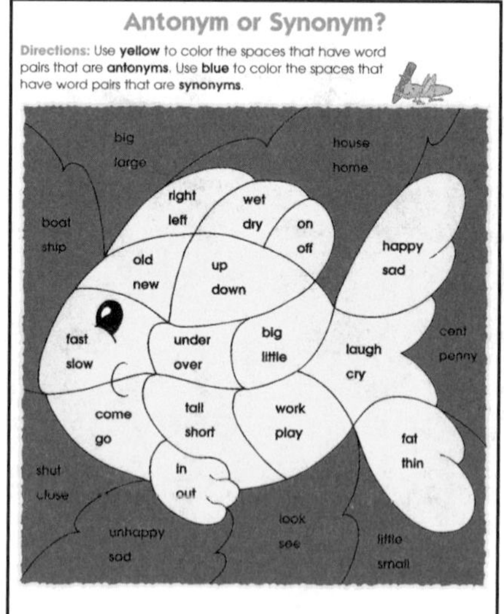

Antonym or Synonym?

Directions: Use **yellow** to color the spaces that have word pairs that are **antonyms**. Use **blue** to color the spaces that have word pairs that are **synonyms**.

75

Answer Key

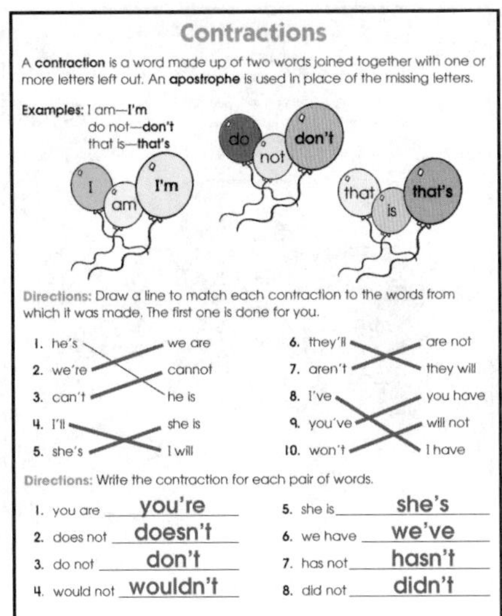

Contractions

A **contraction** is a word made up of two words joined together with one or more letters left out. An **apostrophe** is used in place of the missing letters.

Examples: I am—**I'm**
do not—**don't**
that is—**that's**

Directions: Draw a line to match each contraction to the words from which it was made. The first one is done for you.

1. he's	we are	6. they'll	are not
2. we're	cannot	7. aren't	they will
3. can't	he is	8. I've	you have
4. I'll	she is	9. you've	will not
5. she's	I will	10. won't	I have

Directions: Write the contraction for each pair of words.

1. you are **you're**
2. does not **doesn't**
3. do not **don't**
4. would not **wouldn't**
5. she is **she's**
6. we have **we've**
7. has not **hasn't**
8. did not **didn't**

76

Something Is Missing!

doesn't it's she's don't aren't who's he's didn't that's isn't

Directions: Write the correct contraction for each set of words. Then, circle the letter that was left out when the contraction was made.

1. he is **he's**
2. are not **aren't**
3. do not **don't**
4. who is **who's**
5. is not **isn't**
6. did not **didn't**
7. it is **it's**
8. she is **she's**
9. does not **doesn't**
10. that is **that's**

Directions: Write the missing contraction on the line.

1. **She's** on her way to school.
2. There **isn't** enough time to finish the story.
3. Do you think **it's** too long?
4. We **aren't** going to the party.
5. Donna **doesn't** like the movie.
6. **Who's** going to try for a part in the play?
7. Bob said **he's** going to run in the big race.
8. They **don't** know how to bake a cake.
9. Tom **didn't** want to go skating on Saturday.
10. Look, **that's** where they found the lost watch.

77

Tooth Tales, cont.

Directions: Answer the questions from the story about your teeth.

What are your teeth made of? **enamel**
Highlight where you found the answer.

What is the hardest material in your body? **enamel**
Highlight where you found the answer.

How many different types of teeth are in your mouth? **four**
Highlight where you found the answer.

What are your two very pointy teeth called? **canines**
Highlight where you found the answer.

What teeth are used for grinding food? **molars**
(Hint: The Tooth Fairy likes this type of tooth!)
Highlight where you found the answer.

How many teeth do adults have? **thirty-two**
Highlight where you found the answer.

What teeth are used for biting? **incisors**
Highlight where you found the answer.

How many molars do people have? **twelve**
Highlight where you found the answer.

79

Something's Fruity!

Directions: Find and circle **twelve** things that are wrong with this picture.

80

Clue Caper!

Directions: Read the clues below. Write each child's name under the correct picture. Color the hats using the following clues.

Anna **Talia** **Sara** **Kessia**

- Anna is tall and wearing a green top hat. There is a red baseball cap on top of her top hat!
- Sara is short and wearing a blue polka dotted hat.
- Talia has long hair and is standing between Anna and Sara. Talia is wearing a pretty ribbon in her hair with a flower on it.
- Kessia is standing next to Sara. She is wearing a white baker's hat with a purple veil!

How many hats do you count on the page? **4**

81

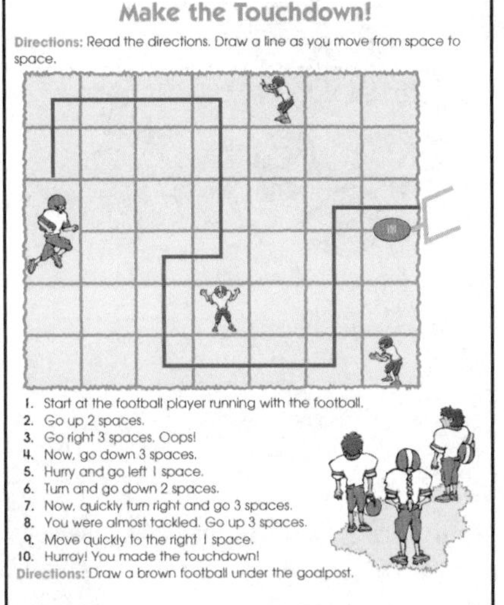

Make the Touchdown!

Directions: Read the directions. Draw a line as you move from space to space.

1. Start at the football player running with the football.
2. Go up 2 spaces.
3. Go right 3 spaces. Oops!
4. Now, go down 3 spaces.
5. Hurry and go left 1 space.
6. Turn and go down 2 spaces.
7. Now, quickly turn right and go 3 spaces.
8. You were almost tackled. Go up 3 spaces.
9. Move quickly to the right 1 space.
10. Hurray! You made the touchdown!

Directions: Draw a brown football under the goalpost.

82

Answer Key

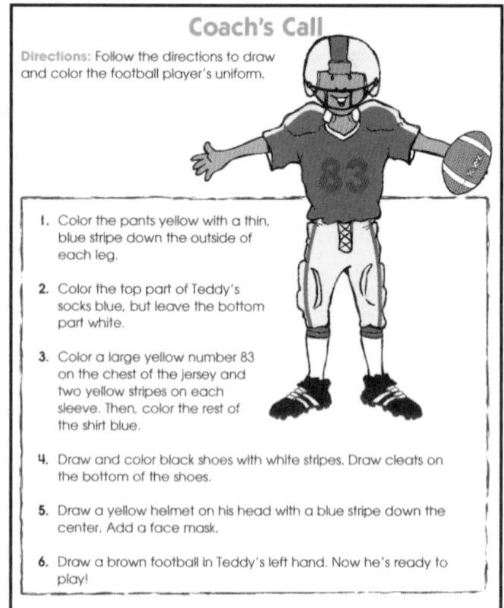

Coach's Call

Directions: Follow the directions to draw and color the football player's uniform.

1. Color the pants yellow with a thin, blue stripe down the outside of each leg.
2. Color the top part of Teddy's socks blue, but leave the bottom part white.
3. Color a large yellow number 83 on the chest of the jersey and two yellow stripes on each sleeve. Then, color the rest of the shirt blue.
4. Draw and color black shoes with white stripes. Draw cleats on the bottom of the shoes.
5. Draw a yellow helmet on his head with a blue stripe down the center. Add a face mask.
6. Draw a brown football in Teddy's left hand. Now he's ready to play!

83

Game Story

Directions: Put the basketball story in order. Write the numbers **1–5** on the blanks to show when each event happened.

4 At the end of the regulation game, the score was tied.
1 The teams warmed up before the game.
3 The score at the half was Cougars, 25; Lions, 20.
2 Kim made the first basket of the game.
5 When the overtime ended, the Lions had won the game 50–49.

84

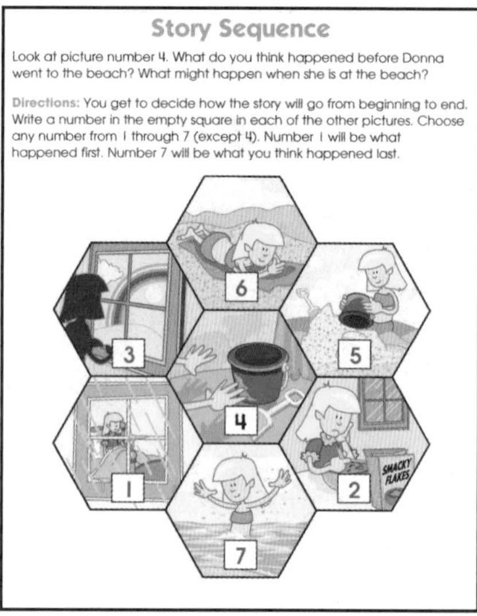

Story Sequence

Look at picture number 4. What do you think happened before Donna went to the beach? What might happen when she is at the beach?

Directions: You get to decide how the story will go from beginning to end. Write a number in the empty square in each of the other pictures. Choose any number from 1 through 7 (except 4). Number 1 will be what happened first. Number 7 will be what you think happened last.

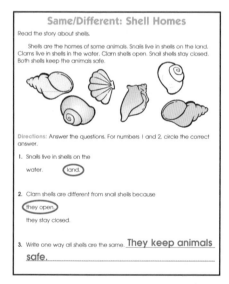

85

Same/Different: Shell Homes

Read the story about shells.

Shells are the homes of some animals. Snails live in shells on the land. Clams live in shells in the water. Clam shells open. Snail shells stay closed. Both shells keep the animals safe.

Directions: Answer the questions. For numbers 1 and 2, circle the correct answer.

1. Snails live in shells on the
   water. (land.)
2. Clam shells are different from snail shells because
   (they open.)
   they stay closed.
3. Write one way all shells are the same. They keep animals safe.

86

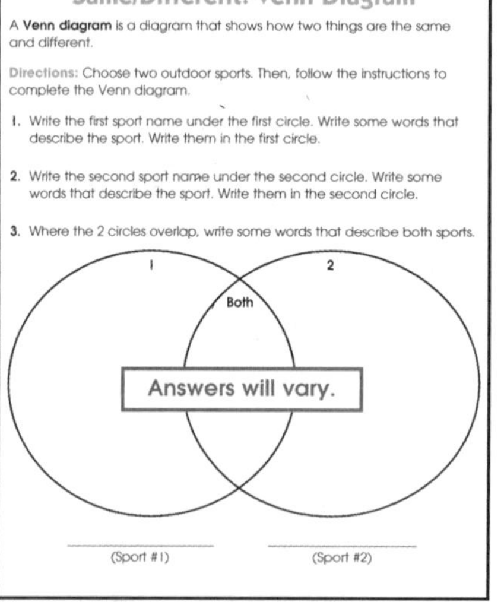

Same/Different: Venn Diagram

A **Venn diagram** is a diagram that shows how two things are the same and different.

Directions: Choose two outdoor sports. Then, follow the instructions to complete the Venn diagram.

1. Write the first sport name under the first circle. Write some words that describe the sport. Write them in the first circle.
2. Write the second sport name under the second circle. Write some words that describe the sport. Write them in the second circle.
3. Where the 2 circles overlap, write some words that describe both sports.

87

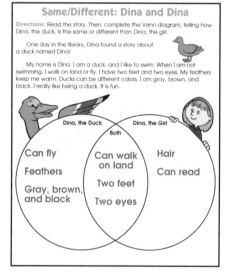

Same/Different: Dina and Dina

Directions: Read the story. Then, complete the Venn diagram, telling how Dina, the duck, is the same or different than Dina, the girl.

One day in the library, Dina found a story about a duck named Dina!

My name is Dina. I am a duck, and I like to swim. When I am not swimming, I walk on land or fly. I have two feet and two eyes. My feathers keep me warm. Ducks can be different colors. I am gray, brown, and black. I really like being a duck. It is fun.

Dina, the Duck	Both	Dina, the Girl
Can fly	Can walk on land	Hair
Feathers	Two feet	Can read
Gray, brown, and black	Two eyes	

88

Answer Key

Same/Different: Marvin and Mugsy

Directions: Read about Marvin and Mugsy. Then, complete the Venn diagram, telling how they are the same and different.

Marcy has two dogs, Marvin and Mugsy. Marvin is a black-and-white spotted Dalmatian. Marvin likes to run after balls in the backyard. His favorite food is Canine Crunchy Crunch. Marcy likes to take Marvin for walks, because dogs need exercise. Marvin loves to sleep in his doghouse. Mugsy is a big, furry brown dog, who wiggles when she is happy. Since she is big, she needs lots of exercise. So, Marcy takes her for walks in the park. Her favorite food is Canine Crunchy Crunch. Mugsy likes to sleep on Marcy's bed.

89

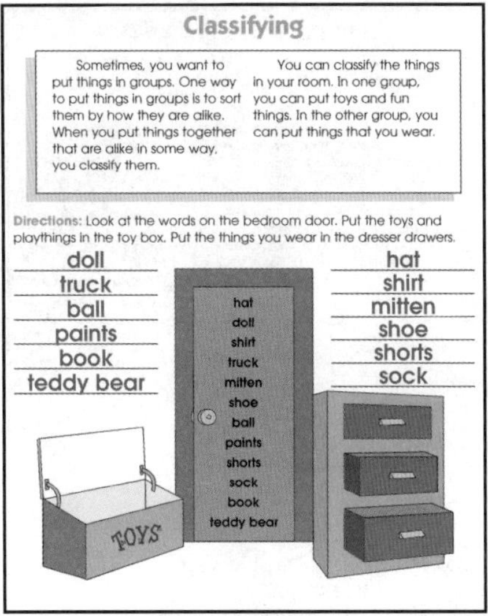

Classifying

Sometimes, you want to put things in groups. One way to put things in groups is to sort them by how they are alike. When you put things together that are alike in some way, you classify them.

You can classify the things in your room. In one group, you can put toys and fun things. In the other group, you can put things that you wear.

Directions: Look at the words on the bedroom door. Put the toys and playthings in the toy box. Put the things you wear in the dresser drawers.

90

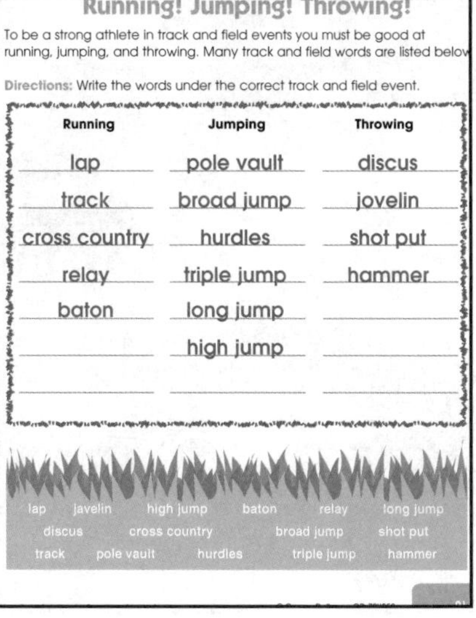

Running! Jumping! Throwing!

To be a strong athlete in track and field events you must be good at running, jumping, and throwing. Many track and field words are listed below.

Directions: Write the words under the correct track and field event.

Running	Jumping	Throwing
lap	pole vault	discus
track	broad jump	jovelin
cross country	hurdles	shot put
relay	triple jump	hammer
baton	long jump	
	high jump	

91

All Animals

There are many kinds of animals. Three kinds of animals are mammals, birds, and reptiles.

Mammals have fur or hair. Baby mammals drink milk from their mothers' bodies. A whale is a mammal.

Birds are the only animals that have feathers. A robin is a bird.

Reptiles have scaly skin. Most reptiles lay eggs on the land. An alligator is a reptile.

Directions: Read the sentences below. Is the animal in the sentence a mammal, bird, or reptile? Put an **M** on the line if it is a mammal, a **B** if it is a bird, or an **R** if it is a reptile.

M 1. Maggie brushes her horse's coat.
R 2. The turtle lays its eggs in the sand.
B 3. Adam cleans the feathers from his pet's cage.
B 4. The baby penguin hides in its father's feathers to stay warm.
M 5. The piglets drink their mother's milk.
R 6. The scaly skin on the snake is dry.
B 7. A blue jay has blue feathers.
M 8. The bunny pulls fur from her body to build a nest.

92

Baby Animal Names

Many animals are called special names when they are young. A baby deer is called a fawn. A baby cat is called a kitten.

Some young animals have the same name as other kinds of baby animals. A baby elephant is a calf. A baby whale is a calf. A baby giraffe is a calf. A baby cow is a calf.

Some baby animals are called cubs. A baby lion, a baby bear, a baby tiger, and a baby fox are all called cubs.

Some baby animals are called colts. A young horse is a colt. A baby zebra is a colt. A baby donkey is a colt.

Directions: Use the story about baby animal names to complete the chart below. Write the kind of animal that belongs with each special baby name.

calf	cub	colt
elephant	lion	horse
whale	bear	zebra
giraffe	tiger	donkey
cow	fox	

93

Winter Sleepers, cont.

Directions: Read all of the word groups. Then, place them under the correct hibernation type. Use the story on page 127.

will shiver to warm itself
body temperature drops a little
hardly breathes at all
seems more dead than alive
moves about and then goes back to sleep
breathing only slows
easily awakens
body temperature drops far below normal

True Hibernator

will shiver to warm itself
body temperature drops far below normal
seems more dead than alive
hardly breathes at all

Light Sleeper

body temperature drops a littler
moves about and then goes back to sleep
breathing only slows
easily awakens

95

Answer Key

Use the Clues

Context clues can help you figure out words you do not know. Read the words around the new word. Think of a word that makes sense.

Kate swam in a ___?___.

Did Kate swim in a cake or a lake? The word **swim** is a context clue.

Directions: Kate wrote this letter from camp. Read the letter. Use context clues to write the missing words from the word box. What clues did you use?

lake	six
pancakes	forest

Dear Mom and Dad,

I woke up at six o'clock and got dressed. My friends and I ate pancakes for breakfast. We went hiking in the forest. Then, we went swimming in the lake. Camp is fun!

Love,
Kate

96

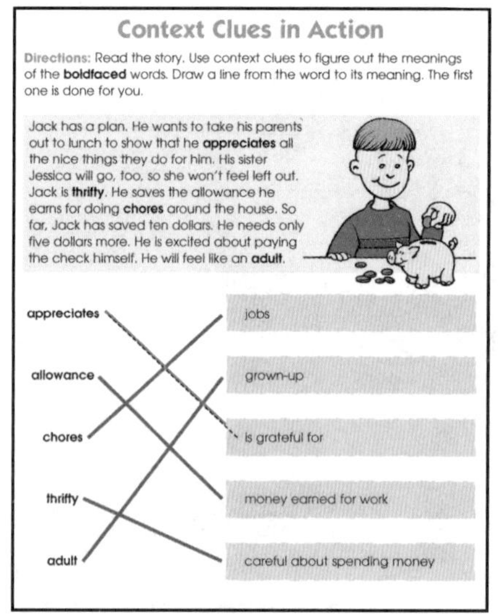

Context Clues in Action

Directions: Read the story. Use context clues to figure out the meanings of the **boldfaced** words. Draw a line from the word to its meaning. The first one is done for you.

Jack has a plan. He wants to take his parents out to lunch to show that he **appreciates** all the nice things they do for him. His sister Jessica will go, too, so she won't feel left out. Jack is **thrifty**. He saves the allowance he earns for doing **chores** around the house. So far, Jack has saved ten dollars. He needs only five dollars more. He is excited about paying the check himself. He will feel like an **adult**.

appreciates	jobs
allowance	grown-up
chores	is grateful for
thrifty	money earned for work
adult	careful about spending money

97

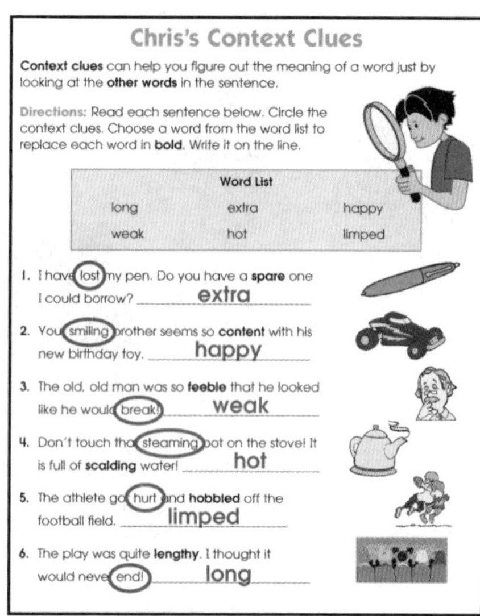

Chris's Context Clues

Context clues can help you figure out the meaning of a word just by looking at the **other words** in the sentence.

Directions: Read each sentence below. Circle the context clues. Choose a word from the word list to replace each word in **bold**. Write it on the line.

Word List		
long	extra	happy
weak	hot	limped

1. I have (lost) my pen. Do you have a **spare** one I could borrow? extra
2. Your (smiling) brother seems so **content** with his new birthday toy. happy
3. The old, old man was so **feeble** that he looked like he would (break). weak
4. Don't touch that (steaming) pot on the stove! It is full of **scalding** water! hot
5. The athlete got (hurt) and **hobbled** off the football field. limped
6. The play was quite **lengthy**. I thought it would never (end)! long

98

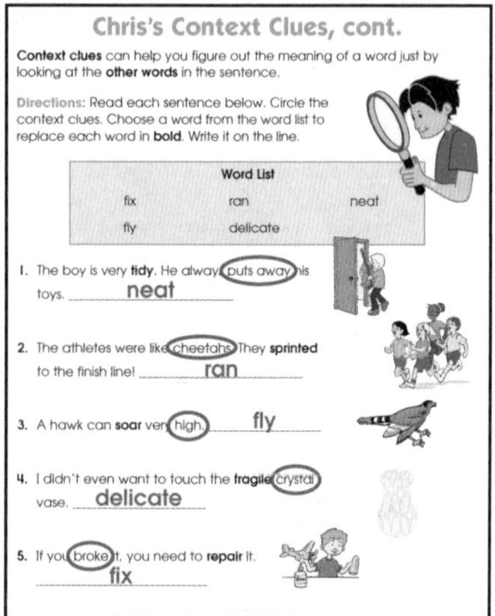

Chris's Context Clues, cont.

Context clues can help you figure out the meaning of a word just by looking at the **other words** in the sentence.

Directions: Read each sentence below. Circle the context clues. Choose a word from the word list to replace each word in **bold**. Write it on the line.

Word List		
fix	ran	neat
fly	delicate	

1. The boy is very **tidy**. He always (puts away) his toys. neat
2. The athletes were like (cheetahs). They **sprinted** to the finish line! ran
3. A hawk can **soar** very (high). fly
4. I didn't even want to touch the **fragile** (crystal) vase. delicate
5. If you (broke) it, you need to **repair** it. fix

99

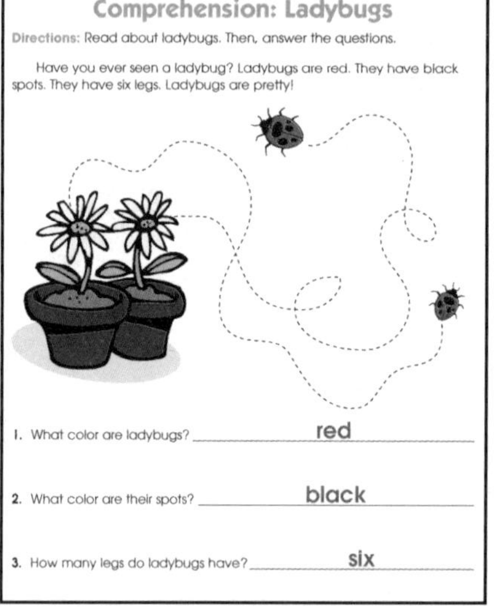

Comprehension: Ladybugs

Directions: Read about ladybugs. Then, answer the questions.

Have you ever seen a ladybug? Ladybugs are red. They have black spots. They have six legs. Ladybugs are pretty!

1. What color are ladybugs? red
2. What color are their spots? black
3. How many legs do ladybugs have? six

100

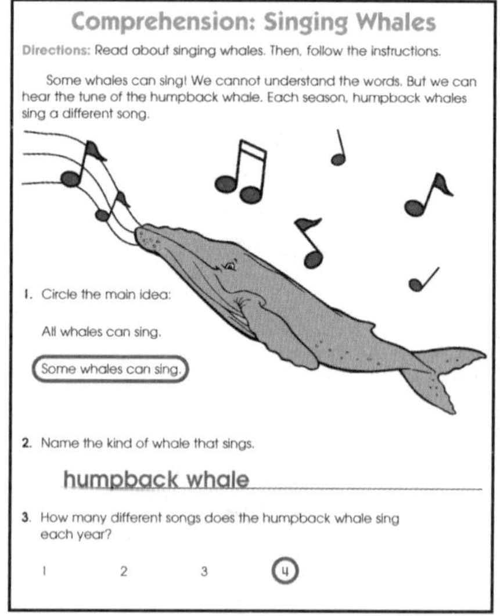

Comprehension: Singing Whales

Directions: Read about singing whales. Then, follow the instructions.

Some whales can sing! We cannot understand the words. But we can hear the tune of the humpback whale. Each season, humpback whales sing a different song.

1. Circle the main idea:

   All whales can sing.

   (Some whales can sing.)

2. Name the kind of whale that sings.

   humpback whale

3. How many different songs does the humpback whale sing each year?

   1 2 3 (4)

101

Answer Key

Hermit Crabs

The hermit crab lives in a shell in or near the ocean. It does not make its own shell. It moves into a shell left by another sea animal. As the hermit crab grows, it gets too big for its shell. It will hunt for a new shell. It will feel the new shell with its claw. If the shell feels just right, the crab will leave its old shell and move into the bigger one. It might even take a shell away from another hermit crab.

Directions: Read about hermit crabs. Use what you learn to finish the sentences.

1. This story is mostly about the **hermit crab**.
2. The hermit crab lives **in a shell**.
3. When it gets too big for its shell, it will **hunt for a new shell**.
4. The crab will feel the shell with its **claw**.
5. It might take a shell away from **another hermit crab**.

102

The Statue of Liberty

The Statue of Liberty is a symbol of the United States. It stands for freedom. It is the tallest statue in the United States.

The statue is of a woman wearing a robe. She is holding a torch in her right hand. She is holding a book in her left hand. She is wearing a crown. The Statue of Liberty was a gift from the country of France.

Each year, people come from all over the world to visit the statue. Not only do they look at it, they can also go inside the statue. At one time, visitors could go all the way up into the arm. In 1916, the arm was closed to visitors because it was too dangerous. The Statue of Liberty is located on an island in New York Harbor.

Directions: Read the facts above. Then, read each sentence below. If it is true, put a **T** on the line. If it is false, put an **F** on the line.

T 1. The Statue of Liberty is a symbol of the United States.
F 2. People cannot go inside the statue.
F 3. The statue was a gift from Mexico.
T 4. People used to be able to climb up into the statue's arm.
F 5. It is a very short statue.
T 6. The woman statue has a torch in her right hand.
T 7. People come from all over to see the statue.

103

Venus Flytraps

Many insects eat plants. There is one kind of plant that eats insects. It is the Venus flytrap. The Venus flytrap works like a trap. Each leaf is shaped like a circle. The circle is in two parts. When the leaf closes, the two parts fold together. The leaf has little spikes all the way around it. Inside the leaf, there are little hairs. If an insect touches the little hairs, the two sides of the Venus flytrap leaf will clap together. The spikes will trap the insect inside. The Venus flytrap will then eat the insect.

Directions: Read about the Venus flytrap. Then, read each sentence below. If it is true, circle the sentence. If it is **not** true, draw an **X** on the sentence.

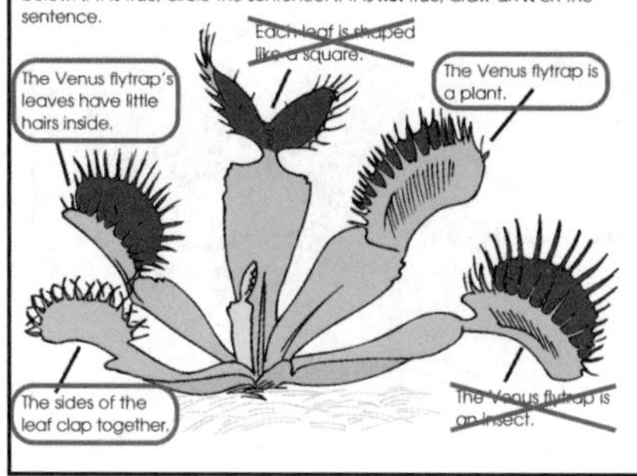

~~Each leaf is shaped like a square.~~
The Venus flytrap's leaves have little hairs inside.
The Venus flytrap is a plant.
The sides of the leaf clap together.
~~The Venus flytrap is an insect.~~

104

Sticklebacks

Sticklebacks are small fish. They have small spines along their backs. The spines keep other fish from trying to swallow them.

Stickleback fish are odd because the male builds the nest for the eggs. He makes the nest out of water plants and sticks. He makes it in the shape of a barrel and glues it together. He uses a thread-like material from his body to glue the nest together.

When the nest is ready, the mother fish comes. She lays her eggs and goes away. The father stays by the nest and guards the eggs. After the eggs hatch, he stays with the baby fish for a few days. If other sea animals try to eat the baby sticklebacks, he will fight them. He keeps the baby fish safe until they can care for themselves.

Directions: Read about the stickleback fish. Use the story to help pick the correct answers to fill in the blanks. Circle the correct answer.

1. The story is mostly about ____.
   spines   enemy sea animals   (stickleback fish)
2. The stickleback is unusual because ____.
   the female lays eggs   (the male builds a nest)   the eggs are in the nest
3. The nest is made of ____.
   mud and grass   (water plants and sticks)   string and glue
4. If an animal tries to eat the baby fish, the stickleback father will ____.
   (fight it off)   swim away   jump out of the water

105

Eagles

Eagles are large birds. They eat small animals such as mice and rabbits. Eagles make their nests in high places such as the tops of trees. Their nests are made of sticks, weeds, and dirt. Eagles can live in the same nest for many years.

The mother eagle lays one or two eggs each year. When she sits on the eggs, the father eagle brings her food. Baby eagles are called *eaglets*.

Directions: Read about eagles. Then, circle the correct ending to each sentence below.

1. Eagles are
   large dogs.   (large birds.)
2. Eagles eat
   (small animals.)
   plants and trees.
3. Eagles
   build a nest each year.
   (live in the same nest for many years.)
4. The mother eagle lays
   (one or two eggs.)
   three or four eggs.
5. Baby eagles are called
   igloos.   (eaglets.)

106

Seals

Seals live in the oceans and on land. They eat different kinds of sea animals, such as fish, shrimp, squid, and krill. They are very good swimmers. They use their flippers to help them move in the water and on the land. They talk to each other by making barking sounds.

Directions: Read the facts above. Then, answer each question using complete sentences.

1. What do seals eat? **fish, shrimp, squid, krill**
2. For what do seals use their flippers? **to help them move in the water and on land**
3. Where do seals live? **in the oceans and on land**
4. How do seals talk? **by making barking sounds**

107

Answer Key

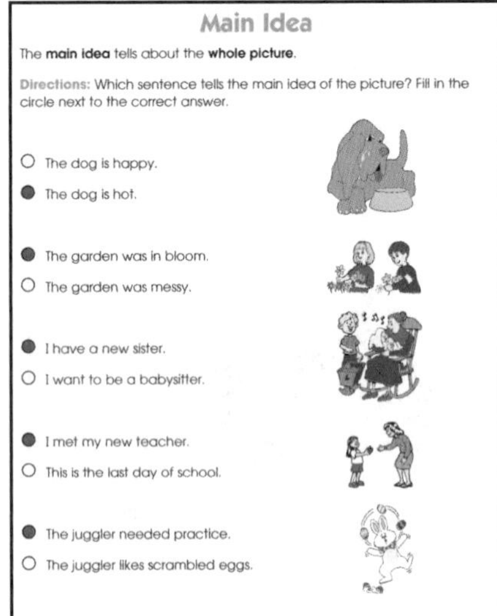

Main Idea

The **main idea** tells about the **whole picture**.

Directions: Which sentence tells the main idea of the picture? Fill in the circle next to the correct answer.

○ The dog is happy.
● The dog is hot.

● The garden was in bloom.
○ The garden was messy.

● I have a new sister.
○ I want to be a babysitter.

● I met my new teacher.
○ This is the last day of school.

● The juggler needed practice.
○ The juggler likes scrambled eggs.

108

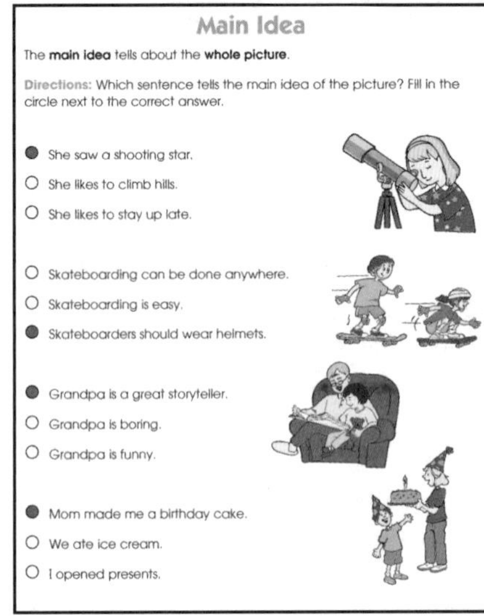

Main Idea

The **main idea** tells about the **whole picture**.

Directions: Which sentence tells the main idea of the picture? Fill in the circle next to the correct answer.

● She saw a shooting star.
○ She likes to climb hills.
○ She likes to stay up late.

○ Skateboarding can be done anywhere.
○ Skateboarding is easy.
● Skateboarders should wear helmets.

● Grandpa is a great storyteller.
○ Grandpa is boring.
○ Grandpa is funny.

● Mom made me a birthday cake.
○ We ate ice cream.
○ I opened presents.

109

What's the Idea?

Directions: Look at the pictures. Read the sentences in the speech balloons. Fill in the circle beside the sentence that tells the main idea.

My tummy hurts.
○ The mouse wants more to eat.
● The mouse ate too much cheese.

My hat is blowing away.
● It is a very windy day.
○ He doesn't want a hat.

I am seven years old today.
○ The cake is very big.
● Today is her birthday.

I can't find my home.
● The cat is lost.
○ The cat has a new home.

110

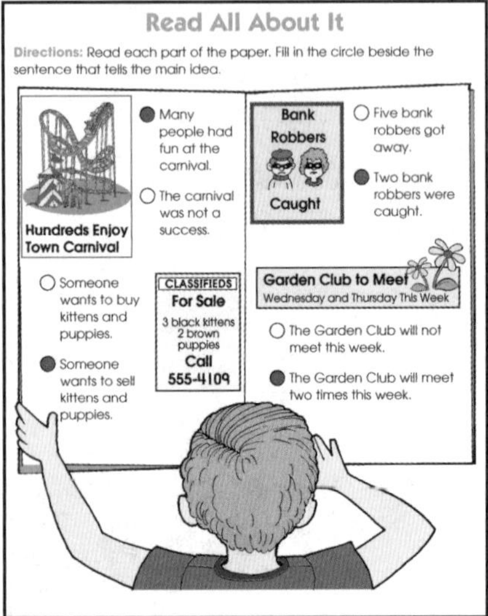

Read All About It

Directions: Read each part of the paper. Fill in the circle beside the sentence that tells the main idea.

Hundreds Enjoy Town Carnival
● Many people had fun at the carnival.
○ The carnival was not a success.

Bank Robbers Caught
○ Five bank robbers got away.
● Two bank robbers were caught.

CLASSIFIEDS
For Sale
3 black kittens
2 brown puppies
Call 555-4109
○ Someone wants to buy kittens and puppies.
● Someone wants to sell kittens and puppies.

Garden Club to Meet
Wednesday and Thursday This Week
○ The Garden Club will not meet this week.
● The Garden Club will meet two times this week.

111

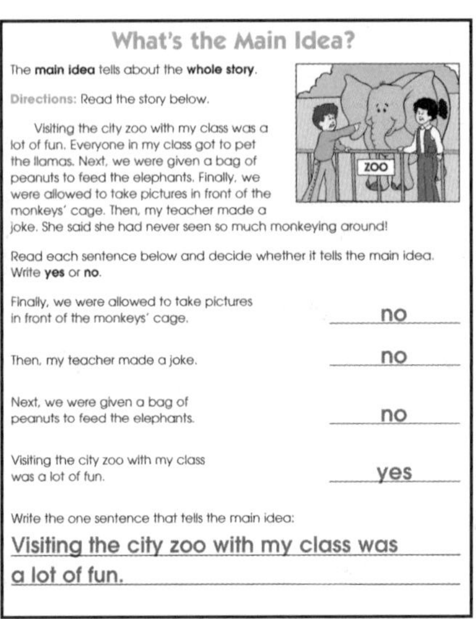

What's the Main Idea?

The **main idea** tells about the **whole story**.

Directions: Read the story below.

Visiting the city zoo with my class was a lot of fun. Everyone in my class got to pet the llamas. Next, we were given a bag of peanuts to feed the elephants. Finally, we were allowed to take pictures in front of the monkeys' cage. Then, my teacher made a joke. She said she had never seen so much monkeying around!

Read each sentence below and decide whether it tells the main idea. Write **yes** or **no**.

Finally, we were allowed to take pictures in front of the monkeys' cage.	no
Then, my teacher made a joke.	no
Next, we were given a bag of peanuts to feed the elephants.	no
Visiting the city zoo with my class was a lot of fun.	yes

Write the one sentence that tells the main idea:

Visiting the city zoo with my class was a lot of fun.

112

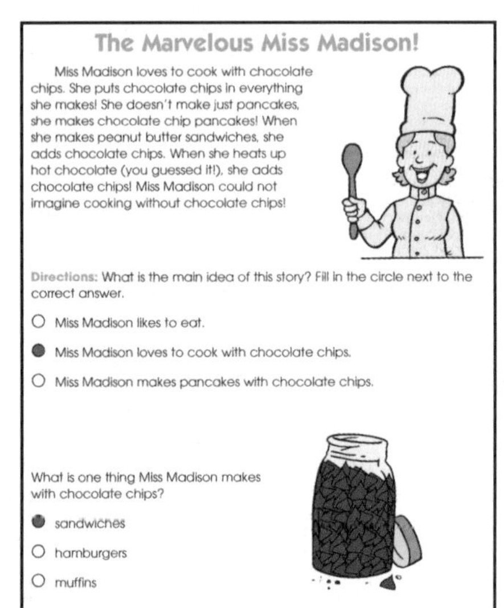

The Marvelous Miss Madison!

Miss Madison loves to cook with chocolate chips. She puts chocolate chips in everything she makes! She doesn't make just pancakes, she makes chocolate chip pancakes! When she makes peanut butter sandwiches, she adds chocolate chips. When she heats up hot chocolate (you guessed it!), she adds chocolate chips! Miss Madison could not imagine cooking without chocolate chips!

Directions: What is the main idea of this story? Fill in the circle next to the correct answer.

○ Miss Madison likes to eat.
● Miss Madison loves to cook with chocolate chips.
○ Miss Madison makes pancakes with chocolate chips.

What is one thing Miss Madison makes with chocolate chips?

● sandwiches
○ hamburgers
○ muffins

113

Answer Key

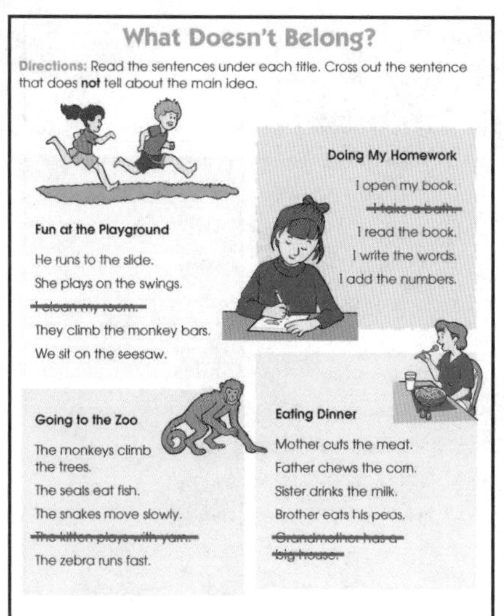

What Doesn't Belong?

Directions: Read the sentences under each title. Cross out the sentence that does **not** tell about the main idea.

Fun at the Playground

He runs to the slide.
She plays on the swings.
~~I clean my room.~~
They climb the monkey bars.
We sit on the seesaw.

Doing My Homework

I open my book.
~~I take a bath.~~
I read the book.
I write the words.
I add the numbers.

Going to the Zoo

The monkeys climb the trees.
The seals eat fish.
The snakes move slowly.
~~The kitten plays with yarn.~~
The zebra runs fast.

Eating Dinner

Mother cuts the meat.
Father chews the corn.
Sister drinks the milk.
Brother eats his peas.
~~Grandmother has a big house.~~

114

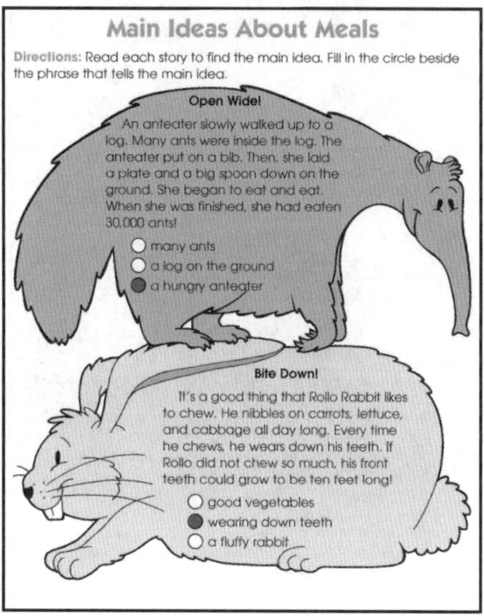

Main Ideas About Meals

Directions: Read each story to find the main idea. Fill in the circle beside the phrase that tells the main idea.

Open Wide!

An anteater slowly walked up to a log. Many ants were inside the log. The anteater put on a bib. Then, she laid a plate and a big spoon down on the ground. She began to eat and eat. When she was finished, she had eaten 30,000 ants!

○ many ants
○ a log on the ground
● a hungry anteater

Bite Down!

It's a good thing that Rollo Rabbit likes to chew. He nibbles on carrots, lettuce, and cabbage all day long. Every time he chews, he wears down his teeth. If Rollo did not chew so much, his front teeth could grow to be ten feet long!

○ good vegetables
● wearing down teeth
○ a fluffy rabbit

115

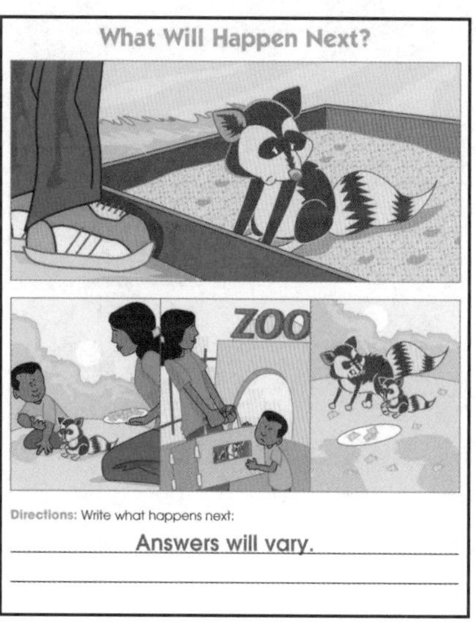

What Will Happen Next?

Directions: Write what happens next:

Answers will vary.

116

What's Next?

Directions: Draw a picture of what will happen next in the boxes below:

Pictures will vary.

117

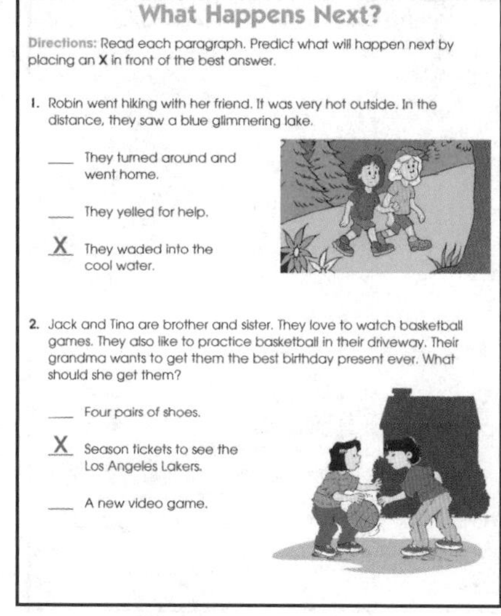

What Happens Next?

Directions: Read each paragraph. Predict what will happen next by placing an **X** in front of the best answer.

1. Robin went hiking with her friend. It was very hot outside. In the distance, they saw a blue glimmering lake.

___ They turned around and went home.
___ They yelled for help.
X They waded into the cool water.

2. Jack and Tina are brother and sister. They love to watch basketball games. They also like to practice basketball in their driveway. Their grandma wants to get them the best birthday present ever. What should she get them?

___ Four pairs of shoes.
X Season tickets to see the Los Angeles Lakers.
___ A new video game.

118

What Will They Do?

Directions: Read each sentence. Fill in the circle beside the best prediction. Then, circle the picture that matches your answer.

The boy is putting on his skates.
○ He will go swimming.
● He will go skating.

The girl fills her glass with milk.
● She will drink the milk.
○ She will drink water.

The woman wrote a letter to her friend.
○ She will call her friend on the phone.
● She will put the letter in the mailbox.

The kids gave Sally a birthday gift.
● She will open the gift.
○ She will throw the gift away.

119

Answer Key

How Will It End?

Directions: Read each story. Fill in the circle beside the sentence that tells what will happen next.

It is a snowy winter night. The lights flicker once, twice, and then they go out. It is cold and dark. Dad finds the flashlight and matches. He brings logs in from outside. What will Dad do?

- ● Dad will make a fire.
- ○ Dad will cook dinner.
- ○ Dad will clean the fireplace.

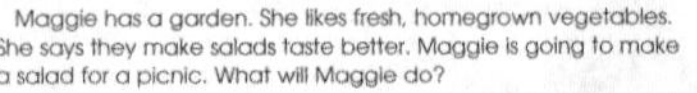

Maggie has a garden. She likes fresh, homegrown vegetables. She says they make salads taste better. Maggie is going to make a salad for a picnic. What will Maggie do?

- ○ Maggie will buy the salad at the store.
- ○ Maggie will buy the vegetables at the store.
- ● Maggie will use vegetables from her garden.

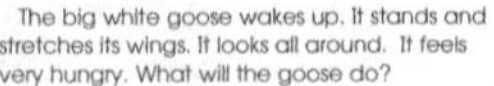

The big white goose wakes up. It stands and stretches its wings. It looks all around. It feels very hungry. What will the goose do?

- ○ The goose will go swimming.
- ● The goose will look for food.
- ○ The goose will go back to sleep.

120

Boa Constrictors

Boa constrictors are very big. They may grow up to 14 feet (4.3 meters) long. A boa kills its prey by squeezing it. Then, the prey is swallowed.

Boas do not eat cows or other large animals. They do eat animals that are larger than their own heads. The bones in their jaws stretch so they can swallow small animals such as rodents and birds.

Boa constrictors hunt while hanging from trees. They watch for their prey. Then, they attack. After eating, they may sleep for a week. Boas do not need to eat often. They can live without food for many months.

Boas are not poisonous. They defend themselves by striking and biting with their sharp teeth.

Boa constrictors give birth to live baby snakes. They do not lay eggs. They may have up to fifty baby snakes at one time.

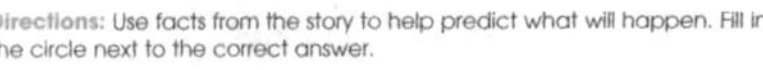

Directions: Use facts from the story to help predict what will happen. Fill in the circle next to the correct answer.

1. A boa is hanging from a tree. Suddenly, a bird hops under it. The boa will ____.
   - ○ strike and bite it
   - ● squeeze it, then swallow it
   - ○ poison it, then eat it
   - ○ sleep for one week
2. The boa is hungry and hunting for food. Which type of prey will the snake most likely eat?
   - ○ cow ○ panther ○ horse ● mouse
3. A boa constrictor is slithering through the grass. Out of the grass comes a hunter walking toward it. The boa will probably ____.
   - ● strike the hunter
   - ○ slither up a tree to sleep
   - ○ squeeze and kill the hunter
   - ○ poison the hunter

121

Fact or Opinion?

In sports, there are many facts and opinions. A **fact** is something that is true. An **opinion** is a belief someone has about something.

Directions: Read the sports sentences below. Next to each sentence, write **F** if it is a fact and **O** if it is an opinion.

1. F In bowling, a poodle is a ball that rolls down the gutter.
2. O I think poodles are cute.
3. O Julio is my favorite football player.
4. F A football player is a person who plays in a football game.
5. F A catcher's mask protects the catcher's face.
6. O My catcher's mask is too tight.
7. O I had a great putt!
8. F A putt is when a golfer hits the ball into the hole on a green.
9. F A referee is a person who enforces the rules in a game.
10. O Josh thought the referee did a good job.
11. O This silly javelin is really hard to throw!
12. F A metal spear that is thrown for a distance is called a javelin.
13. O Jake said, "The defense tried its best to block the ball."

122

Fact and Opinion: Games!

A **fact** is something that can be proven. An **opinion** is a feeling or belief about something and cannot be proven.

Directions: Read these sentences about different games. Then, write **F** next to each fact and **O** next to each opinion.

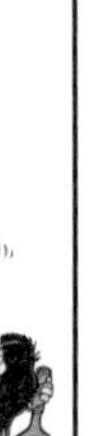

1. O Tennis is cool!
2. F There are red and black markers in a Checkers game.
3. F In football, a touchdown is worth six points.
4. O Being a goalie in soccer is easy.
5. F A yo-yo moves on a string.
6. O June's sister looks like the queen on the card.
7. F The six kids need three more players for a baseball team.
8. O Table tennis is more fun than court tennis.
9. F Hide-and-Seek is a game that can be played outdoors or indoors.
10. F Play money is used in many board games.

123

Fact and Opinion: A Bounty of Birds

Directions: Read the story. Then, follow the instructions.

Tashi's family likes to go to the zoo. Her favorite animals are all the different kinds of birds. Tashi likes birds because they can fly, they have colorful feathers, and they make funny noises.

Write F next to each fact and O next to each opinion.

1. F Birds have two feet.
2. F All birds lay eggs.
3. O Parrots are too noisy.
4. F All birds have feathers and wings.
5. O It would be great to be a bird and fly south for the winter.
6. F Birds have hard beaks or bills instead of teeth.
7. O Pigeons are fun to watch.
8. F Some birds cannot fly.
9. O Parakeets make good pets.
10. F A penguin is a bird.

124

Fact and Opinion: Henrietta the Humpback

Directions: Read the story. Then, follow the instructions.

My name is Henrietta, and I am a humpback whale. I live in cold seas in the summer and warm seas in the winter. My long flippers are used to move forward and backward. I like to eat fish. Sometimes, I show off by leaping out of the water. Would you like to be a humpback whale?

Write **F** next to each fact and **O** next to each opinion.

1. O Being a humpback whale is fun.
2. F Humpback whales live in cold seas during the summer.
3. O Whales are fun to watch.
4. F Humpback whales use their flippers to move forward and backward.
5. O Henrietta is a great name for a whale.
6. O Leaping out of water would be hard.
7. F Humpback whales like to eat fish.
8. F Humpback whales show off by leaping out of the water.

125

Answer Key

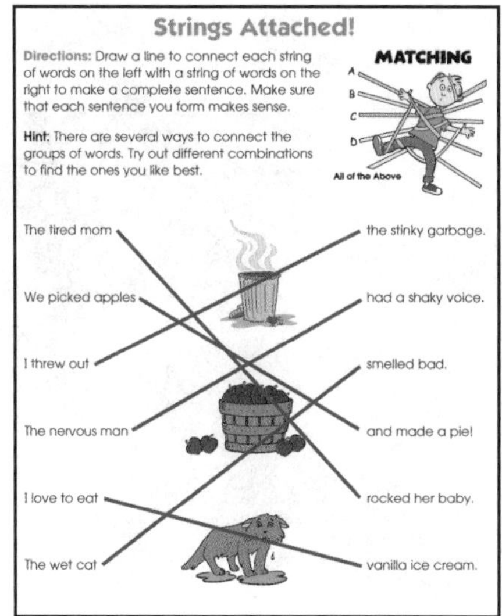

Strings Attached!

Directions: Draw a line to connect each string of words on the left with a string of words on the right to make a complete sentence. Make sure that each sentence you form makes sense.

Hint: There are several ways to connect the groups of words. Try out different combinations to find the ones you like best.

The tired mom — the stinky garbage.
We picked apples — had a shaky voice.
I threw out — smelled bad.
The nervous man — and made a pie!
I love to eat — rocked her baby.
The wet cat — vanilla ice cream.

126

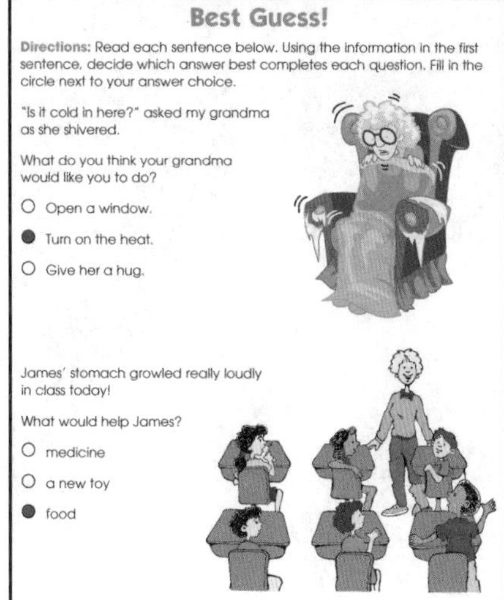

Best Guess!

Directions: Read each sentence below. Using the information in the first sentence, decide which answer best completes each question. Fill in the circle next to your answer choice.

"Is it cold in here?" asked my grandma as she shivered.

What do you think your grandma would like you to do?

- ○ Open a window.
- ● Turn on the heat.
- ○ Give her a hug.

James' stomach growled really loudly in class today!

What would help James?

- ○ medicine
- ○ a new toy
- ● food

127

It Isn't!

Directions: Finish the sentences about the stories.

Something is inside the kitchen cabinet. It isn't a **crocodile**.

can vase crocodile

I smell something delicious in the kitchen. It isn't **dirty socks**.

a cherry pie dirty socks a plate of brownies

I touch something soft and fluffy. It isn't **sand paper**.

sand paper a kitten a bath towel

I taste something sour. It isn't a **chocolate bar**.

lemon chocolate bar

I hear something making noise. It isn't **a book**.

a dog a squirrel a book

128

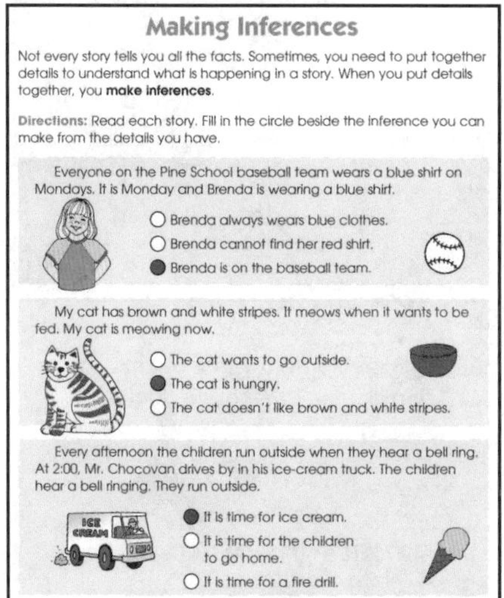

Making Inferences

Not every story tells you all the facts. Sometimes, you need to put together details to understand what is happening in a story. When you put details together, you **make inferences**.

Directions: Read each story. Fill in the circle beside the inference you can make from the details you have.

Everyone on the Pine School baseball team wears a blue shirt on Mondays. It is Monday and Brenda is wearing a blue shirt.

- ○ Brenda always wears blue clothes.
- ○ Brenda cannot find her red shirt.
- ● Brenda is on the baseball team.

My cat has brown and white stripes. It meows when it wants to be fed. My cat is meowing now.

- ○ The cat wants to go outside.
- ● The cat is hungry.
- ○ The cat doesn't like brown and white stripes.

Every afternoon the children run outside when they hear a bell ring. At 2:00, Mr. Chocovan drives by in his ice-cream truck. The children hear a bell ringing. They run outside.

- ● It is time for ice cream.
- ○ It is time for the children to go home.
- ○ It is time for a fire drill.

129

Inferences About Characters

Directions: Read this story. Look for clues about Tom. Then, follow the directions below the story.

"You can't get me!" Goldie teased Tom when she saw him looking at her.

"I never said that I wanted to get you, anyway," answered Tom, knowing that Goldie was right. He walked away, waving his fluffy tail proudly.

Although Goldie had once been afraid of Tom, she now liked to tease him.

"It's fun to tease Tom. When he is upset, all his fur stands straight up," she thought.

Soon Goldie heard noises. Someone else was home. "It is almost time for dinner," thought Goldie. "I'm really glad to be a goldfish. I'm safe and sound and very well fed."

What does Tom look like? Draw a picture of Tom.

Drawing will vary.

Circle the picture that tells how Goldie feels.

130

Mind-Reading Tricks

Samantha thought of a good joke. She bragged that she could read Maria's mind. She put her hand on Maria's head, closed her eyes, and said, "You had red punch with your lunch!"

"Wow! You're right!" replied Maria, not realizing that she had a little red ring around her lips.

"That was easy. But I bet you can't tell me what I just ate," said Thomas.

"That's a bunch of baloney," answered Samantha.

"How did you know?" gasped Thomas.

"It's my little secret," said Samantha, with a sigh of relief.

"Here comes your mom," said Maria. "Can you read her mind, too?"

Samantha looked down at her watch. She should have been home half an hour ago. As she ran to meet her mother, she yelled back, "Yes, I know exactly what she's thinking!"

Directions: Make inferences about Samantha's mind-reading tricks. Fill in the circle beside the correct inference.

1. Was Samantha sure that Thomas had eaten bologna for lunch?
   - ● No, she was just lucky.
   - ○ Yes, she saw him eat his bologna sandwich.
2. What was Samantha's mother probably thinking?
   - ○ Samantha was a great mind reader.
   - ● Samantha was late.

131

Answer Key

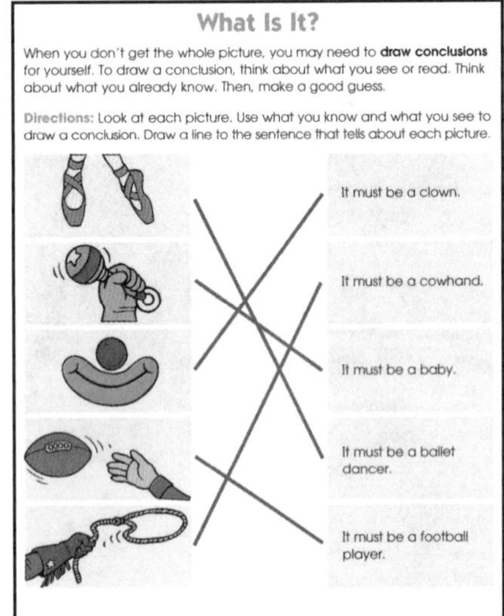

What Is It?

When you don't get the whole picture, you may need to **draw conclusions** for yourself. To draw a conclusion, think about what you see or read. Think about what you already know. Then, make a good guess.

Directions: Look at each picture. Use what you know and what you see to draw a conclusion. Draw a line to the sentence that tells about each picture.

It must be a clown.

It must be a cowhand.

It must be a baby.

It must be a ballet dancer.

It must be a football player.

132

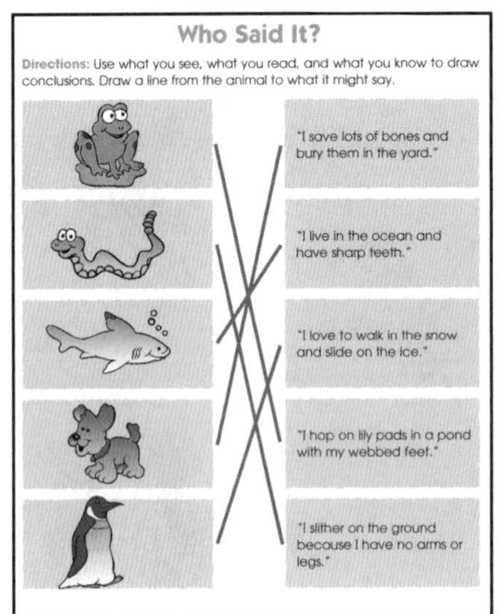

Who Said It?

Directions: Use what you see, what you read, and what you know to draw conclusions. Draw a line from the animal to what it might say.

"I save lots of bones and bury them in the yard."

"I live in the ocean and have sharp teeth."

"I love to walk in the snow and slide on the ice."

"I hop on lily pads in a pond with my webbed feet."

"I slither on the ground because I have no arms or legs."

133

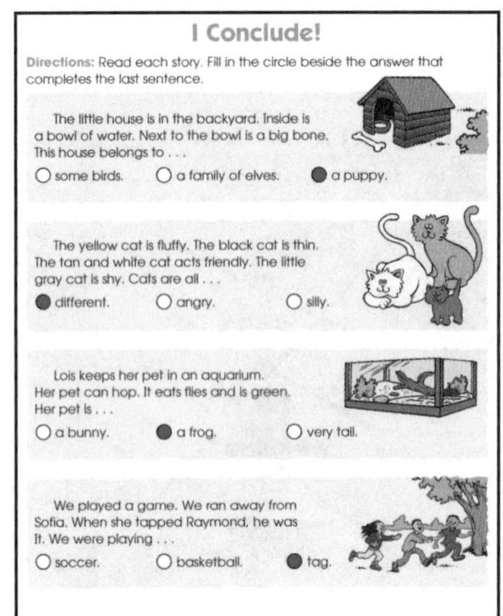

I Conclude!

Directions: Read each story. Fill in the circle beside the answer that completes the last sentence.

The little house is in the backyard. Inside is a bowl of water. Next to the bowl is a big bone. This house belongs to . . .

○ some birds. ○ a family of elves. ● a puppy.

The yellow cat is fluffy. The black cat is thin. The tan and white cat acts friendly. The little gray cat is shy. Cats are all . . .

● different. ○ angry. ○ silly.

Lois keeps her pet in an aquarium. Her pet can hop. It eats flies and is green. Her pet is . . .

○ a bunny. ● a frog. ○ very tall.

We played a game. We ran away from Sofia. When she tapped Raymond, he was It. We were playing . . .

○ soccer. ○ basketball. ● tag.

134

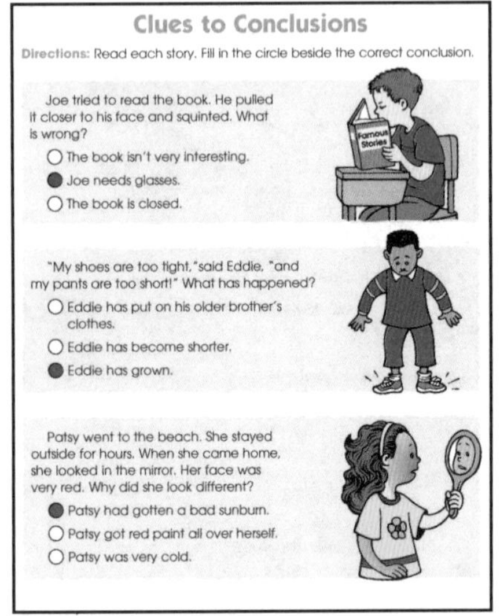

Clues to Conclusions

Directions: Read each story. Fill in the circle beside the correct conclusion.

Joe tried to read the book. He pulled it closer to his face and squinted. What is wrong?

○ The book isn't very interesting.
● Joe needs glasses.
○ The book is closed.

"My shoes are too tight," said Eddie, "and my pants are too short!" What has happened?

○ Eddie has put on his older brother's clothes.
○ Eddie has become shorter.
● Eddie has grown.

Patsy went to the beach. She stayed outside for hours. When she came home, she looked in the mirror. Her face was very red. Why did she look different?

● Patsy had gotten a bad sunburn.
○ Patsy got red paint all over herself.
○ Patsy was very cold.

135

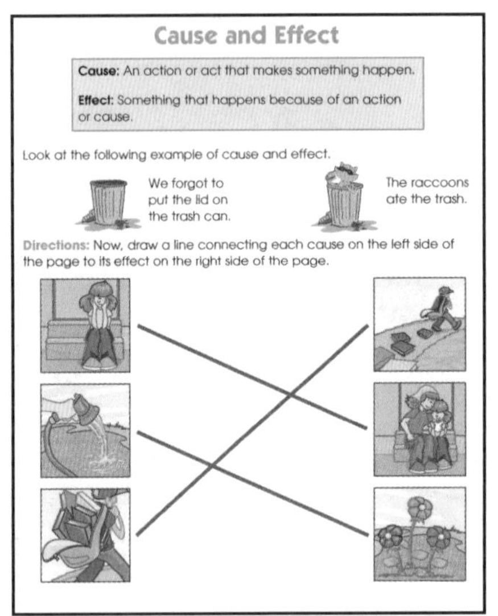

Cause and Effect

Cause: An action or act that makes something happen.

Effect: Something that happens because of an action or cause.

Look at the following example of cause and effect.

We forgot to put the lid on the trash can. The raccoons ate the trash.

Directions: Now, draw a line connecting each cause on the left side of the page to its effect on the right side of the page.

136

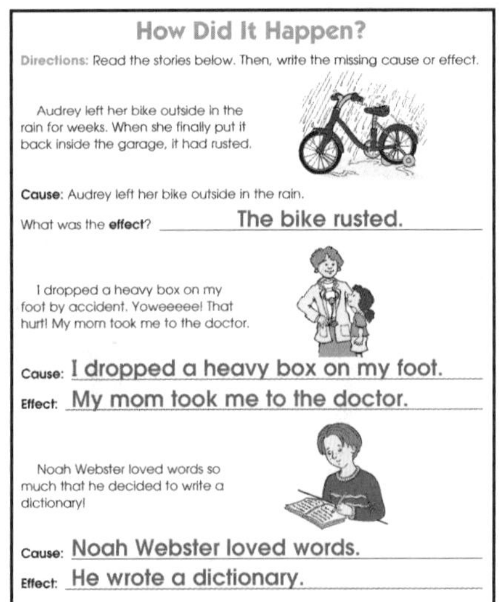

How Did It Happen?

Directions: Read the stories below. Then, write the missing cause or effect.

Audrey left her bike outside in the rain for weeks. When she finally put it back inside the garage, it had rusted.

Cause: Audrey left her bike outside in the rain.

What was the **effect**? The bike rusted.

I dropped a heavy box on my foot by accident. Yoweeeee! That hurt! My mom took me to the doctor.

Cause: I dropped a heavy box on my foot.

Effect: My mom took me to the doctor.

Noah Webster loved words so much that he decided to write a dictionary!

Cause: Noah Webster loved words.

Effect: He wrote a dictionary.

137

Answer Key

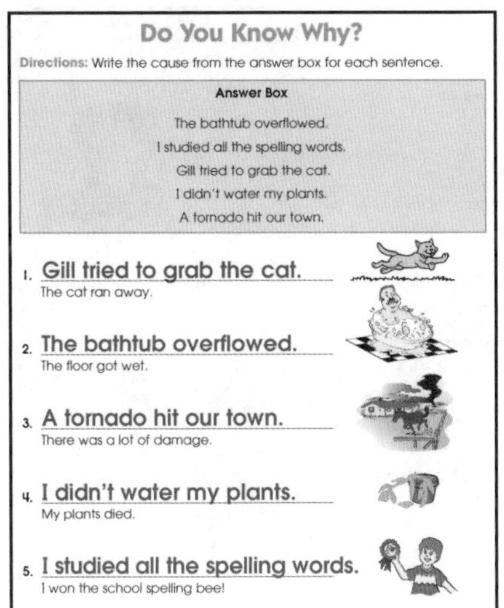

Do You Know Why?

Directions: Write the cause from the answer box for each sentence.

Answer Box

The bathtub overflowed.
I studied all the spelling words.
Gill tried to grab the cat.
I didn't water my plants.
A tornado hit our town.

1. Gill tried to grab the cat.
The cat ran away.
2. The bathtub overflowed.
The floor got wet.
3. A tornado hit our town.
There was a lot of damage.
4. I didn't water my plants.
My plants died.
5. I studied all the spelling words.
I won the school spelling bee!

138

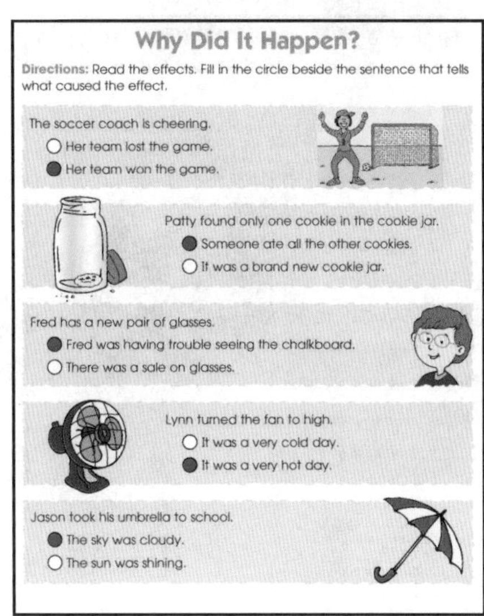

Why Did It Happen?

Directions: Read the effects. Fill in the circle beside the sentence that tells what caused the effect.

The soccer coach is cheering.
○ Her team lost the game.
● Her team won the game.

Patty found only one cookie in the cookie jar.
● Someone ate all the other cookies.
○ It was a brand new cookie jar.

Fred has a new pair of glasses.
● Fred was having trouble seeing the chalkboard.
○ There was a sale on glasses.

Lynn turned the fan to high.
○ It was a very cold day.
● It was a very hot day.

Jason took his umbrella to school.
● The sky was cloudy.
○ The sun was shining.

139

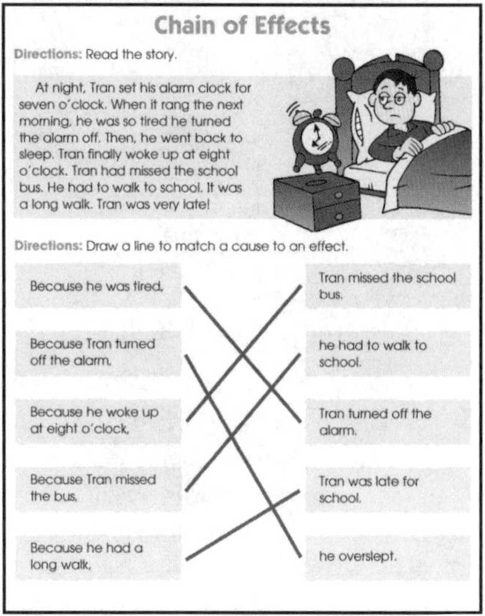

Chain of Effects

Directions: Read the story.

At night, Tran set his alarm clock for seven o'clock. When it rang the next morning, he was so tired he turned the alarm off. Then, he went back to sleep. Tran finally woke up at eight o'clock. Tran had missed the school bus. He had to walk to school. It was a long walk. Tran was very late!

Directions: Draw a line to match a cause to an effect.

Cause	Effect
Because he was tired,	Tran missed the school bus.
Because Tran turned off the alarm,	he had to walk to school.
Because he woke up at eight o'clock,	Tran turned off the alarm.
Because Tran missed the bus,	Tran was late for school.
Because he had a long walk,	he overslept.

140

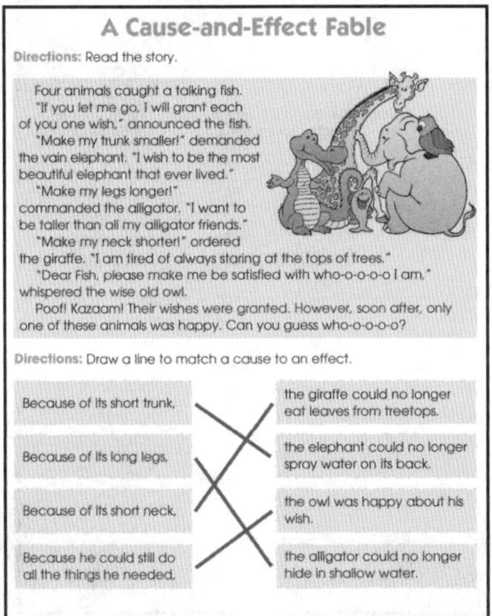

A Cause-and-Effect Fable

Directions: Read the story.

Four animals caught a talking fish.
"If you let me go, I will grant each of you one wish," announced the fish.
"Make my trunk smaller!" demanded the vain elephant. "I wish to be the most beautiful elephant that ever lived."
"Make my legs longer!" commanded the alligator. "I want to be taller than all my alligator friends."
"Make my neck shorter!" ordered the giraffe. "I am tired of always staring at the tops of trees."
"Dear Fish, please make me be satisfied with who-o-o-o-o I am," whispered the wise old owl.
Poof! Kazaam! Their wishes were granted. However, soon after, only one of these animals was happy. Can you guess who-o-o-o-o?

Directions: Draw a line to match a cause to an effect.

Cause	Effect
Because of its short trunk,	the giraffe could no longer eat leaves from treetops.
Because of its long legs,	the elephant could no longer spray water on its back.
Because of its short neck,	the owl was happy about his wish.
Because he could still do all the things he needed,	the alligator could no longer hide in shallow water.

141

Fiction or Nonfiction?

Some stories are made up and some are true. **Fiction** stories are made up, and **nonfiction** stories are true.

Directions: Read the passages below. Then, write if they are **fiction** or **nonfiction**.

Following a balanced diet is important for good health. Your body needs many kinds of vitamins and minerals found in different types of food. For example, oranges provide vitamin C, and bananas are a good source of the mineral potassium.

nonfiction

We call my dog the alphabet dog. Why? Because my dog can sing the alphabet! That's right! My dog, Smarty Pants, is a dog genius! Smarty Pants can sing the entire alphabet! "S.P.," as we sometimes call her, is also starting her own dog academy to teach other dogs how to sing the alphabet. You should sign up your dog for classes with Smarty Pants today!

fiction

142

Nonfiction: Tornado Tips

Directions: Read about tornadoes. Then, follow the instructions.

A tornado begins over land with strong winds and thunderstorms. The spinning air becomes a funnel. It can cause damage. If you are inside, go to the lowest floor of the building. A basement is a safe place. A bathroom or closet in the middle of a building can be a safe place, too. If you are outside, lie in a ditch. Remember, tornadoes are dangerous.

Write five facts about tornadoes.

1. A tornado begins over land.
2. Spinning air becomes a funnel.
3. Tornadoes can cause damage.
4. A basement is a safe place to be in a tornado.
5. If you are outside during a tornado, you should lie in a ditch.

143

Answer Key

Fiction: Hercules

The **setting** is where a story takes place. The **characters** are the people in a story or play.

Directions: Read about Hercules. Then, answer the questions.

Hercules was born in the warm Atlantic Ocean. He was a very small and weak baby. He wanted to be the strongest hurricane in the world. But he had one problem. He couldn't blow 75-mile-per-hour winds. Hercules blew and blew in the ocean, until one day, his sister, Hola, told him it would be more fun to be a breeze than a hurricane. Hercules agreed. It was a breeze to be a breeze!

1. What is the setting of the story? Atlantic Ocean
2. Who are the characters? Hercules, Hola
3. What is the problem? Hercules couldn't blow 75 mile-per-hour winds.
4. How does Hercules solve his problem? He decides that it is more fun to be a breeze than a hurricane.

144

Fiction and Nonfiction: Which Is It?

Directions: Read about fiction and nonfiction books. Then, follow the instructions.

There are many kinds of books. Some books have make-believe stories about princesses and dragons. Some books contain poetry and rhymes, like Mother Goose. These are fiction.

Some books contain facts about space and plants. And still other books have stories about famous people in history like Abraham Lincoln. These are nonfiction.

Write **F** for **fiction** and **NF** for **nonfiction**.

F 1. nursery rhyme
F 2. fairy tale
NF 3. true life story of a famous athlete
F 4. Aesop's fables
NF 5. dictionary entry about foxes
NF 6. weather report
F 7. story about a talking tree
NF 8. story about how a tadpole becomes a frog
NF 9. story about animal habitats
F 10. riddles and jokes

145

Character, cont.

First, authors must decide who their main character is going to be. Next, they decide what their main character looks like. Then, they reveal the character's personality by:

what the character does

what the character says

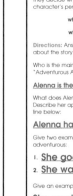

Directions: Answer the questions about the story you just read.

Who is the main character in "Adventurous Alenna!"?

Alenna is the main character.

What does Alenna look like? Describe her appearance on the line below:

Alenna had long, blond hair and sea-green eyes.

Give two examples of what Alenna **does** that shows that she is adventurous:

1. She goes on long bike rides.
2. She water-skis.

Give an example of what Alenna **says** that reveals she is adventurous.

She wants to go snorkeling.

147

Setting—Place

Every story has a **setting**. The setting is the **place** where the story happens. Think of a place that you know well. It could be your room, your kitchen, your backyard, your classroom, or an imaginary place.

Directions: Brainstorm some words and ideas about that place. Think about what you see, hear, smell, taste, or feel in that place.

Brainstorm your ideas for a setting below:

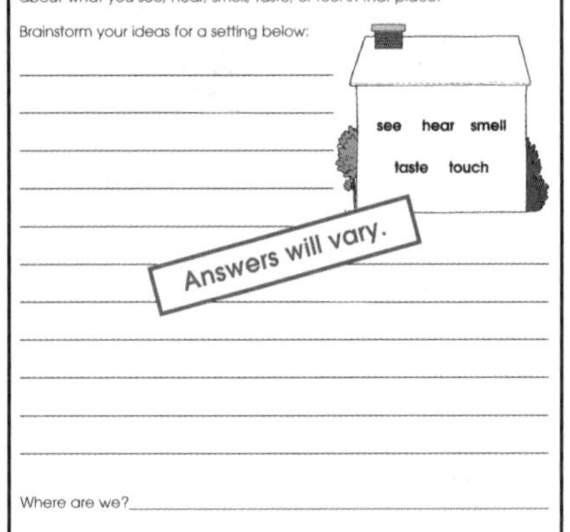

Answers will vary.

Where are we?

148

Setting—Time

The **setting** is the **place** where the story happens. The setting is also the **time** in which the story happens. A reader needs to know **when** the story is happening. Does it take place at night? On a sunny day? In the future? During the winter?

Time can be:

 time of day
 a holiday
 a season of the year
 a time in the future
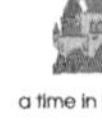 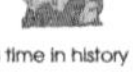 a time in history

Directions: Read the following story. Then, answer the questions below.

Knock, Knock!

One windy fall night there was a knock at the door. "Who is it?" I asked.

"It's your dog, Max. Please let me in," Max said.

"Oh, good. I was getting worried about you!" I said. Then, I let Max inside.

I thought to myself how glad I was that scientists had invented voice boxes for dogs. How did people in the olden days ever know when to let their dogs inside if their dogs couldn't talk? The Doggie Voice Box is such a wonderful invention. I'm so happy that I live in the year 2090!

What time of day is it? It was night.

What season is it? It was fall.

What year does this story take place? The story takes place in 2090.

149

Extra! Extra! Read All About It!

Newspaper reporters have very important jobs. They have to catch a reader's attention and, at the same time, **tell the facts**.

Newspaper reporters write their stories by answering **who**, **what**, **where**, **when**, **why**, and **how**.

Directions: Think about a book you just read and answer the questions below.

Who: **Who** is the story about?

What: **What** happened to the main character?

Where: **Where** do[...]

When: **When** does the story take place?

Why: **Why** do these story events happen?

How: **How** do these events happen?

Answers will vary.

150

Answer Key

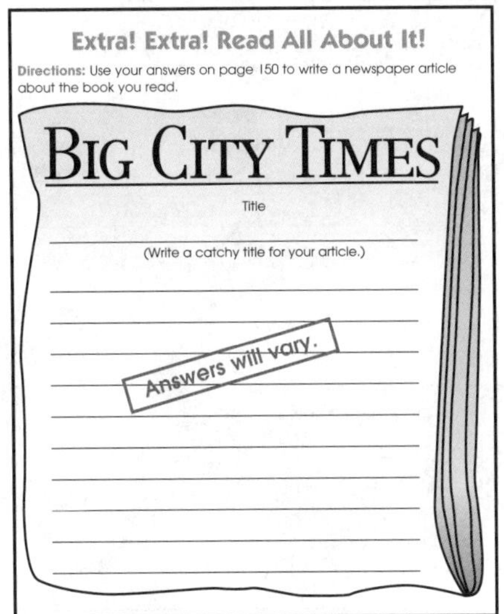

Extra! Extra! Read All About It!

Directions: Use your answers on page 150 to write a newspaper article about the book you read.

BIG CITY TIMES

Title

(Write a catchy title for your article.)

Answers will vary.

151

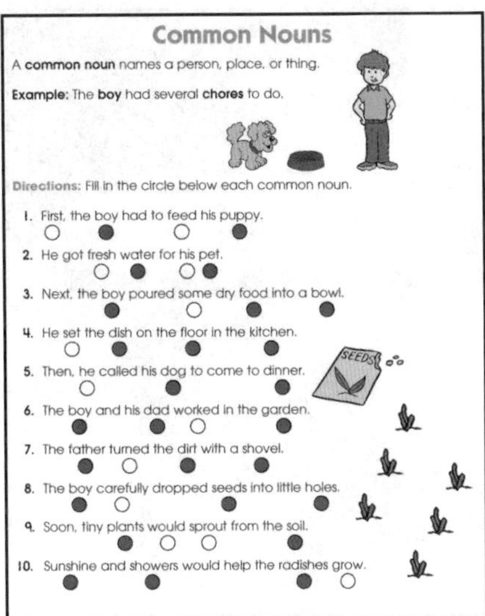

Common Nouns

A **common noun** names a person, place, or thing.

Example: The **boy** had several **chores** to do.

Directions: Fill in the circle below each common noun.

1. First, the boy had to feed his puppy.
2. He got fresh water for his pet.
3. Next, the boy poured some dry food into a bowl.
4. He set the dish on the floor in the kitchen.
5. Then, he called his dog to come to dinner.
6. The boy and his dad worked in the garden.
7. The father turned the dirt with a shovel.
8. The boy carefully dropped seeds into little holes.
9. Soon, tiny plants would sprout from the soil.
10. Sunshine and showers would help the radishes grow.

152

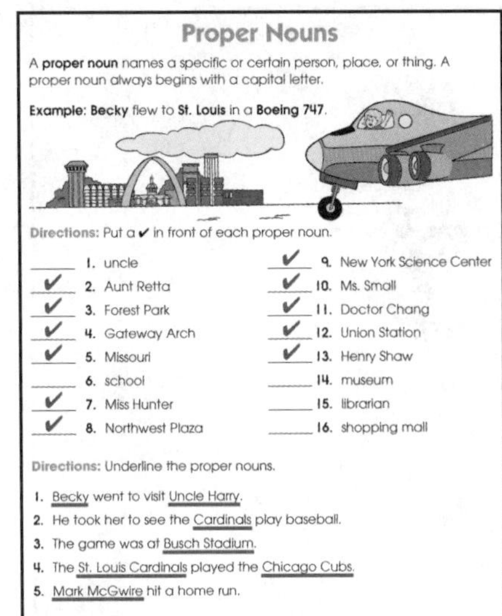

Proper Nouns

A **proper noun** names a specific or certain person, place, or thing. A proper noun always begins with a capital letter.

Example: Becky flew to **St. Louis** in a **Boeing 747**.

Directions: Put a ✔ in front of each proper noun.

	1. uncle	✔	9. New York Science Center
✔	2. Aunt Retta	✔	10. Ms. Small
✔	3. Forest Park	✔	11. Doctor Chang
✔	4. Gateway Arch	✔	12. Union Station
✔	5. Missouri	✔	13. Henry Shaw
	6. school		14. museum
✔	7. Miss Hunter		15. librarian
✔	8. Northwest Plaza		16. shopping mall

Directions: Underline the proper nouns.

1. Becky went to visit Uncle Harry.
2. He took her to see the Cardinals play baseball.
3. The game was at Busch Stadium.
4. The St. Louis Cardinals played the Chicago Cubs.
5. Mark McGwire hit a home run.

153

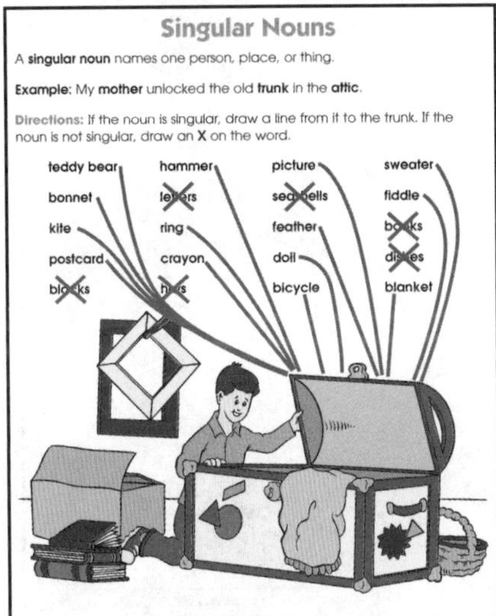

Singular Nouns

A **singular noun** names one person, place, or thing.

Example: My **mother** unlocked the old **trunk** in the **attic**.

Directions: If the noun is singular, draw a line from it to the trunk. If the noun is not singular, draw an **X** on the word.

teddy bear, hammer, picture, sweater, bonnet, letters (X), seashells (X), fiddle, kite, ring, feather, books (X), postcard, crayon, doll, dishes (X), blocks (X), hats (X), bicycle, blanket

154

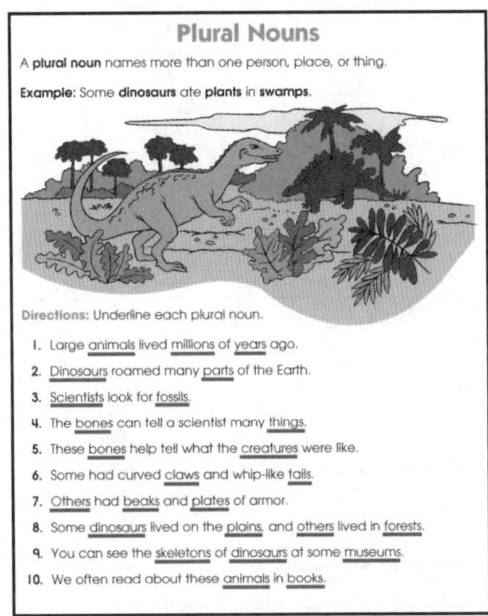

Plural Nouns

A **plural noun** names more than one person, place, or thing.

Example: Some **dinosaurs** ate **plants** in **swamps**.

Directions: Underline each plural noun.

1. Large animals lived millions of years ago.
2. Dinosaurs roamed many parts of the Earth.
3. Scientists look for fossils.
4. The bones can tell a scientist many things.
5. These bones help tell what the creatures were like.
6. Some had curved claws and whip-like tails.
7. Others had beaks and plates of armor.
8. Some dinosaurs lived on the plains, and others lived in forests.
9. You can see the skeletons of dinosaurs at some museums.
10. We often read about these animals in books.

155

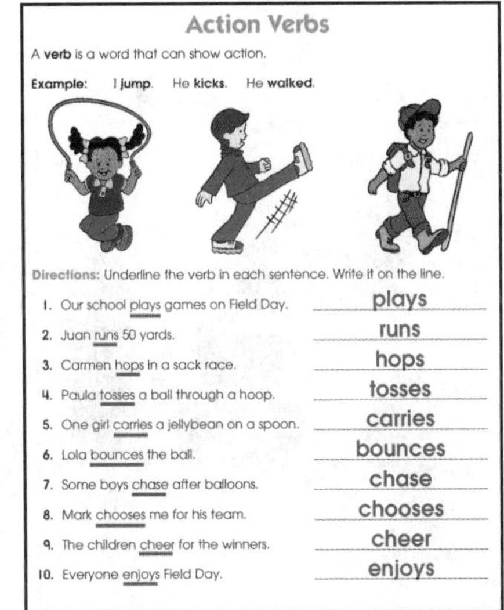

Action Verbs

A **verb** is a word that can show action.

Example: I **jump**. He **kicks**. He **walked**.

Directions: Underline the verb in each sentence. Write it on the line.

1. Our school plays games on Field Day. plays
2. Juan runs 50 yards. runs
3. Carmen hops in a sack race. hops
4. Paula tosses a ball through a hoop. tosses
5. One girl carries a jellybean on a spoon. carries
6. Lola bounces the ball. bounces
7. Some boys chase after balloons. chase
8. Mark chooses me for his team. chooses
9. The children cheer for the winners. cheer
10. Everyone enjoys Field Day. enjoys

156

Answer Key

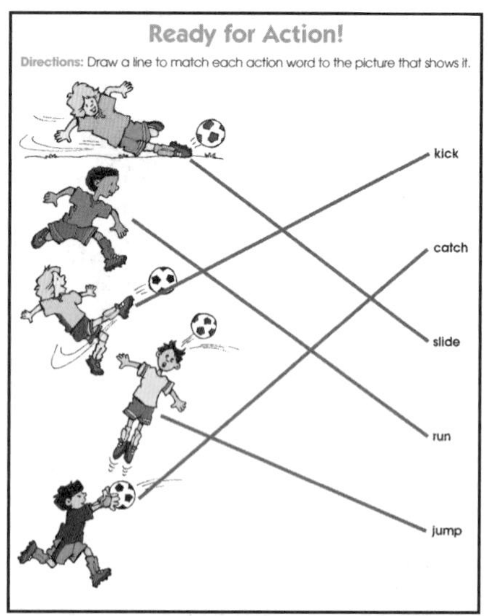

Ready for Action!

Directions: Draw a line to match each action word to the picture that shows it.

kick

catch

slide

run

jump

157

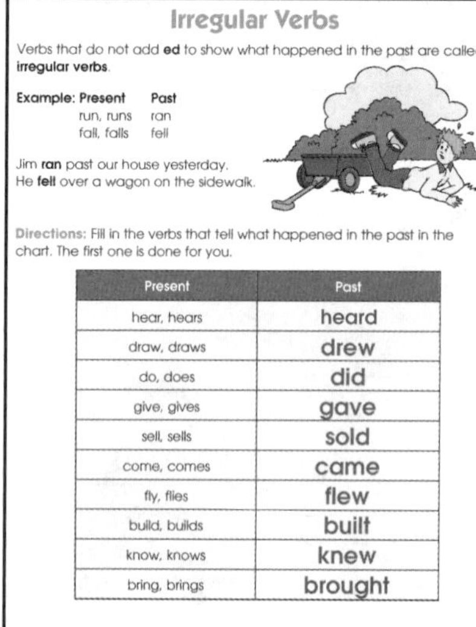

Irregular Verbs

Verbs that do not add **ed** to show what happened in the past are called **irregular verbs**.

Example: Present | **Past**
run, runs | ran
fall, falls | fell

Jim **ran** past our house yesterday.
He **fell** over a wagon on the sidewalk.

Directions: Fill in the verbs that tell what happened in the past in the chart. The first one is done for you.

Present	Past
hear, hears	heard
draw, draws	drew
do, does	did
give, gives	gave
sell, sells	sold
come, comes	came
fly, flies	flew
build, builds	built
know, knows	knew
bring, brings	brought

158

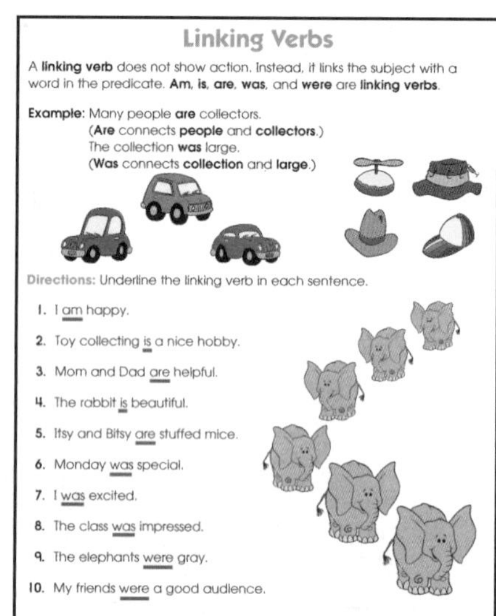

Linking Verbs

A **linking verb** does not show action. Instead, it links the subject with a word in the predicate. **Am**, **is**, **are**, **was**, and **were** are **linking verbs**.

Example: Many people **are** collectors.
(**Are** connects **people** and **collectors**.)
The collection **was** large.
(**Was** connects **collection** and **large**.)

Directions: Underline the linking verb in each sentence.

1. I am happy.
2. Toy collecting is a nice hobby.
3. Mom and Dad are helpful.
4. The rabbit is beautiful.
5. Itsy and Bitsy are stuffed mice.
6. Monday was special.
7. I was excited.
8. The class was impressed.
9. The elephants were gray.
10. My friends were a good audience.

159

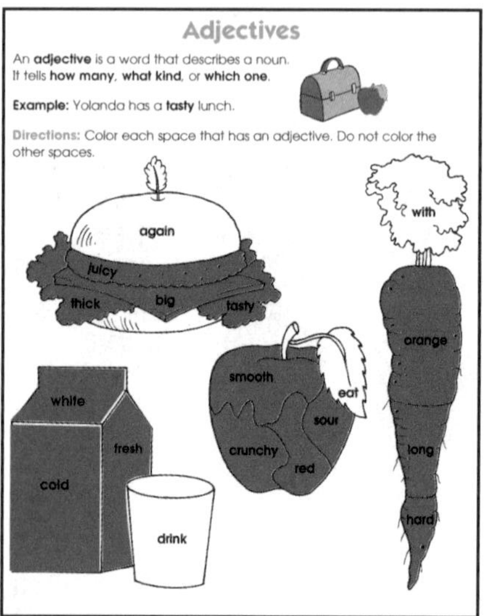

Adjectives

An **adjective** is a word that describes a noun. It tells **how many**, **what kind**, or **which one**.

Example: Yolanda has a **tasty** lunch.

Directions: Color each space that has an adjective. Do not color the other spaces.

160

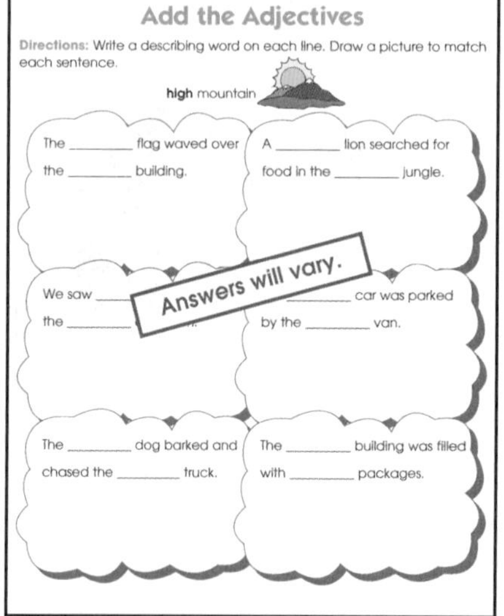

Add the Adjectives

Directions: Write a describing word on each line. Draw a picture to match each sentence.

high mountain

The ________ flag waved over the ________ building.

A ________ lion searched for food in the ________ jungle.

We saw ________ the ________.

________ car was parked by the ________ van.

The ________ dog barked and chased the ________ truck.

The ________ building was filled with ________ packages.

Answers will vary.

161

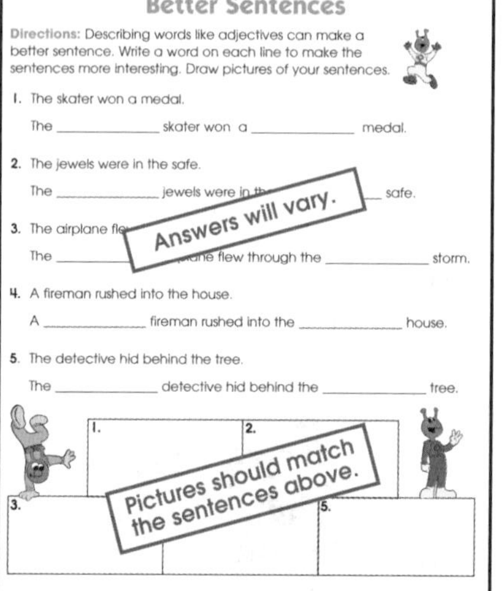

Better Sentences

Directions: Describing words like adjectives can make a better sentence. Write a word on each line to make the sentences more interesting. Draw pictures of your sentences.

1. The skater won a medal.
 The ____________ skater won a ____________ medal.
2. The jewels were in the safe.
 The ____________ jewels were in the ____________ safe.
3. The airplane flew through the storm.
 The ____________ plane flew through the ____________ storm.
4. A fireman rushed into the house.
 A ____________ fireman rushed into the ____________ house.
5. The detective hid behind the tree.
 The ____________ detective hid behind the ____________ tree.

1. 2. 3. 4. 5.

Answers will vary.

Pictures should match the sentences above.

162

Answer Key

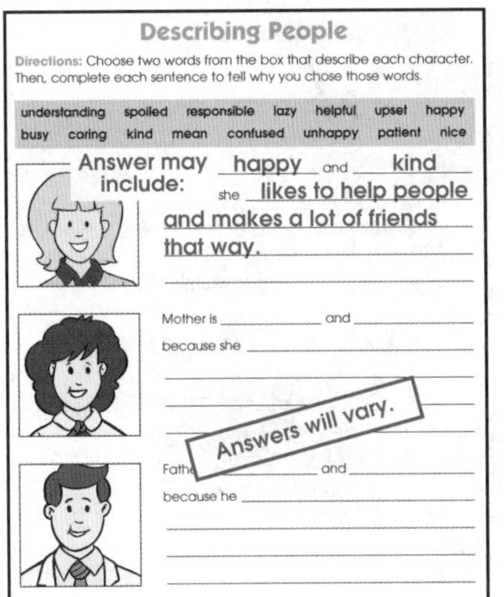

Describing People

Directions: Choose two words from the box that describe each character. Then, complete each sentence to tell why you chose those words.

understanding	spoiled	responsible	lazy	helpful	upset	happy
busy	caring	kind	mean	confused	unhappy	patient	nice

Answer may include: happy and kind

she likes to help people and makes a lot of friends that way.

Mother is ________ and ________ because she ________

Answers will vary.

Father is ________ and ________ because he ________

163

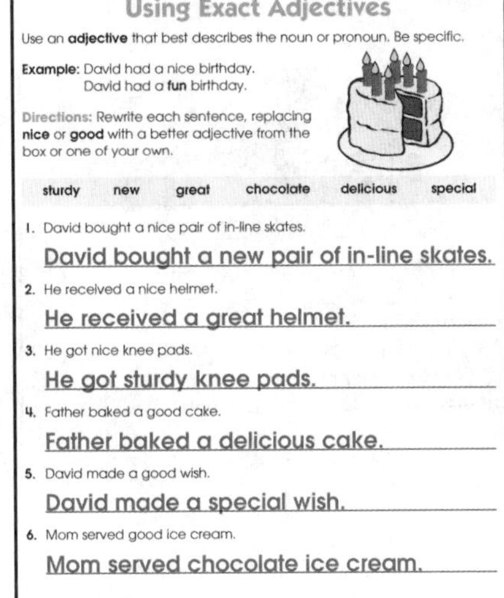

Using Exact Adjectives

Use an **adjective** that best describes the noun or pronoun. Be specific.

Example: David had a nice birthday.
David had a **fun** birthday.

Directions: Rewrite each sentence, replacing **nice** or **good** with a better adjective from the box or one of your own.

sturdy	new	great	chocolate	delicious	special

1. David bought a nice pair of in-line skates.
   David bought a new pair of in-line skates.
2. He received a nice helmet.
   He received a great helmet.
3. He got nice knee pads.
   He got sturdy knee pads.
4. Father baked a good cake.
   Father baked a delicious cake.
5. David made a good wish.
   David made a special wish.
6. Mom served good ice cream.
   Mom served chocolate ice cream.

164

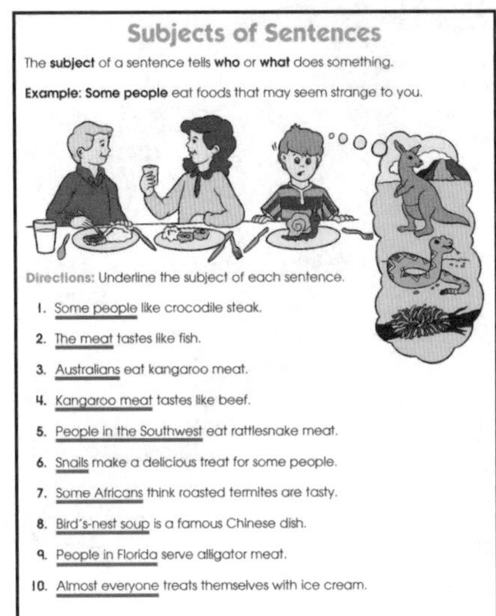

Subjects of Sentences

The **subject** of a sentence tells **who** or **what** does something.

Example: Some people eat foods that may seem strange to you.

Directions: Underline the subject of each sentence.

1. Some people like crocodile steak.
2. The meat tastes like fish.
3. Australians eat kangaroo meat.
4. Kangaroo meat tastes like beef.
5. People in the Southwest eat rattlesnake meat.
6. Snails make a delicious treat for some people.
7. Some Africans think roasted termites are tasty.
8. Bird's-nest soup is a famous Chinese dish.
9. People in Florida serve alligator meat.
10. Almost everyone treats themselves with ice cream.

165

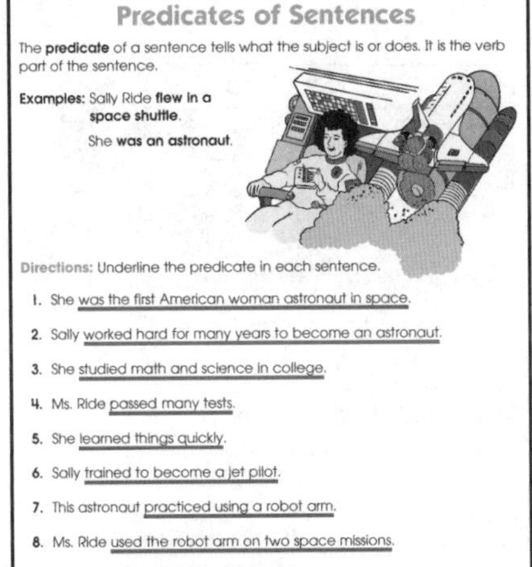

Predicates of Sentences

The **predicate** of a sentence tells what the subject is or does. It is the verb part of the sentence.

Examples: Sally Ride **flew in a space shuttle**.
She **was an astronaut**.

Directions: Underline the predicate in each sentence.

1. She was the first American woman astronaut in space.
2. Sally worked hard for many years to become an astronaut.
3. She studied math and science in college.
4. Ms. Ride passed many tests.
5. She learned things quickly.
6. Sally trained to become a jet pilot.
7. This astronaut practiced using a robot arm.
8. Ms. Ride used the robot arm on two space missions.
9. She conducted experiments with it.
10. The robot arm is called a remote manipulator.

166

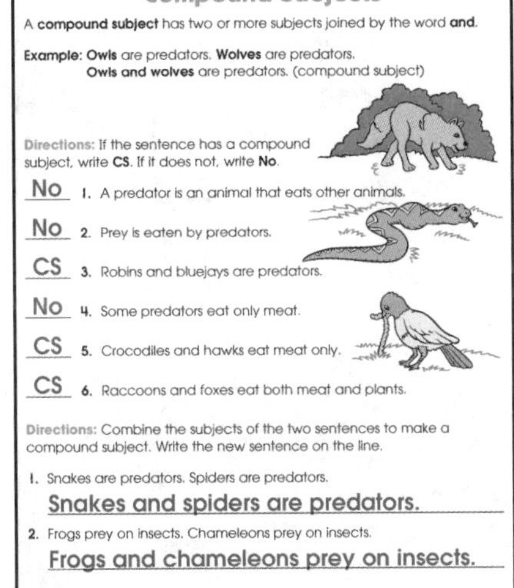

Compound Subjects

A **compound subject** has two or more subjects joined by the word **and**.

Example: Owls are predators. **Wolves** are predators.
Owls and wolves are predators. (compound subject)

Directions: If the sentence has a compound subject, write **CS**. If it does not, write **No**.

No 1. A predator is an animal that eats other animals.
No 2. Prey is eaten by predators.
CS 3. Robins and bluejays are predators.
No 4. Some predators eat only meat.
CS 5. Crocodiles and hawks eat meat only.
CS 6. Raccoons and foxes eat both meat and plants.

Directions: Combine the subjects of the two sentences to make a compound subject. Write the new sentence on the line.

1. Snakes are predators. Spiders are predators.
   Snakes and spiders are predators.
2. Frogs prey on insects. Chameleons prey on insects.
   Frogs and chameleons prey on insects.

169

Compound Predicates

A **compound predicate** has two or more predicates joined by the word **and**.

Example: Abe Lincoln was born in Kentucky. Abe Lincoln lived in a log cabin there.
Abe Lincoln **was born in Kentucky and lived in a log cabin there**.

Directions: If the sentence has a compound predicate, write **CP**. If it does not, write **No**.

CP 1. Abe Lincoln cut trees and chopped wood.
No 2. Abe and his sister walked to a spring for water.
CP 3. Abe's family packed up and left Kentucky.
No 4. They crossed the Ohio River to Indiana.
No 5. Abe's father built a new home.
CP 6. Abe's mother became sick and died.
No 7. Mr. Lincoln married again.
CP 8. Abe's new mother loved Abe and his sister and cared for them.

170

Answer Key

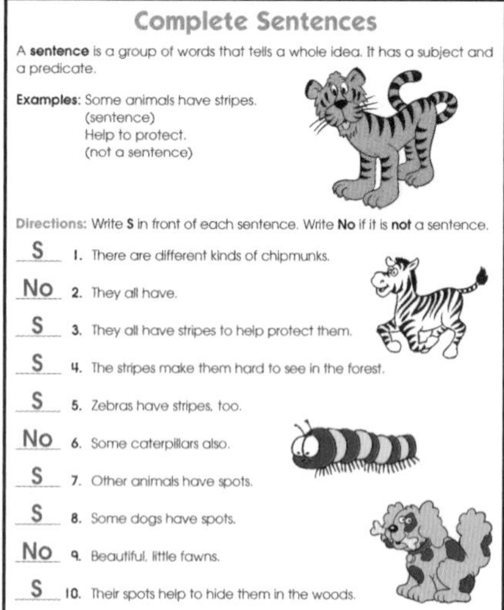

Complete Sentences

A **sentence** is a group of words that tells a whole idea. It has a subject and a predicate.

Examples: Some animals have stripes.
(sentence)
Help to protect.
(not a sentence)

Directions: Write **S** in front of each sentence. Write **No** if it is **not** a sentence.

S 1. There are different kinds of chipmunks.
No 2. They all have.
S 3. They all have stripes to help protect them.
S 4. The stripes make them hard to see in the forest.
S 5. Zebras have stripes, too.
No 6. Some caterpillars also.
S 7. Other animals have spots.
S 8. Some dogs have spots.
No 9. Beautiful, little fawns.
S 10. Their spots help to hide them in the woods.

171

Summer Camp

A **statement** is a telling sentence. It begins with a capital letter and ends with a period.

Directions: Write each statement correctly on the lines.

1. everyone goes to breakfast at 6:30 each morning
   Everyone goes to breakfast at 6:30 each morning.
2. only three people can ride in one canoe
   Only three people can ride in one canoe.
3. each person must help clean the cabins
   Each person must help clean the cabins.
4. older campers should help younger campers
   Older campers should help younger campers.
5. all lights are out by 9:00 each night
   All lights are out by 9:00 each night.
6. everyone should write home at least once a week
   Everyone should write home at least once a week.

172

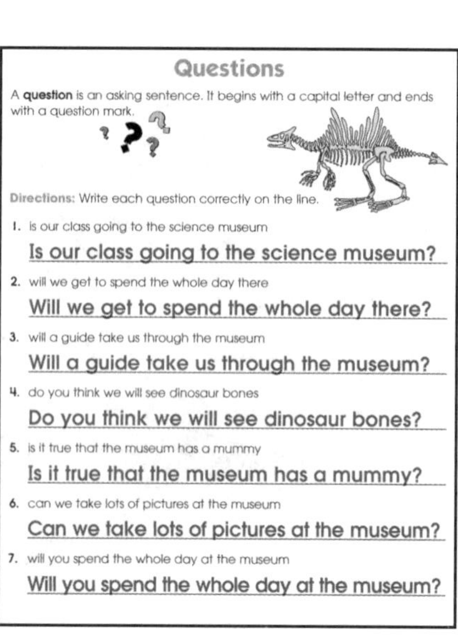

Questions

A **question** is an asking sentence. It begins with a capital letter and ends with a question mark.

Directions: Write each question correctly on the line.

1. is our class going to the science museum
   Is our class going to the science museum?
2. will we get to spend the whole day there
   Will we get to spend the whole day there?
3. will a guide take us through the museum
   Will a guide take us through the museum?
4. do you think we will see dinosaur bones
   Do you think we will see dinosaur bones?
5. is it true that the museum has a mummy
   Is it true that the museum has a mummy?
6. can we take lots of pictures at the museum
   Can we take lots of pictures at the museum?
7. will you spend the whole day at the museum
   Will you spend the whole day at the museum?

173

More Questions

Directions: Write five questions about the picture.

Blue
Yellow

Example: What color is she painting the front door?

174

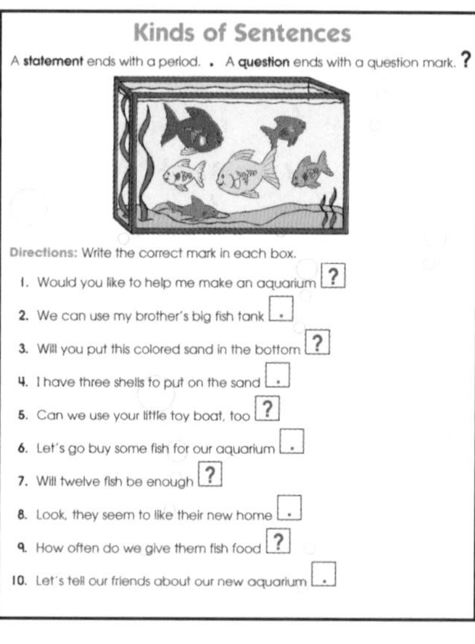

Kinds of Sentences

A **statement** ends with a period. **.** A **question** ends with a question mark. **?**

Directions: Write the correct mark in each box.

1. Would you like to help me make an aquarium ?
2. We can use my brother's big fish tank .
3. Will you put this colored sand in the bottom ?
4. I have three shells to put on the sand .
5. Can we use your little toy boat, too ?
6. Let's go buy some fish for our aquarium .
7. Will twelve fish be enough ?
8. Look, they seem to like their new home .
9. How often do we give them fish food ?
10. Let's tell our friends about our new aquarium .

175

Writing Sentences

Every sentence begins with a capital letter.

Come to the Fourth of July Picnic.
Town Park—All Day

Directions: Write three statements about the picture.

Example: The red airplane is pulling a sign.

Directions: Write three questions about the picture.

Example: Will the boy catch a fish?

176

Answer Key

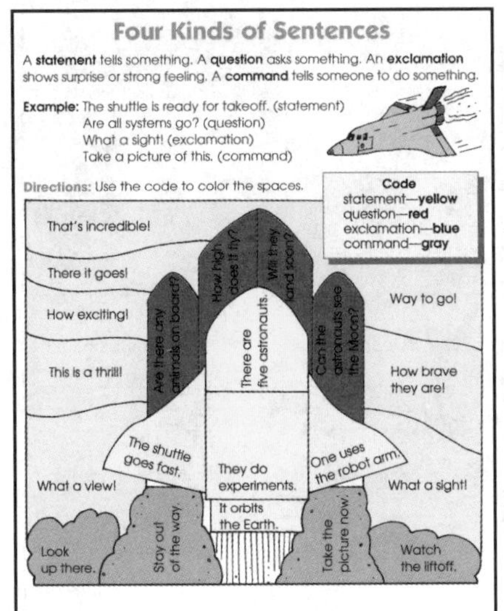

Four Kinds of Sentences

A **statement** tells something. A **question** asks something. An **exclamation** shows surprise or strong feeling. A **command** tells someone to do something.

Example: The shuttle is ready for takeoff. (statement)
Are all systems go? (question)
What a sight! (exclamation)
Take a picture of this. (command)

Directions: Use the code to color the spaces.

Code
statement—**yellow**
question—**red**
exclamation—**blue**
command—**gray**

That's incredible!
There it goes!
How exciting!
This is a thrill!
How high does it fly?
Will they land soon?
Are there any animals on board?
There are five astronauts.
Can the astronauts see the Moon?
Way to go!
How brave they are!
The shuttle goes fast.
They do experiments.
One uses the robot arm.
What a view!
What a sight!
It orbits the Earth.
Look up there.
Stay out of the way.
Take the picture now.
Watch the liftoff.

177

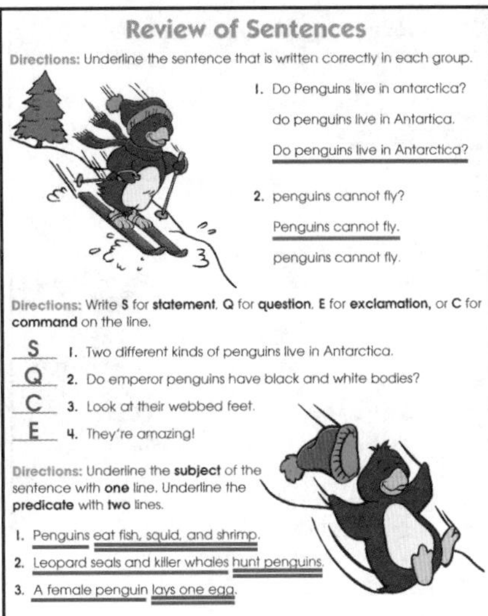

Review of Sentences

Directions: Underline the sentence that is written correctly in each group.

1. Do Penguins live in antarctica?
   do penguins live in Antartica.
   Do penguins live in Antarctica?
2. penguins cannot fly?
   Penguins cannot fly.
   penguins cannot fly.

Directions: Write **S** for **statement**, **Q** for **question**, **E** for **exclamation**, or **C** for **command** on the line.

S 1. Two different kinds of penguins live in Antarctica.
Q 2. Do emperor penguins have black and white bodies?
C 3. Look at their webbed feet.
E 4. They're amazing!

Directions: Underline the **subject** of the sentence with **one** line. Underline the **predicate** with **two** lines.

1. Penguins eat fish, squid, and shrimp.
2. Leopard seals and killer whales hunt penguins.
3. A female penguin lays one egg.

178

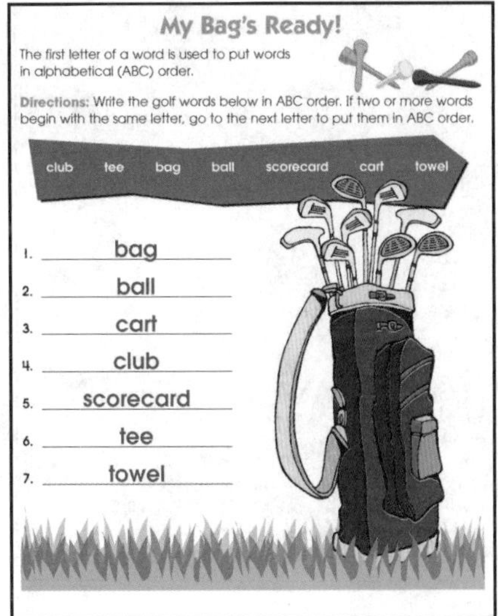

My Bag's Ready!

The first letter of a word is used to put words in alphabetical (ABC) order.

Directions: Write the golf words below in ABC order. If two or more words begin with the same letter, go to the next letter to put them in ABC order.

club tee bag ball scorecard cart towel

1. bag
2. ball
3. cart
4. club
5. scorecard
6. tee
7. towel

179

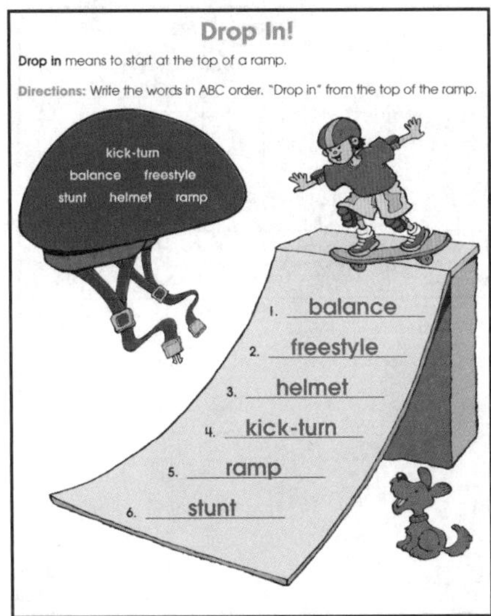

Drop In!

Drop in means to start at the top of a ramp.

Directions: Write the words in ABC order. "Drop in" from the top of the ramp.

kick-turn balance freestyle stunt helmet ramp

1. balance
2. freestyle
3. helmet
4. kick-turn
5. ramp
6. stunt

180

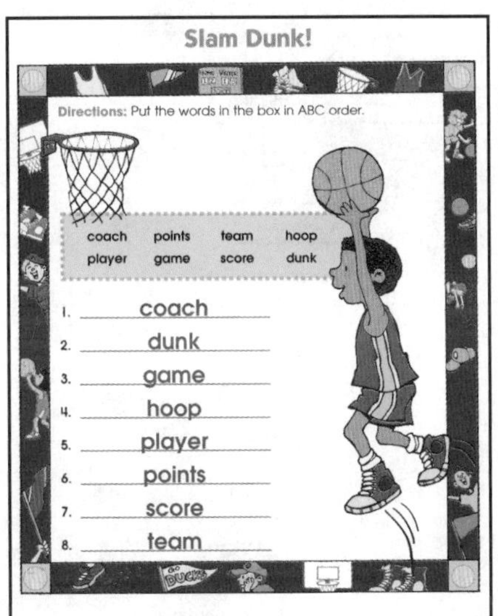

Slam Dunk!

Directions: Put the words in the box in ABC order.

coach points team hoop player game score dunk

1. coach
2. dunk
3. game
4. hoop
5. player
6. points
7. score
8. team

181

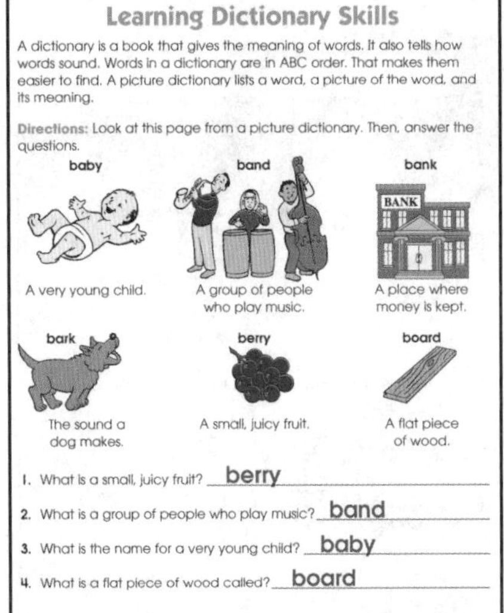

Learning Dictionary Skills

A dictionary is a book that gives the meaning of words. It also tells how words sound. Words in a dictionary are in ABC order. That makes them easier to find. A picture dictionary lists a word, a picture of the word, and its meaning.

Directions: Look at this page from a picture dictionary. Then, answer the questions.

baby — A very young child.
band — A group of people who play music.
bank — A place where money is kept.
bark — The sound a dog makes.
berry — A small, juicy fruit.
board — A flat piece of wood.

BANK

1. What is a small, juicy fruit? berry
2. What is a group of people who play music? band
3. What is the name for a very young child? baby
4. What is a flat piece of wood called? board

182

Answer Key

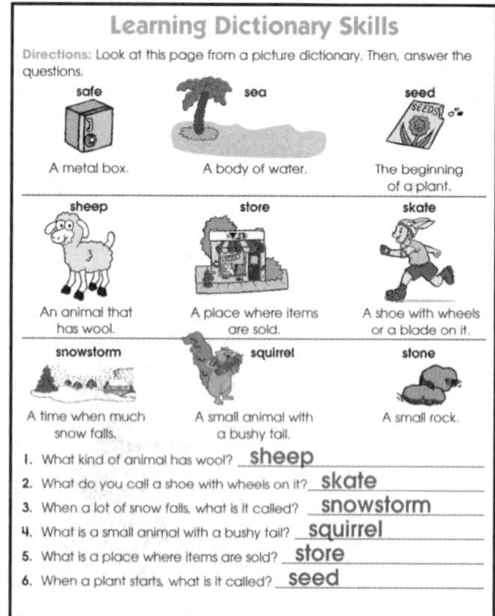

Learning Dictionary Skills

Directions: Look at this page from a picture dictionary. Then, answer the questions.

safe	sea	seed
A metal box.	A body of water.	The beginning of a plant.

sheep	store	skate
An animal that has wool.	A place where items are sold.	A shoe with wheels or a blade on it.

snowstorm	squirrel	stone
A time when much snow falls.	A small animal with a bushy tail.	A small rock.

1. What kind of animal has wool? sheep
2. What do you call a shoe with wheels on it? skate
3. When a lot of snow falls, what is it called? snowstorm
4. What is a small animal with a bushy tail? squirrel
5. What is a place where items are sold? store
6. When a plant starts, what is it called? seed

183

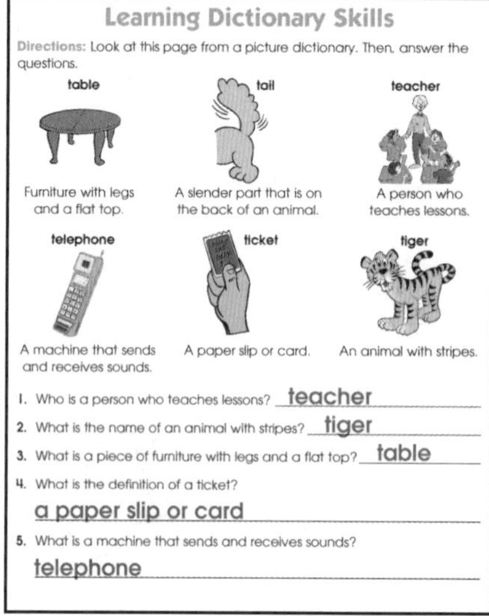

Learning Dictionary Skills

Directions: Look at this page from a picture dictionary. Then, answer the questions.

table	tail	teacher
Furniture with legs and a flat top.	A slender part that is on the back of an animal.	A person who teaches lessons.

telephone	ticket	tiger
A machine that sends and receives sounds.	A paper slip or card.	An animal with stripes.

1. Who is a person who teaches lessons? teacher
2. What is the name of an animal with stripes? tiger
3. What is a piece of furniture with legs and a flat top? table
4. What is the definition of a ticket?
   a paper slip or card
5. What is a machine that sends and receives sounds?
   telephone

184

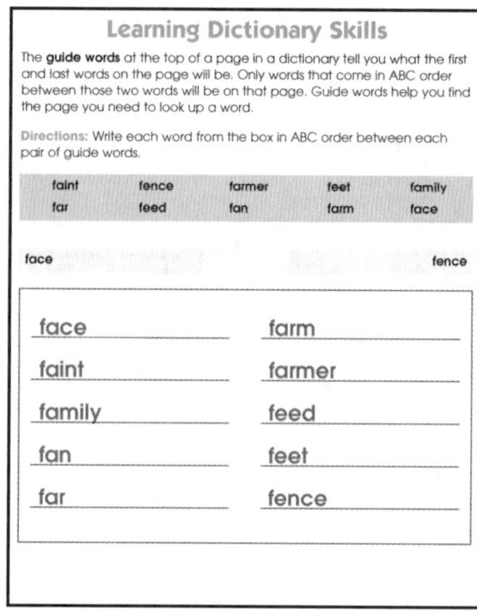

Learning Dictionary Skills

The **guide words** at the top of a page in a dictionary tell you what the first and last words on the page will be. Only words that come in ABC order between those two words will be on that page. Guide words help you find the page you need to look up a word.

Directions: Write each word from the box in ABC order between each pair of guide words.

faint	fence	farmer	feet	family
far	feed	fan	farm	face

face — fence

face	farm
faint	farmer
family	feed
fan	feet
far	fence

185

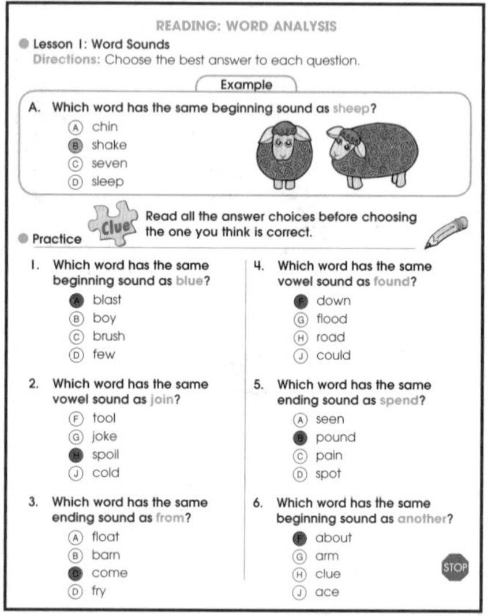

READING: WORD ANALYSIS

Lesson 1: Word Sounds

Directions: Choose the best answer to each question.

Example

A. Which word has the same beginning sound as sheep?
(A) chin
(B) shake
(C) seven
(D) sleep

Practice

Clue: Read all the answer choices before choosing the one you think is correct.

1. Which word has the same beginning sound as blue?
   (A) blast
   (B) boy
   (C) brush
   (D) few
2. Which word has the same vowel sound as join?
   (F) tool
   (G) joke
   (H) spoil
   (J) cold
3. Which word has the same ending sound as from?
   (A) float
   (B) barn
   (C) come
   (D) fry
4. Which word has the same vowel sound as found?
   (F) down
   (G) flood
   (H) road
   (J) could
5. Which word has the same ending sound as spend?
   (A) seen
   (B) pound
   (C) pain
   (D) spot
6. Which word has the same beginning sound as another?
   (F) about
   (G) arm
   (H) clue
   (J) ace

STOP

188

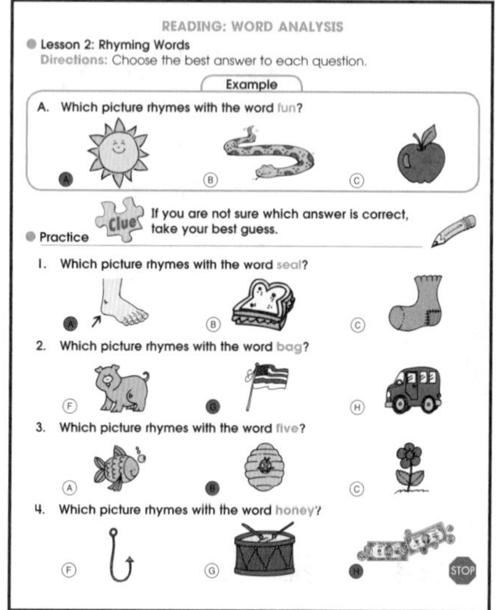

READING: WORD ANALYSIS

Lesson 2: Rhyming Words

Directions: Choose the best answer to each question.

Example

A. Which picture rhymes with the word fun?
(A) (B) (C)

Practice

Clue: If you are not sure which answer is correct, take your best guess.

1. Which picture rhymes with the word seal?
   (A) (B) (C)
2. Which picture rhymes with the word bag?
   (F) **(G)** (H)
3. Which picture rhymes with the word five?
   (A) **(B)** (C)
4. Which picture rhymes with the word honey?
   (F) (G) **(H)**

STOP

189

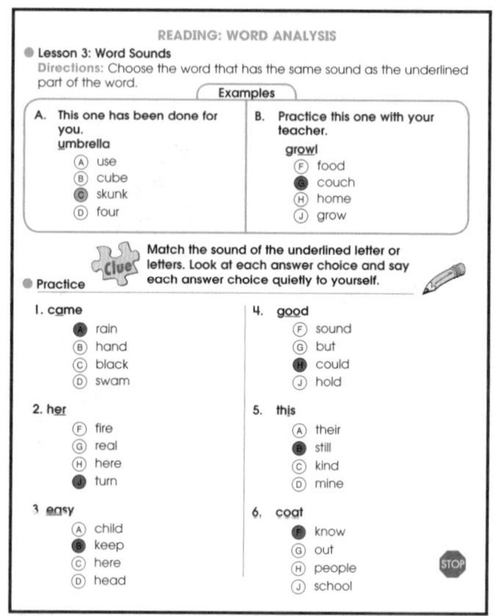

READING: WORD ANALYSIS

Lesson 3: Word Sounds

Directions: Choose the word that has the same sound as the underlined part of the word.

Examples

A. This one has been done for you.
umbrella
(A) use
(B) cube
(C) skunk
(D) four

B. Practice this one with your teacher.
growl
(F) food
(G) couch
(H) home
(J) grow

Practice

Clue: Match the sound of the underlined letter or letters. Look at each answer choice and say each answer choice quietly to yourself.

1. came
   (A) rain
   (B) hand
   (C) black
   (D) swam
2. her
   (F) fire
   (G) real
   (H) here
   (J) turn
3. easy
   (A) child
   (B) keep
   (C) here
   (D) head
4. good
   (F) sound
   (G) but
   (H) could
   (J) hold
5. this
   (A) their
   (B) still
   (C) kind
   (D) mine
6. coat
   (F) know
   (G) out
   (H) people
   (J) school

STOP

190

Answer Key

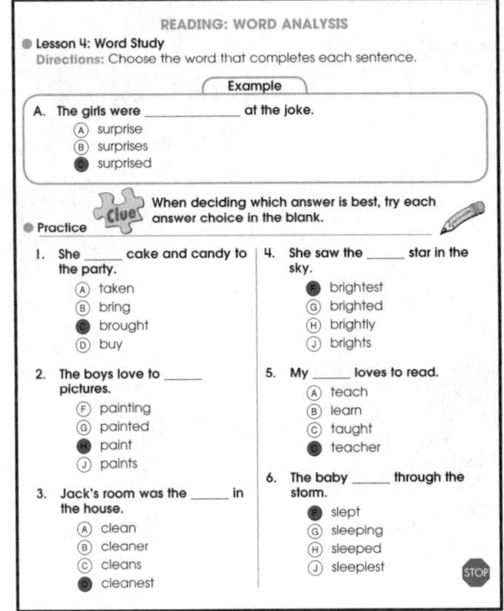

READING: WORD ANALYSIS

Lesson 4: Word Study

Directions: Choose the word that completes each sentence.

Example

A. The girls were ____________ at the joke.
- (A) surprise
- (B) surprises
- ● surprised

Clue: When deciding which answer is best, try each answer choice in the blank.

Practice

1. She _____ cake and candy to the party.
   - (A) taken
   - (B) bring
   - ● brought
   - (D) buy
2. The boys love to _____ pictures.
   - (F) painting
   - (G) painted
   - ● paint
   - (J) paints
3. Jack's room was the _____ in the house.
   - (A) clean
   - (B) cleaner
   - (C) cleans
   - ● cleanest
4. She saw the _____ star in the sky.
   - ● brightest
   - (G) brighted
   - (H) brightly
   - (J) brights
5. My _____ loves to read.
   - (A) teach
   - (B) learn
   - (C) taught
   - ● teacher
6. The baby _____ through the storm.
   - ● slept
   - (G) sleeping
   - (H) sleeped
   - (J) sleepiest

STOP

191

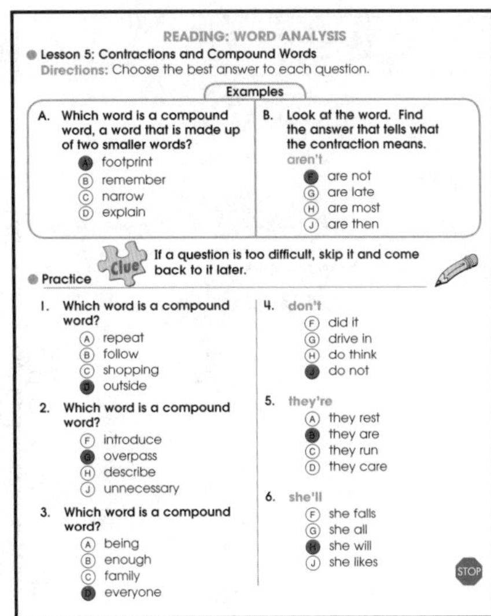

READING: WORD ANALYSIS

Lesson 5: Contractions and Compound Words

Directions: Choose the best answer to each question.

Examples

A. Which word is a compound word, a word that is made up of two smaller words?
- ● footprint
- (B) remember
- (C) narrow
- (D) explain

B. Look at the word. Find the answer that tells what the contraction means.
aren't
- ● are not
- (G) are late
- (H) are most
- (J) are then

Clue: If a question is too difficult, skip it and come back to it later.

Practice

1. Which word is a compound word?
   - (A) repeat
   - (B) follow
   - (C) shopping
   - ● outside
2. Which word is a compound word?
   - (F) introduce
   - ● overpass
   - (H) describe
   - (J) unnecessary
3. Which word is a compound word?
   - (A) being
   - (B) enough
   - (C) family
   - ● everyone
4. don't
   - (F) did it
   - (G) drive in
   - (H) do think
   - ● do not
5. they're
   - (A) they rest
   - ● they are
   - (C) they run
   - (D) they care
6. she'll
   - (F) she falls
   - (G) she all
   - ● she will
   - (J) she likes

STOP

192

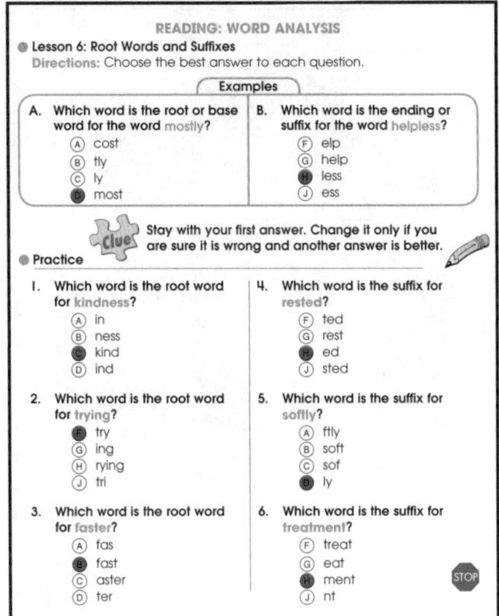

READING: WORD ANALYSIS

Lesson 6: Root Words and Suffixes

Directions: Choose the best answer to each question.

Examples

A. Which word is the root or base word for the word mostly?
- (A) cost
- (B) tly
- (C) ly
- ● most

B. Which word is the ending or suffix for the word helpless?
- (F) elp
- (G) help
- ● less
- (J) ess

Clue: Stay with your first answer. Change it only if you are sure it is wrong and another answer is better.

Practice

1. Which word is the root word for kindness?
   - (A) in
   - (B) ness
   - ● kind
   - (D) ind
2. Which word is the root word for trying?
   - ● try
   - (G) ing
   - (H) rying
   - (J) tri
3. Which word is the root word for faster?
   - (A) fas
   - ● fast
   - (C) aster
   - (D) ter
4. Which word is the suffix for rested?
   - (F) ted
   - (G) rest
   - ● ed
   - (J) sted
5. Which word is the suffix for softly?
   - (A) ftly
   - (B) soft
   - (C) sof
   - ● ly
6. Which word is the suffix for treatment?
   - (F) treat
   - (G) eat
   - ● ment
   - (J) nt

STOP

193

READING: VOCABULARY

Lesson 7: Picture Vocabulary

Directions: Choose the word that matches the picture.

Examples

A. This one has been done for you.
- (A) bottle
- ● pour
- (C) glass
- (D) spill

B. Practice this one with your teacher.
- ● sleep
- (G) baby
- (H) blanket
- (J) awake

Clue: Look at the picture carefully and then read the choices.

Practice

1.
   - (A) clean
   - (B) sing
   - ● blow
   - (D) eat
2.
   - ● crying
   - (G) happy
   - (H) smiling
   - (J) talking
3.
   - (A) baby
   - (B) stand
   - (C) come
   - ● crib
4.
   - (F) out
   - (G) whisper
   - ● shout
   - (J) laugh

STOP

194

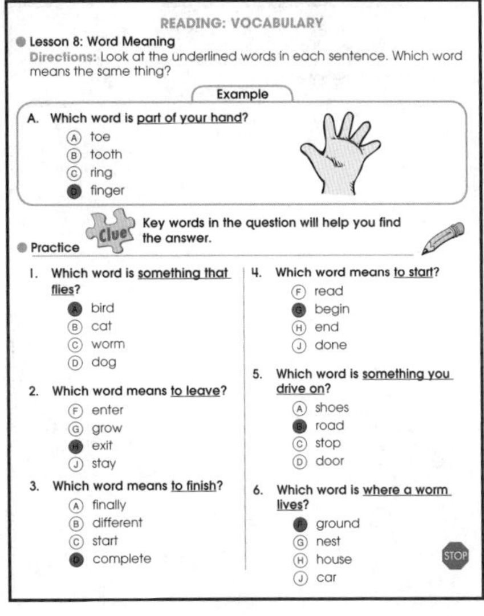

READING: VOCABULARY

Lesson 8: Word Meaning

Directions: Look at the underlined words in each sentence. Which word means the same thing?

Example

A. Which word is part of your hand?
- (A) toe
- (B) tooth
- (C) ring
- ● finger

Clue: Key words in the question will help you find the answer.

Practice

1. Which word is something that flies?
   - ● bird
   - (B) cat
   - (C) worm
   - (D) dog
2. Which word means to leave?
   - (F) enter
   - (G) grow
   - ● exit
   - (J) stay
3. Which word means to finish?
   - (A) finally
   - (B) different
   - (C) start
   - ● complete
4. Which word means to start?
   - (F) read
   - ● begin
   - (H) end
   - (J) done
5. Which word is something you drive on?
   - (A) shoes
   - ● road
   - (C) stop
   - (D) door
6. Which word is where a worm lives?
   - ● ground
   - (G) nest
   - (H) house
   - (J) car

STOP

195

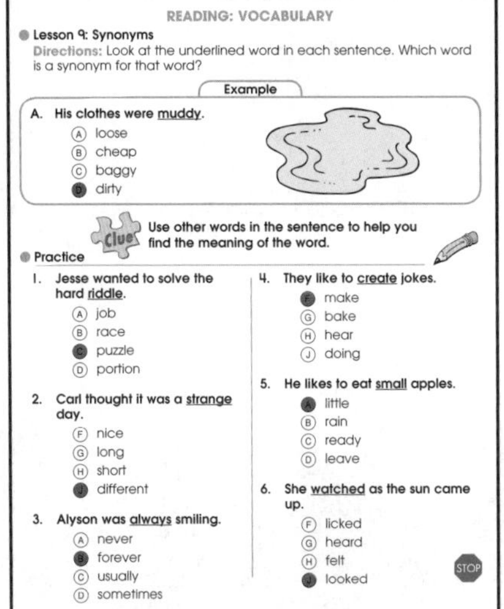

READING: VOCABULARY

Lesson 9: Synonyms

Directions: Look at the underlined word in each sentence. Which word is a synonym for that word?

Example

A. His clothes were muddy.
- (A) loose
- (B) cheap
- (C) baggy
- ● dirty

Clue: Use other words in the sentence to help you find the meaning of the word.

Practice

1. Jesse wanted to solve the hard riddle.
   - (A) job
   - (B) race
   - ● puzzle
   - (D) portion
2. Carl thought it was a strange day.
   - (F) nice
   - (G) long
   - (H) short
   - ● different
3. Alyson was always smiling.
   - (A) never
   - ● forever
   - (C) usually
   - (D) sometimes
4. They like to create jokes.
   - ● make
   - (G) bake
   - (H) hear
   - (J) doing
5. He likes to eat small apples.
   - ● little
   - (B) rain
   - (C) ready
   - (D) leave
6. She watched as the sun came up.
   - (F) licked
   - (G) heard
   - (H) felt
   - ● looked

STOP

196

Answer Key

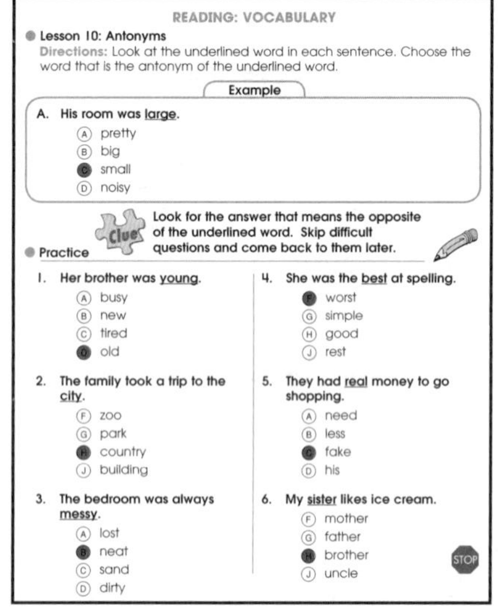

READING: VOCABULARY

Lesson 10: Antonyms

Directions: Look at the underlined word in each sentence. Choose the word that is the antonym of the underlined word.

Example

A. His room was large.
(A) pretty
(B) big
● small
(D) noisy

Clue: Look for the answer that means the opposite of the underlined word. Skip difficult questions and come back to them later.

Practice

1. Her brother was young.
(A) busy
(B) new
(C) tired
● old

2. The family took a trip to the city.
(F) zoo
(G) park
● country
(J) building

3. The bedroom was always messy.
(A) lost
● neat
(C) sand
(D) dirty

4. She was the best at spelling.
● worst
(G) simple
(H) good
(J) rest

5. They had real money to go shopping.
(A) need
(B) less
● fake
(D) his

6. My sister likes ice cream.
(F) mother
(G) father
● brother
(J) uncle

STOP

197

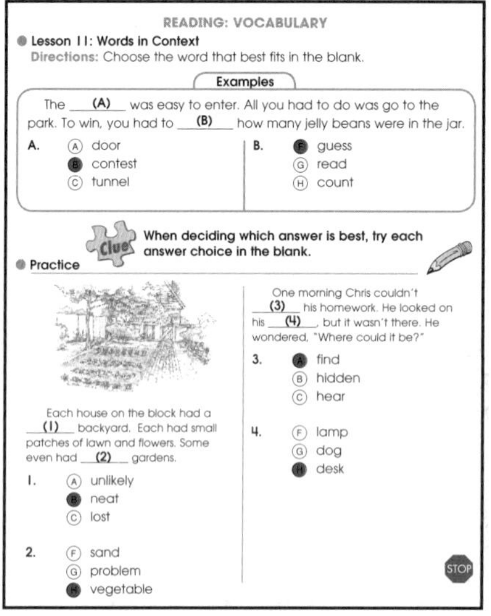

READING: VOCABULARY

Lesson 11: Words in Context

Directions: Choose the word that best fits in the blank.

Examples

The __(A)__ was easy to enter. All you had to do was go to the park. To win, you had to __(B)__ how many jelly beans were in the jar.

A. (A) door
● contest
(C) tunnel

B. ● guess
(G) read
(H) count

Clue: When deciding which answer is best, try each answer choice in the blank.

Practice

Each house on the block had a __(1)__ backyard. Each had small patches of lawn and flowers. Some even had __(2)__ gardens.

1. (A) unlikely
● neat
(C) lost

2. (F) sand
(G) problem
● vegetable

One morning Chris couldn't __(3)__ his homework. He looked on his __(4)__, but it wasn't there. He wondered, "Where could it be?"

3. ● find
(B) hidden
(C) hear

4. (F) lamp
(G) dog
● desk

STOP

198

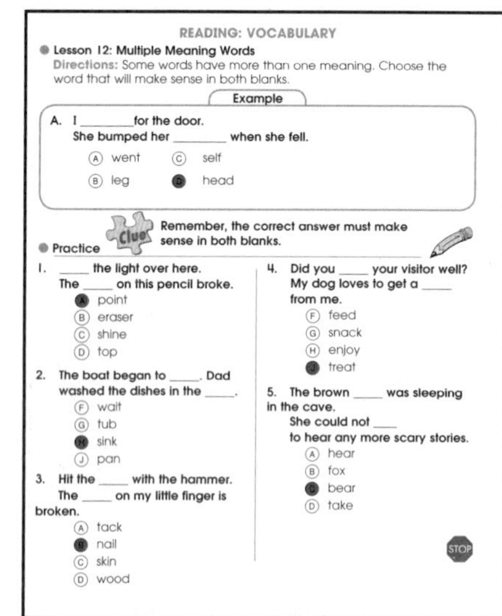

READING: VOCABULARY

Lesson 12: Multiple Meaning Words

Directions: Some words have more than one meaning. Choose the word that will make sense in both blanks.

Example

A. I ________ for the door.
She bumped her ________ when she fell.
(A) went
(C) self
(B) leg
● head

Clue: Remember, the correct answer must make sense in both blanks.

Practice

1. _____ the light over here.
The _____ on this pencil broke.
● point
(B) eraser
(C) shine
(D) top

2. The boat began to _____. Dad washed the dishes in the _____.
(F) wait
(G) tub
● sink
(J) pan

3. Hit the _____ with the hammer.
The _____ on my little finger is broken.
(A) tack
● nail
(C) skin
(D) wood

4. Did you _____ your visitor well?
My dog loves to get a _____ from me.
(F) feed
(G) snack
(H) enjoy
● treat

5. The brown _____ was sleeping in the cave.
She could not _____ to hear any more scary stories.
(A) hear
(B) fox
● bear
(D) take

STOP

199

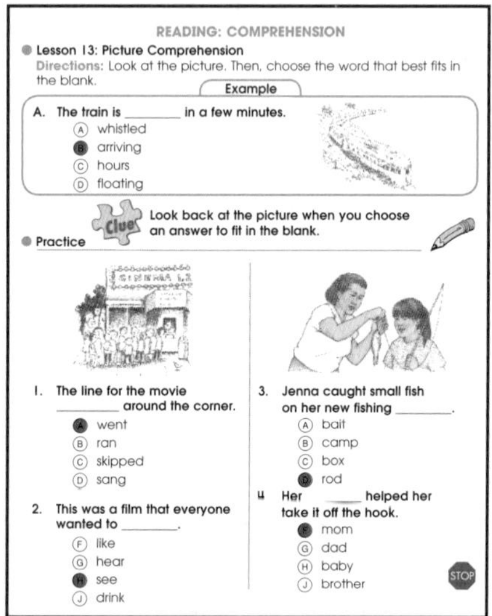

READING: COMPREHENSION

Lesson 13: Picture Comprehension

Directions: Look at the picture. Then, choose the word that best fits in the blank.

Example

A. The train is ________ in a few minutes.
(A) whistled
● arriving
(C) hours
(D) floating

Clue: Look back at the picture when you choose an answer to fit in the blank.

Practice

1. The line for the movie ________ around the corner.
● went
(B) ran
(C) skipped
(D) sang

2. This was a film that everyone wanted to ________.
(F) like
(G) hear
● see
(J) drink

3. Jenna caught small fish on her new fishing ________.
(A) bait
(B) camp
(C) box
● rod

4. Her ______ helped her take it off the hook.
● mom
(G) dad
(H) baby
(J) brother

STOP

200

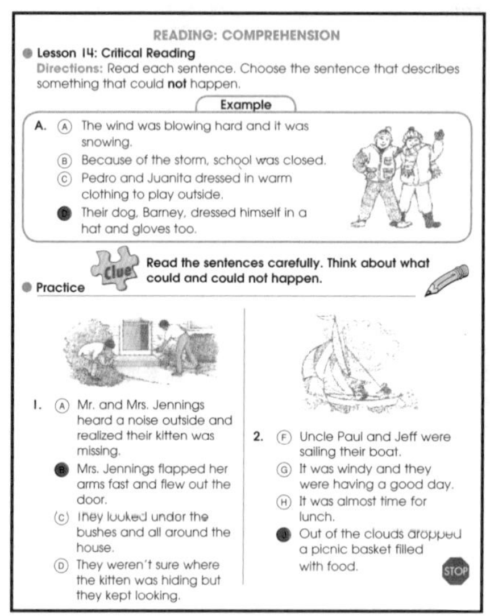

READING: COMPREHENSION

Lesson 14: Critical Reading

Directions: Read each sentence. Choose the sentence that describes something that could **not** happen.

Example

A. (A) The wind was blowing hard and it was snowing.
(B) Because of the storm, school was closed.
(C) Pedro and Juanita dressed in warm clothing to play outside.
● Their dog, Barney, dressed himself in a hat and gloves too.

Clue: Read the sentences carefully. Think about what could and could not happen.

Practice

1. (A) Mr. and Mrs. Jennings heard a noise outside and realized their kitten was missing.
● Mrs. Jennings flapped her arms fast and flew out the door.
(C) They looked under the bushes and all around the house.
(D) They weren't sure where the kitten was hiding but they kept looking.

2. (F) Uncle Paul and Jeff were sailing their boat.
(G) It was windy and they were having a good day.
(H) It was almost time for lunch.
● Out of the clouds dropped a picnic basket filled with food.

STOP

201

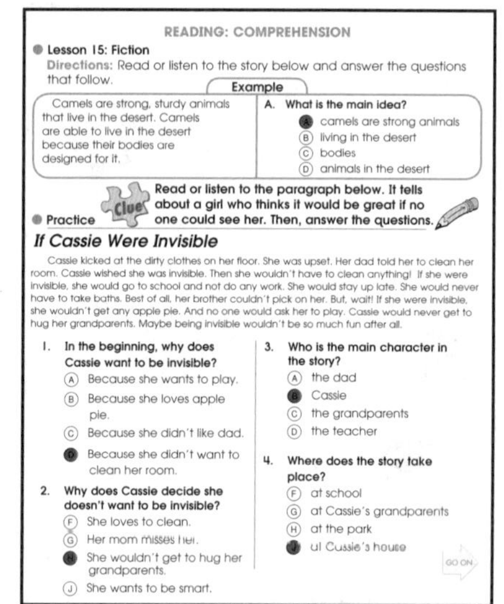

READING: COMPREHENSION

Lesson 15: Fiction

Directions: Read or listen to the story below and answer the questions that follow.

Example

Camels are strong, sturdy animals that live in the desert. Camels are able to live in the desert because their bodies are designed for it.

A. What is the main idea?
● camels are strong animals
(B) living in the desert
(C) bodies
(D) animals in the desert

Clue: Read or listen to the paragraph below. It tells about a girl who thinks it would be great if no one could see her. Then, answer the questions.

Practice

If Cassie Were Invisible

Cassie kicked at the dirty clothes on her floor. She was upset. Her dad told her to clean her room. Cassie wished she was invisible. Then she wouldn't have to clean anything! If she were invisible, she would go to school and not do any work. She would stay up late. She would never have to take baths. Best of all, her brother couldn't pick on her. But, wait! If she were invisible, she wouldn't get any apple pie. And no one would ask her to play. Cassie would never get to hug her grandparents. Maybe being invisible wouldn't be so much fun after all.

1. In the beginning, why does Cassie want to be invisible?
(A) Because she wants to play.
(B) Because she loves apple pie.
(C) Because she didn't like dad.
● Because she didn't want to clean her room.

2. Why does Cassie decide she doesn't want to be invisible?
(F) She loves to clean.
(G) Her mom misses her.
● She wouldn't get to hug her grandparents.
(J) She wants to be smart.

3. Who is the main character in the story?
(A) the dad
● Cassie
(C) the grandparents
(D) the teacher

4. Where does the story take place?
(F) at school
(G) at Cassie's grandparents
(H) at the park
● at Cassie's house

GO ON

202

Answer Key

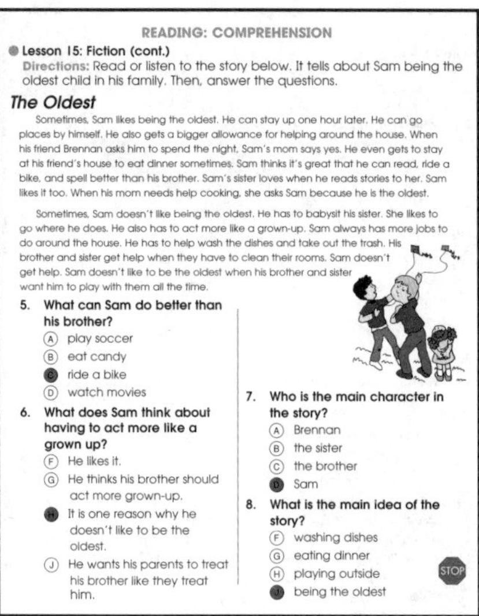

READING: COMPREHENSION

● Lesson 15: Fiction (cont.)

Directions: Read or listen to the story below. It tells about Sam being the oldest child in his family. Then, answer the questions.

The Oldest

Sometimes, Sam likes being the oldest. He can stay up one hour later. He can go places by himself. He also gets a bigger allowance for helping around the house. When his friend Brennan asks him to spend the night, Sam's mom says yes. He even gets to stay at his friend's house to eat dinner sometimes. Sam thinks it's great that he can read, ride a bike, and spell better than his brother. Sam's sister loves when he reads stories to her. Sam likes it too. When his mom needs help cooking, she asks Sam because he is the oldest.

Sometimes, Sam doesn't like being the oldest. He has to babysit his sister. She likes to go where he does. He also has to act more like a grown-up. Sam always has more jobs to do around the house. He has to help wash the dishes and take out the trash. His brother and sister get help when they have to clean their rooms. Sam doesn't get help. Sam doesn't like to be the oldest when his brother and sister want him to play with them all the time.

5. What can Sam do better than his brother?
   - Ⓐ play soccer
   - Ⓑ eat candy
   - ● ride a bike
   - Ⓓ watch movies

6. What does Sam think about having to act more like a grown up?
   - Ⓕ He likes it.
   - Ⓖ He thinks his brother should act more grown-up.
   - ● It is one reason why he doesn't like to be the oldest.
   - Ⓙ He wants his parents to treat his brother like they treat him.

7. Who is the main character in the story?
   - Ⓐ Brennan
   - Ⓑ the sister
   - Ⓒ the brother
   - ● Sam

8. What is the main idea of the story?
   - Ⓕ washing dishes
   - Ⓖ eating dinner
   - Ⓗ playing outside
   - ● being the oldest

STOP

203

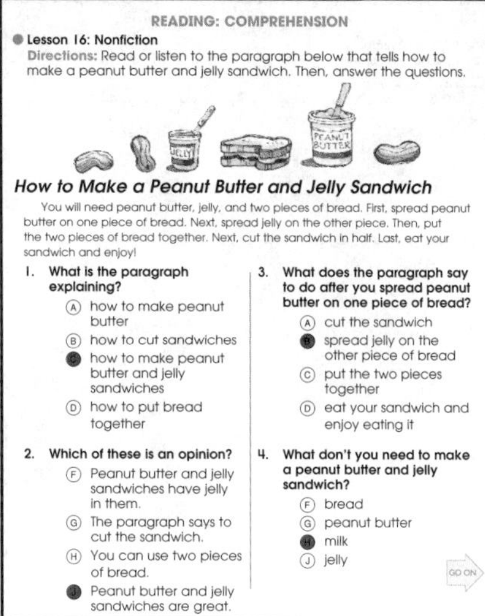

READING: COMPREHENSION

● Lesson 16: Nonfiction

Directions: Read or listen to the paragraph below that tells how to make a peanut butter and jelly sandwich. Then, answer the questions.

How to Make a Peanut Butter and Jelly Sandwich

You will need peanut butter, jelly, and two pieces of bread. First, spread peanut butter on one piece of bread. Next, spread jelly on the other piece. Then, put the two pieces of bread together. Next, cut the sandwich in half. Last, eat your sandwich and enjoy!

1. What is the paragraph explaining?
   - Ⓐ how to make peanut butter
   - Ⓑ how to cut sandwiches
   - ● how to make peanut butter and jelly sandwiches
   - Ⓓ how to put bread together

2. Which of these is an opinion?
   - Ⓕ Peanut butter and jelly sandwiches have jelly in them.
   - Ⓖ The paragraph says to cut the sandwich.
   - Ⓗ You can use two pieces of bread.
   - ● Peanut butter and jelly sandwiches are great.

3. What does the paragraph say to do after you spread peanut butter on one piece of bread?
   - Ⓐ cut the sandwich
   - ● spread jelly on the other piece of bread
   - Ⓒ put the two pieces together
   - Ⓓ eat your sandwich and enjoy eating it

4. What don't you need to make a peanut butter and jelly sandwich?
   - Ⓕ bread
   - Ⓖ peanut butter
   - ● milk
   - Ⓙ jelly

GO ON

204

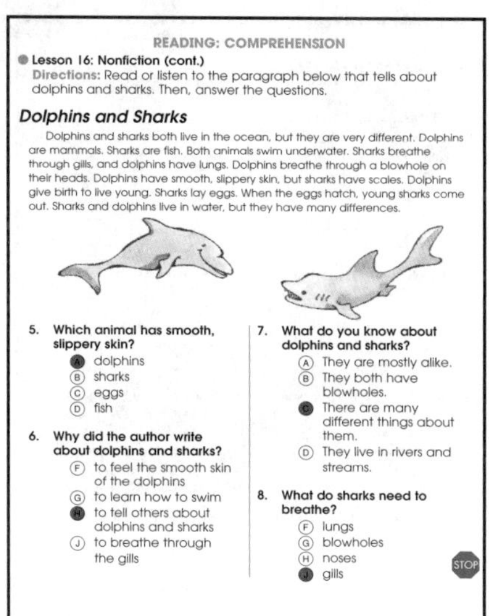

READING: COMPREHENSION

● Lesson 16: Nonfiction (cont.)

Directions: Read or listen to the paragraph below that tells about dolphins and sharks. Then, answer the questions.

Dolphins and Sharks

Dolphins and sharks both live in the ocean, but they are very different. Dolphins are mammals. Sharks are fish. Both animals swim underwater. Sharks breathe through gills, and dolphins have lungs. Dolphins breathe through a blowhole on their heads. Dolphins have smooth, slippery skin, but sharks have scales. Dolphins give birth to live young. Sharks lay eggs. When the eggs hatch, young sharks come out. Sharks and dolphins live in water, but they have many differences.

5. Which animal has smooth, slippery skin?
   - ● dolphins
   - Ⓑ sharks
   - Ⓒ eggs
   - Ⓓ fish

6. Why did the author write about dolphins and sharks?
   - Ⓕ to feel the smooth skin of the dolphins
   - Ⓖ to learn how to swim
   - ● to tell others about dolphins and sharks
   - Ⓙ to breathe through the gills

7. What do you know about dolphins and sharks?
   - Ⓐ They are mostly alike.
   - Ⓑ They both have blowholes.
   - ● There are many different things about them.
   - Ⓓ They live in rivers and streams.

8. What do sharks need to breathe?
   - Ⓕ lungs
   - Ⓖ blowholes
   - Ⓗ noses
   - ● gills

STOP

205

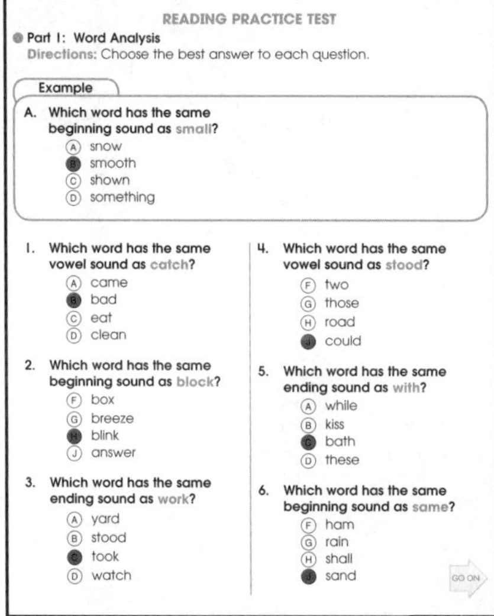

READING PRACTICE TEST

● Part 1: Word Analysis

Directions: Choose the best answer to each question.

Example

A. Which word has the same beginning sound as **small**?
   - Ⓐ snow
   - ● smooth
   - Ⓒ shown
   - Ⓓ something

1. Which word has the same vowel sound as **catch**?
   - Ⓐ came
   - ● bad
   - Ⓒ eat
   - Ⓓ clean

2. Which word has the same beginning sound as **block**?
   - Ⓕ box
   - Ⓖ breeze
   - ● blink
   - Ⓙ answer

3. Which word has the same ending sound as **work**?
   - Ⓐ yard
   - Ⓑ stood
   - ● took
   - Ⓓ watch

4. Which word has the same vowel sound as **stood**?
   - Ⓕ two
   - Ⓖ those
   - Ⓗ road
   - ● could

5. Which word has the same ending sound as **with**?
   - Ⓐ while
   - Ⓑ kiss
   - ● bath
   - Ⓓ these

6. Which word has the same beginning sound as **same**?
   - Ⓕ ham
   - Ⓖ rain
   - Ⓗ shall
   - ● sand

GO ON

207

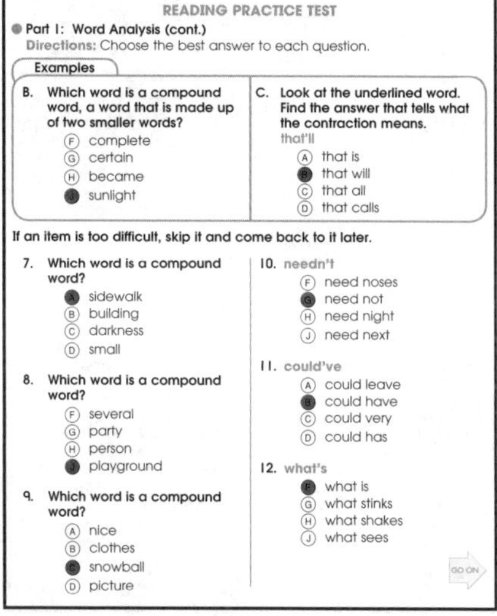

READING PRACTICE TEST

● Part 1: Word Analysis (cont.)

Directions: Choose the best answer to each question.

Examples

B. Which word is a compound word, a word that is made up of two smaller words?
   - Ⓕ complete
   - Ⓖ certain
   - Ⓗ became
   - ● sunlight

C. Look at the underlined word. Find the answer that tells what the contraction means. **that'll**
   - Ⓐ that is
   - ● that will
   - Ⓒ that all
   - Ⓓ that calls

If an item is too difficult, skip it and come back to it later.

7. Which word is a compound word?
   - ● sidewalk
   - Ⓑ building
   - Ⓒ darkness
   - Ⓓ small

8. Which word is a compound word?
   - Ⓕ several
   - Ⓖ party
   - Ⓗ person
   - ● playground

9. Which word is a compound word?
   - Ⓐ nice
   - Ⓑ clothes
   - ● snowball
   - Ⓓ picture

10. **needn't**
   - Ⓕ need noses
   - ● need not
   - Ⓗ need night
   - Ⓙ need next

11. **could've**
   - Ⓐ could leave
   - ● could have
   - Ⓒ could very
   - Ⓓ could has

12. **what's**
   - ● what is
   - Ⓖ what stinks
   - Ⓗ what shakes
   - Ⓙ what sees

GO ON

208

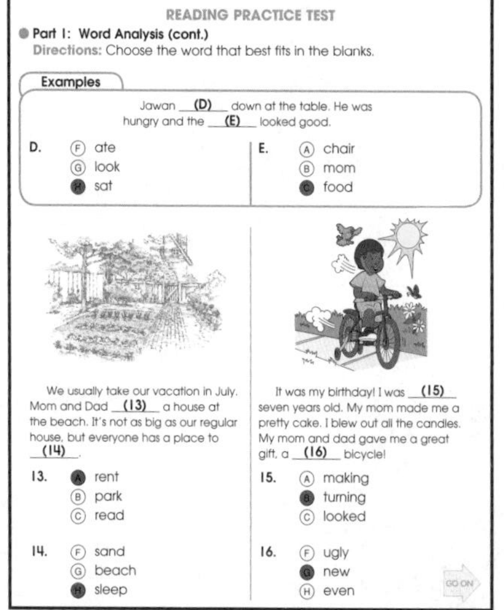

READING PRACTICE TEST

● Part 1: Word Analysis (cont.)

Directions: Choose the word that best fits in the blanks.

Examples

Jawan __(D)__ down at the table. He was hungry and the __(E)__ looked good.

D.
   - Ⓕ ate
   - Ⓖ look
   - ● sat

E.
   - Ⓐ chair
   - Ⓑ mom
   - ● food

We usually take our vacation in July. Mom and Dad __(13)__ a house at the beach. It's not as big as our regular house, but everyone has a place to __(14)__.

13.
   - ● rent
   - Ⓑ park
   - Ⓒ read

14.
   - Ⓕ sand
   - Ⓖ beach
   - ● sleep

It was my birthday! I was __(15)__ seven years old. My mom made me a pretty cake. I blew out all the candles. My mom and dad gave me a great gift, a __(16)__ bicycle!

15.
   - Ⓐ making
   - ● turning
   - Ⓒ looked

16.
   - Ⓕ ugly
   - ● new
   - Ⓗ even

GO ON

209

Answer Key

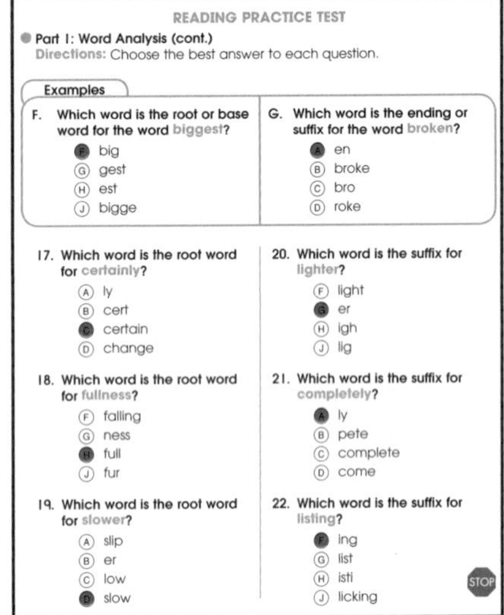

READING PRACTICE TEST

Part 1: Word Analysis (cont.)

Directions: Choose the best answer to each question.

Examples

F. Which word is the root or base word for the word biggest?
- big
- gest
- est
- bigge

G. Which word is the ending or suffix for the word broken?
- en
- broke
- bro
- roke

17. Which word is the root word for certainly?
- ly
- cert
- certain
- change

18. Which word is the root word for fullness?
- falling
- ness
- full
- fur

19. Which word is the root word for slower?
- slip
- er
- low
- slow

20. Which word is the suffix for lighter?
- light
- er
- igh
- lig

21. Which word is the suffix for completely?
- ly
- pete
- complete
- come

22. Which word is the suffix for listing?
- ing
- list
- isti
- licking

STOP

210

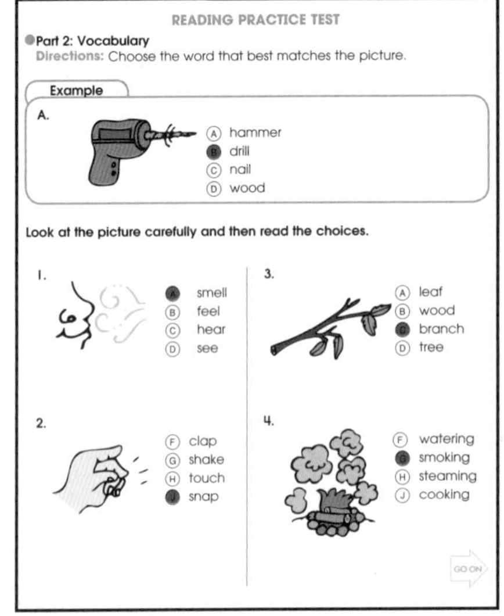

READING PRACTICE TEST

Part 2: Vocabulary

Directions: Choose the word that best matches the picture.

Example

A.
- hammer
- drill
- nail
- wood

Look at the picture carefully and then read the choices.

1.
- smell
- feel
- hear
- see

2.
- clap
- shake
- touch
- snap

3.
- leaf
- wood
- branch
- tree

4.
- watering
- smoking
- steaming
- cooking

GO ON

211

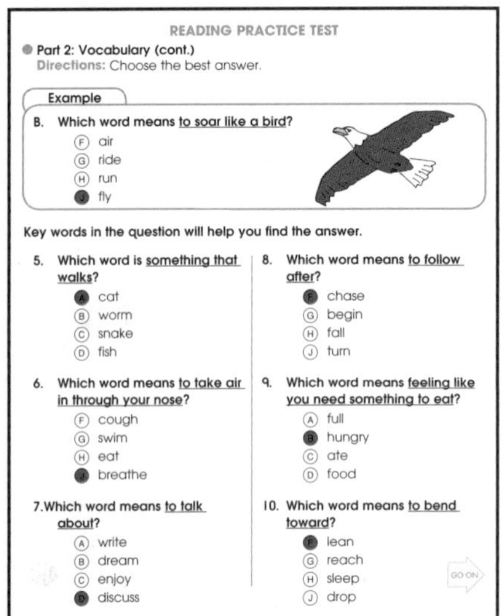

READING PRACTICE TEST

Part 2: Vocabulary (cont.)

Directions: Choose the best answer.

Example

B. Which word means to soar like a bird?
- air
- ride
- run
- fly

Key words in the question will help you find the answer.

5. Which word is something that walks?
- cat
- worm
- snake
- fish

6. Which word means to take air in through your nose?
- cough
- swim
- eat
- breathe

7. Which word means to talk about?
- write
- dream
- enjoy
- discuss

8. Which word means to follow after?
- chase
- begin
- fall
- turn

9. Which word means feeling like you need something to eat?
- full
- hungry
- ate
- food

10. Which word means to bend toward?
- lean
- reach
- sleep
- drop

GO ON

212

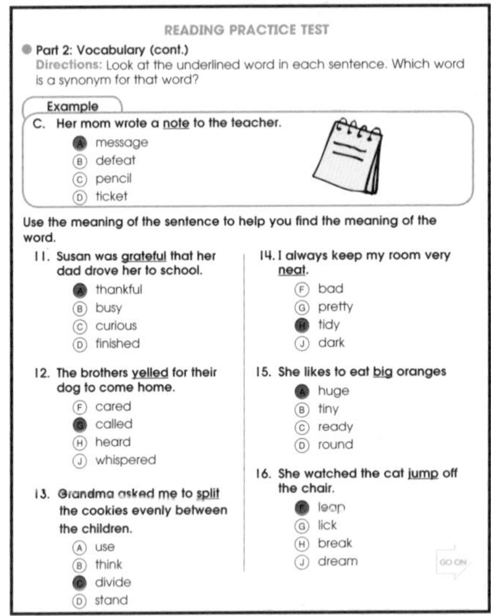

READING PRACTICE TEST

Part 2: Vocabulary (cont.)

Directions: Look at the underlined word in each sentence. Which word is a synonym for that word?

Example

C. Her mom wrote a note to the teacher.
- message
- defeat
- pencil
- ticket

Use the meaning of the sentence to help you find the meaning of the word.

11. Susan was grateful that her dad drove her to school.
- thankful
- busy
- curious
- finished

12. The brothers yelled for their dog to come home.
- cared
- called
- heard
- whispered

13. Grandma asked me to split the cookies evenly between the children.
- use
- think
- divide
- stand

14. I always keep my room very neat.
- bad
- pretty
- tidy
- dark

15. She likes to eat big oranges
- huge
- tiny
- ready
- round

16. She watched the cat jump off the chair.
- leap
- lick
- break
- dream

GO ON

213

Answer Key

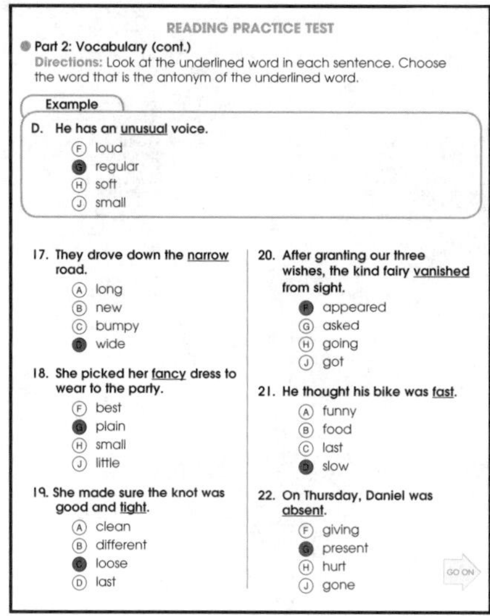

READING PRACTICE TEST

Part 2: Vocabulary (cont.)

Directions: Look at the underlined word in each sentence. Choose the word that is the antonym of the underlined word.

Example

D. He has an unusual voice.
- Ⓕ loud
- ● regular
- Ⓗ soft
- Ⓙ small

17. They drove down the narrow road.
- Ⓐ long
- Ⓑ new
- Ⓒ bumpy
- ● wide

18. She picked her fancy dress to wear to the party.
- Ⓕ best
- ● plain
- Ⓗ small
- Ⓙ little

19. She made sure the knot was good and tight.
- Ⓐ clean
- Ⓑ different
- ● loose
- Ⓓ last

20. After granting our three wishes, the kind fairy vanished from sight.
- ● appeared
- Ⓖ asked
- Ⓗ going
- Ⓙ got

21. He thought his bike was fast.
- Ⓐ funny
- Ⓑ food
- Ⓒ last
- ● slow

22. On Thursday, Daniel was absent.
- Ⓕ giving
- ● present
- Ⓗ hurt
- Ⓙ gone

GO ON

214

READING PRACTICE TEST

Part 2: Vocabulary (cont.)

Directions: Choose the word that best fits in each blank.

Examples

Mr. Jennings went __(E)__ after work. He bought food for dinner and then he went __(F)__.

E.
- ● shopping
- Ⓑ walking
- Ⓒ driving

F.
- Ⓕ soon
- Ⓖ fast
- ● home

When deciding which answer is best, try each answer choice in the blank.

Our neighbor is a gardener. One of her __(23)__ trees recently died. She said it was because of a bug that likes to eat __(24)__.

23.
- Ⓐ girl
- Ⓑ half
- ● small

24.
- Ⓕ each
- ● leaves
- Ⓗ dirt

One sunny June day, a man __(25)__ too fast down the road. A police officer stopped him and gave him a __(26)__.

25.
- ● drove
- Ⓑ paced
- Ⓒ ran

26.
- Ⓕ picture
- ● ticket
- Ⓗ rest

There are many different __(27)__ of bats. One kind is the brown bat.

27.
- Ⓐ only
- Ⓑ paper
- ● kinds

__(28)__ brown bats eat insects. One bat can eat 600 mosquitoes in just an hour.

28.
- Ⓕ second
- ● little
- Ⓗ sleep

GO ON

215

READING PRACTICE TEST

Part 2: Vocabulary (cont.)

Directions: Some words have more than one meaning. Choose the word that will make sense in both blanks.

Example

G. My mom gets to take ________ at work. I get mad when my brother________ my toys.
- Ⓐ misses
- ● breaks
- Ⓒ picks
- Ⓓ walks

29. He carried his________to the baseball field. The ________ was hanging in the cave.
- ● bat
- Ⓑ men
- Ⓒ ball
- Ⓓ sheep

30. In the ________ my mom plants all of her flowers. The ________ next to the mountain had fresh water.
- Ⓕ picnic
- Ⓖ fall
- ● spring
- Ⓙ snow

31. Did you go to the ______ with your friends? Where should I ______ the car?
- Ⓐ party
- Ⓑ school
- ● park
- Ⓓ drive

32. A bear had a heavy ______. My mom bought me a new ______ for winter.
- Ⓕ hat
- Ⓖ fur
- Ⓗ enjoy
- ● coat

33. The river ______ into two seperate streams. The ______ on the tree swayed in the wind
- Ⓐ leaves
- ● branches
- Ⓒ wanted
- Ⓓ goes

34. Cinderella was the most beautiful girl at the ______. Hunter's grandma bought him a red ______ for his birthday.
- Ⓕ party
- Ⓖ gift
- ● ball
- Ⓙ bike

STOP

216

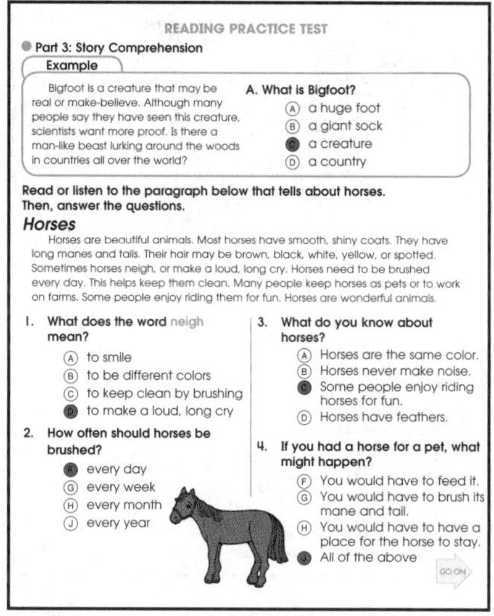

READING PRACTICE TEST

Part 3: Story Comprehension

Example

Bigfoot is a creature that may be real or make-believe. Although many people say they have seen this creature, scientists want more proof. Is there a man-like beast lurking around the woods in countries all over the world?

A. What is Bigfoot?
- Ⓐ a huge foot
- Ⓑ a giant sock
- ● a creature
- Ⓓ a country

Read or listen to the paragraph below that tells about horses. Then, answer the questions.

Horses

Horses are beautiful animals. Most horses have smooth, shiny coats. They have long manes and tails. Their hair may be brown, black, white, yellow, or spotted. Sometimes horses neigh, or make a loud, long cry. Horses need to be brushed every day. This helps keep them clean. Many people keep horses as pets or to work on farms. Some people enjoy riding them for fun. Horses are wonderful animals.

1. What does the word neigh mean?
- Ⓐ to smile
- Ⓑ to be different colors
- Ⓒ to keep clean by brushing
- ● to make a loud, long cry

2. How often should horses be brushed?
- ● every day
- Ⓖ every week
- Ⓗ every month
- Ⓙ every year

3. What do you know about horses?
- Ⓐ Horses are the same color.
- Ⓑ Horses never make noise.
- ● Some people enjoy riding horses for fun.
- Ⓓ Horses have feathers.

4. If you had a horse for a pet, what might happen?
- Ⓕ You would have to feed it.
- Ⓖ You would have to brush its mane and tail.
- Ⓗ You would have to have a place for the horse to stay.
- ● All of the above

GO ON

217

Answer Key

READING PRACTICE TEST

● Part 3: Story Comprehension (cont.)

Directions: Read or listen to the paragraphs below that tell about stars. Then, answer the questions.

Stars

(1) When you look up on a clear, dark night, you can see small points of light called stars. Actually, stars are not small at all. Some stars may be 50 million miles across! Stars just look like points of light because they are so far from Earth. Our sun is a star. It looks bigger than other stars in the sky because it is closer to us. A star's brightness depends on its mass and distance from Earth. Bigger stars are brighter than smaller ones. Stars also look brighter when they are closer.

(2) To make it easier to study, people have grouped stars into patterns. The patterns are called constellations. They may be large or small. They may have bright or dim stars. Sometimes in a constellation, the bright stars may be in the shape of a person or animal.

(3) Stars, unlike planets, make their own heat and light. The color of a star's light can tell us how much heat it has. The cooler stars give off a reddish light. The hottest stars look blue or blue-white in color. Stars do not last the same amount of time. They all will eventually burn out.

5. What does the word constellation mean?
- (A) large and in space
- (B) different stars people see from Mars
- (C) different color stars we can see from the earth
- ● (D) a pattern of stars that are grouped together

6. Which of the following is an opinion?
- ● (F) Stars are fun to look at every night.
- (G) Our sun is a star.
- (H) Stars look brighter when they are closer.
- (J) Cooler stars give off a reddish light.

7. What is a supporting detail for paragraph 2?
- (A) Colors of stars help us to know how hot they are.
- (B) Our sun is a star.
- ● (C) It takes imagination to find when different patterns in the sky look like people or animals.
- (D) When stars burn out they turn into new kinds of stars.

8. What would happen if you traveled through space and got closer and closer to a star?
- (F) You would see it get smaller.
- (G) It would look like a rainbow.
- ● (H) It would get brighter.
- (J) All of the above

GO ON

218

READING PRACTICE TEST

● Part 3: Story Comprehension (cont.)

Directions: Read or listen to the paragraph below. It tells about honey and bees. Then, answer the questions.

Sweet as Honey

Honey is sweet and thick. Honeybees make it. First, they fly from flower to flower. At each flower, they collect nectar. Nectar is watery. It is found inside flower blossoms. The bees sip the nectar from flowers. Next, they store it in their bodies. It is kept in their honey bags. Then, the nectar in the honey bags changes. It changes into two kinds of sugars. The bees fly back to their hives. Finally, they put the nectar into their hives. While it is there, most of the water leaves or evaporates. All that is left is the sweet, thick honey inside the honeycomb. People who collect honey remove the combs. Last, the sweet honey is sold for us to eat.

9. What is nectar?
- (A) a flower
- ● (B) a watery substance that bees sip from flowers
- (C) another name for honey
- (D) a part of a bee's body that makes honey

10. What would happen if the bees didn't have honey bags?
- ● (F) They couldn't make honey.
- (G) They would fly in circles.
- (H) They couldn't find flowers.
- (J) They wouldn't be able to see.

11. What happens after the bees put the nectar into their hives?
- (A) They fly from flower to flower.
- (B) They collect the nectar.
- (C) The bees sip the nectar from flowers.
- ● (D) Most of the water leaves or evaporates.

12. If you were a honey collector, where would you go to find honey?
- (F) in the store
- ● (G) in the honeybees' hive
- (H) in your house
- (J) in the sand

GO ON

219

READING PRACTICE TEST

● Part 3: Story Comprehension (cont.)

Directions: Read or listen to the paragraphs below that tell about a mom who lost her spaghetti. Then, answer the questions.

The Investigation

The bowl sat empty. "Oh, no! My spaghetti is missing!" shrieked Mom. "I was supposed to take it to the school potluck tonight. What am I going to do?"

I decided to help my mom find her lost spaghetti. "Don't panic Mom, I'll look for clues," I said as I started looking around. The spaghetti had been in the bowl, on the counter, near the sink. First, I ran outside to check for footprints. There were none! It must have been an inside job.

Who would be my first suspect? I went to my baby sister Laurie's room. I checked in her crib, in her toy box, and in the closet. There was no sign of the spaghetti.

Next, I went to question my second suspect. I asked Dad if he had seen anything unusual. He had been mowing the lawn and didn't know anything about the case.

My leads seemed to be vanishing. Could a thief have come into our house and helped himself to dinner? Had aliens zapped it aboard their spaceship?

I looked around. Suddenly, I noticed through the open window two birds carrying long, red-and-white worms in their beaks. The Case of the Missing Spaghetti was closed!

13. What is the solution to The Case of the Missing Spaghetti?
- (A) Dad took the spaghetti.
- (B) Laurie ate the spaghetti.
- ● (C) Birds took the spaghetti.
- (D) Mom had put the spaghetti in the fridge.

14. Who was the second suspect?
- (F) baby Laurie
- (G) Mom
- ● (H) Dad
- (J) the birds

15. How do you know Dad didn't take the spaghetti?
- ● (A) He was mowing the lawn.
- (B) He was watching Laurie.
- (C) He liked pizza better.
- (D) Dad didn't like to investigate.

16. Why might the birds have taken the spaghetti?
- (F) They liked Italian food.
- ● (G) They thought they were worms.
- (H) They wanted to try something different.
- (J) They needed to make a nest.

GO ON

220

READING PRACTICE TEST

● Part 3: Story Comprehension (cont.)

Directions: Read or listen to the paragraphs below that tell about a boy who builds a robot. Then, answer the questions.

Bert, the Inventor

Every day after school, Bert locked himself in his bedroom. He was working on a secret project. He didn't tell anyone what he was doing. Not even his best friend Larry.

Bert finally finished. He had made a robot that looked exactly like himself. The robot had orange hair, freckles, and glasses. The robot and Bert both talked in a squeaky voice. "Life is going to be easy now!" exclaimed Bert. "I'm going to send my robot to school while I stay home and play."

The next morning the robot ate breakfast. Then, he rode the bus to school. After school the bus dropped the robot back home. The robot knocked on the door.

"Sweetie, I am so glad you're home. I really missed you!" said Mom. Then, she took the robot into the kitchen and gave him a snack before dinner.

"We had lots of fun at school today," said the robot. "We went to the space museum. I got to try on a real space suit. It was too big for me but the teacher took my picture."

Bert was listening outside the kitchen. He was sad. He wanted to be an astronaut someday. He decided this wasn't a good idea. So the next day, Bert went to school himself.

17. What did Bert look like?
- (A) He had curly hair and was tall.
- (B) He had red hair and wore a cap.
- (C) He was short with blonde hair.
- ● (D) He had orange hair, freckles, and glasses.

18. Why did Bert decide to go to school himself?
- (F) He missed his mom's smile.
- ● (G) He missed going to the space museum.
- (H) He missed his friend Larry.
- (J) He missed eating breakfast and going to school.

19. Where does this story take place?
- (A) at school
- (B) at the grocery store
- (C) at Larry's house
- ● (D) at Bert's house

20. Why did Bert create the robot?
- ● (F) He wanted to make life easier and have the robot go to school for him.
- (G) His mom was feeling sick and needed help cleaning.
- (H) He didn't want to be friends with Larry anymore.
- (J) He was sad that he didn't have any brothers.

STOP

221